Seattle
UNCOVERED

Jo Ann Roe

Library of Congress Cataloging-in-Publication Data

Roe, Jo Ann
    Seattle Uncovered / Jo Ann Roe.
      p. cm.
    Includes bibliographical references and Index.
    ISBN 1-55622-394-3
    1. Seattle (Wash.)--History.   2. Seattle (Wash.)--Social life and customs.
    I. Title.
    F899.S457R64   1995
    979.7'772--dc20   95-20834
                                      CIP

Seaside Press is an imprint of Wordware Publishing, Inc.

No part of this book may be reproduced in any form or by
any means without permission in writing from
Wordware Publishing, Inc.

Printed in the United States of America

ISBN 1-55622-394-3
10 9 8 7 6 5 4 3 2 1
9508

All inquiries for volume purchases of this book should be addressed to
Wordware Publishing, Inc., at 1506 Capital Avenue, Plano, Texas 75074.
Telephone inquiries may be made by calling:

(214) 423-0090

Contents

Acknowledgments

I am grateful to the editor, Mary Goldman, for assigning the project to me. In assembling the book, which touches on so many varied topics, casual conversations with Seattleites contributed to the material. Seattleites furnished leads about unusual places or events that I could subsequently research. I want to thank fellow writers such as Archie Satterfield, Dan Peterson, Rich Berner, Junius Rochester, and others for comparing notes. George Mortenson, former investor in many downtown buildings, was helpful in showing the buildings belonging to his former company to me and reminiscing about their uses and appearances in past days. My sympathies to Lawrence Kreisman for his frustration in dealing with me on architectural questions. If I still have made errors, they are my own. I especially want to thank Richard Engeman and Carla Rickerson of Special Collections, University of Washington Libraries, for enduring my endless questions and leading me to research materials. I was helped greatly by Rick Caldwell of the Museum of History and Industry (MOHAI), who guided me to pertinent files. Thanks to the Bellingham Public Library staff for obtaining endless (it seemed) rolls of microfilm and books through inter-library loans. Thanks go to the public relations staffs of the Seahawks, Mariners, and SuperSonics for reading portions of the Sports Page; to Joe Leduca for advice about the Longacres chapter; and to Dan Peterson for reading parts of the historical chapters. Finally, a big thanks to Seattleites for molding an interesting and diverse city.

Introduction

It is difficult to pigeonhole Seattle. The city perches at the outer northwest limits of the "lower 48," seemingly at a frontier. Yet it is a highly cosmopolitan city, as much at ease with the Orient, Alaska, Canada, and the South Pacific as it is with New York. Seattle's people are equally at home, muddy and chilled, digging in the sand for clams and, gowned and suited, attending an opera.

This book is for the newcomer, a crash course in Seattle lore and history. *Seattle Uncovered* is for the Seattleites, too, a reminder of people and events half-forgotten, the rogues and the builders, and a look at the stories behind familiar, modern topics such as Seafair, the floating bridges, Seattle's preoccupation with coffee, and microbrews. Reading *Seattle Uncovered* is like sampling wines. The reader may delve more deeply into a subject of particular interest, just as the wine taster may buy the whole bottle of an appealing wine.

What Do You Know About Seattle?

1. What was the name of the festival that preceded Seafair?

2. Who was the cartoon character "Weatherman" modeled after?

3. What do the letters AYP stand for, and what was it?

4. Between what two towns did the Seattle and Walla Walla Railroad operate?

5. Was there ever an Ivar's on Broadway?

6. From which hotel could one fish from the hotel room windows?

7. Where was Du-Wamps?

8. Do you know where Belltown would be today?

9. Who was Noodles Smith?

10. In Seattle, when you refer to the "Dawgs" and the "Cats," are you referring to the animal shelter?

11. What are the "Fives?"

12. Where is "Pill Hill?"

13. What is liquid sunshine?

14. Where is the "Cut?"

Answers:

1. The Potlatch Festival.

2. Roy Olmsted, because he invented the umbrella hat. Others say it was Robert Patton.

3. The Alaska-Yukon Exposition held in 1909 to showcase Seattle's charms and business climate.

4. Gotcha, too easy. The railroad never got beyond Newcastle, where the coal mines operated, running the 22 miles from Seattle.

5. Yes, for nineteen years serving Mexican, Chinese, and seafood, even hamburgers.

6. The Edgewater Hotel.

7. It was the original name of Seattle, listed on territorial records.

8. More or less between Bell and Denny Way along Elliott.

9. The owner of the well-attended Black and Tan Club in the International District, Twelfth and Jackson, that operated into the 1950s.

10. No, the "Dawgs" are the University of Washington's Huskies and the "Cats" are Washington State's Cougars—both football teams.

11. I-5 and I-405. Radio announcers giving traffic information to listeners refer to them as the "Fives."

12. On First Hill where so many medical facilities are located.

13. Fine rain coming down over Seattle.

14. The channel between Lake Washington and Lake Union.

CHAPTER 1

Uniquely Seattle

The Seattle Spirit

Whatever "spirit" means, Seattleites are supposed to have it. To many early timers it meant making the most of an opportunity. Seattle is unusual in that magnates were conspicuously absent from its early economic life. Ordinary people saw the possibilities and took advantage of the area's natural assets, making lots of money in the process, but, by gosh, they were ordinary people and don't you forget it.

In 1911 writer L. Byrd Mock tried to identify the Seattle Spirit, saying it was "a combination of energy, determination and optimism." It was an attitude that, whatever the adversity, we can triumph. James R. Meikle of the Seattle Chamber of Commerce identified "Seattle Spirit" during the 1903 Semi-Centennial of Seattle as "the spirit that takes hold of everyone who becomes a resident of this city and inspires him with energy, enterprise, and enthusiasm." One saw Seattleites marching, torches high, into the future fearless, confident, dauntless in the face of difficulty. Author Gerald B. Nelson observed "The Seattle Spirit. Its soft, sweet blanket covers only achievers; the rest do not belong." Mark Twain defined it more as a "Horatio Alger" approach.

Achievers, yes. Audacious, definitely. What other pioneer village the size of Seattle would have gotten a bill locating the territorial university within its environs? Arthur Denny did in 1861, and it was the first public university chartered west of the Rocky Mountains. Daniel Bagley, John Webster, and Edmund Carr were appointed university commissioners the day after passage of the bill. The University of Washington was established on ten acres of tangled underbrush on a knoll now between Seneca and Union, Fourth to Sixth. The land was cleared by volunteers and laborers paid with donated funds, at first, then supported by selling lands granted to the territorial university. When the cornerstone was laid near today's Four Seasons Hotel, the pioneers put a Bible inside that had two whole sections missing—Genesis and Revelation, the beginning and the end. Perhaps it was significant in some way.

And don't forget . . . we are ordinary people.

Perhaps not so ordinary. The bachelors of Seattle, desperate for wives and families, sent Asa Mercer to New England in the fall of 1863 to encourage single women, some orphaned because of the Civil War deaths, to come to Seattle as teachers, seamstresses, etc. Of course, he made it clear that there were plenty of potential suitors, too, eagerly awaiting them. Eleven brave and educated young women accepted the challenge, embued with the spirit that typified Seattleites, and came West in May 1864. All found jobs and, within a short time, all but one married. That hold-out, Lizzie Ordway, a beautiful woman, single by choice, became Seattle's first public school teacher and later the superintendent of Kitsap County schools. Women from ordinary backgrounds but perhaps more likely extraordinary.

It was this independent spirit later on that drove maverick leaders like Dave Beck of the labor movement to bushwhack their way through political forests to gain their ends. Ordinary people. Bill Boeing who built an aviation empire when lesser visionaries laughed behind his back at the uselessness of building flying machines. Can-do people who climbed aboard even the leakiest vessel bound for the Yukon to seek gold in 1897. We can overcome the weather, the very seas, and bring home riches. Robert Moran, the shipbuilder, who was told he wouldn't live out the year, bought San Juan Island property, built an estate, and fooled his gloomy doctors by living almost forever—even surviving the bad attitude of his house guests when he played the pipe organ at dawn.

That same energy and fierce independence survive today. The talk at social occasions is of skiing, boating, fishing, rock climbing, hurtling down wild rivers. Sure, there is a vigorous arts community and several prestigious universities, but still, if you don't know what a stem christie is or can't discuss the merits of harbors in Hood Canal versus the San Juan Islands, you are pretty silent at parties. Then there is the eternal "in" topic of how to cook salmon. The devotees of brown sugar glaze, of alder-smoking salmon, of slow-cooking the feast Indian-style, how long should it be cooked, which salmon is the best—silvers or chinook. The scorn heaped on non-Northwesterners who overcook salmon and wouldn't know a good fish if it leaped into their laps.

Not only salmon, but clams, oysters, scallops, the feasts one can gather from the sea. Then there is coffee . . . and microbrews. Seattleites seem to think they invented both. Every imaginable type of coffee, latte, espresso, and regular brew is available. When you ask for a cup of coffee you have to specify what exact kind. The same with beer and Washington wines.

Seattleites are so filled with delight at the extraordinary beauty of their surroundings—the mountains, the lovely maritime ambience—that they become protective of it, as if they personally invented the place. While Seattle really has

3

weeks and months of fine weather, its denizens complain loudly about the rain to discourage outsiders from crowding in—outsiders who have to shovel their precipitation. On the rare occasions when an errant storm system brings unusual cold and ice, or an inch or so of snow, even briefly, the city comes to a halt, for it's a city with virtually no snowplows (although it has lots of sand and salt for the hilly streets).

Seattle's spirit includes fanatic support of the University of Washington Huskies football team and intense intrastate rivalry with Washington State University. Some fans even travel from downtown to Husky Stadium on a cruise boat, partying all the way. The Husky tailgate parties have gained wide renown.

With all the recreation, one would imagine that the current Seattleites have forgotten the sober Seattle Spirit that revered work and enterprise—the stern Arthur Denny approach. But Seattleites work hard and play hard in the city that sees itself as a hub of the Pacific Rim trading partnership. Not a few businesspeople speak Japanese or Chinese. Young business people from Japan, especially, come to special schools in Seattle to learn American business practices, while Northwest youths go to Japan to fathom the nuances of business dealings. Students from the Orient at Seattle universities and colleges fall right into that Seattle Spirit—the belief that ordinary people who work hard can prosper.

The City Called New York-Alki

Dogs barked, the smoke from cooking fires hung low over the Indian campsite, and native families watched with amazement the landing of the ship *Exact* November 13,

1851. Seattle's founding families were aboard—Denny, Boren, Terry, Low, Bell. To the Indians they looked pale and sickly, especially the blonde Rollie Denny, then two months old. "Memaloose, memaloose" (Die, die), they predicted. But Denny lived to be eighty-seven years old.

The families settled in with the Indians for protection against the fierce North Coast raiders who came regularly to carry off Duwampsh as slaves. The Indians figured the settlers' guns would help them drive the hostiles away; the settlers reckoned that large numbers couldn't hurt.

The growing community was dubbed New York-Alki by the settlers, who predicted it would grow to be a big city "by and by," the Indian word Alki. As it turned out, Elliott Bay was a far better natural harbor and the whole town picked up and moved. Although settlers thought of themselves as the New York of the Pacific, New York-Alki never happened.

Doctor David S. Maynard, one of Alki's first settlers, moved to Elliott Bay or Seattle and sold his 314 acres at Alki for $450 to Knute Olson—who just happened to be the grandfather of Seattle's beloved character Ivar Haglund.

The Naming of Seattle

The city of Seattle was named by pioneers that included Doc Maynard and Arthur Denny on January 6, 1853, honoring Chief Seattle of the Suquamish. The spelling is closer to the spoken word than the word "Sealth" often used by historians.

Right after the declaration, Maynard went off to the territorial legislature at Oregon City and, while there, had his land claim registered as Seattle, King County's seat. The

Oregon Territorial Legislature thereafter passed a law making the name official.

Seattle was a staunch friend and defender of the pioneer settlement—even during the Indian uprisings of 1855-56. He set down firm rules for his people: no murder, no lying, no cheating, no drinking.

Chief Seattle was so well respected that, upon his death in June 1866, four hundred white men joined the Indians who attended his funeral rites. His son said, "Seattle fear no man. He worship only *Hyas Tyee* above the stars (the Christian God, for he had been converted by Father Demers to Catholicism)." He is buried near the site of an old Suquamish longhouse called Oleman House at today's village of Suquamish (Port Madison Indian Reservation).

Twenty-five years after his death, Arthur Denny, Hillory Butler, and Samuel L. Crawford erected a memorial to him at Fifth and Denny Way with an inscription:

SEATTLE
Chief of the Suquamish and Allied Tribes
Died June 7, 1866
The Firm Friend of the Whites
For Him Seattle Was Named By Its Founders

The bronze statue was affixed to a granite pedestal and was originally set above a drinking trough for horses, now a fountain.

Why the Streets Are Crooked

Henry Yesler built the first wharf of Seattle's waterfront in 1854, one that was so flimsy and short that ships could not use it at low tide. Quite logically, he built his wharf perpendicularly to the shoreline and so did the subsequent builders. Seattle's waterfront, however, was curved and the wharves began to make a pattern like the game "pick up sticks."

Worse yet, paths and then streets grew in line with the piers, creating a maze farther inland. Extending the pier oceanward, it was inevitable that the distance between two piers would eventually meet. On shore, if streets extended from piers, street A would be one block from street B at the waterfront and a mile distant farther inland. Independent pioneer builders laid out and filed plats before streets even existed. It was a real mess.

After statehood in 1889, there was an attempt to make sense out of the waterfront ownership, resulting in the 1895 plat that assigned lands to owners using the alignment of the hodge-podge of piers as a guide. Obviously, that made matters even worse, and ownership of virtually the entire waterfront had to be sorted out.

Meantime, since the fire of 1889 burned all the wharves, every one, the owners rebuilt them at about a 45-degree angle to shore. Some said it was because they could gain longer piers by driving pilings into the shallower water closer to shore. Others said that ships approaching approximately from the northwest would not have to tack.

So the system along the waterfront grew up with streets leading down to the wharves—approximately northwest-southeast. Arthur Denny decided to lay out other streets accordingly, despite the protests of Doc Maynard that streets universally were to be established north/south and east/west, as Maynard's properties were platted. Both men stuck to their viewpoints.

Following adoption of the tideland plat in 1895, city engineer R.H. Thomson sided with Maynard. It seems there was a mandate from the federal government that American streets should be so arranged, although no one was able to find it.

However, Denny was not about to change "HIS" streets, and forever after the original plat and later ones had to match up at odd angles.

Seattle Covered

Seattle's first site was on a knoll not far above high tide centered around today's First and Yesler, sloping down to marshy ground and deep water. The founding fathers—the Denny brothers, Boren, Maynard— were more interested in setting up shop adjacent to deep water ports than in aesthetics. Hence, the first flimsy, wooden structures, some on pilings, threatened to float away during unusually high tides or storms. Pigs would have thrived in the muddy streets.

Seattle's waterfront today is several hundred feet west of the original high tide mark, because of extensive landfill. Early advocates encouraged visiting ships to dump their ballast along Seattle's tidelands and at least two entire derelict ships are buried under what became known as Ballast Island. The island disappeared, too, during the great cover-up . . . but that was later.

The stingy, flat beachlands were backed up to serious 200-foot cliffs where grew magnificent cedar, hemlock, and fir trees. Furnishing Henry Yesler's waterfront sawmill

(1853) was simply a matter of cutting down trees and sliding them down the steep slope in a funnel-shaped guide, called Mill Street then Skid Road, Yesler Way today. The term has been corrupted over time to "Skid Row," adopted as a designation by towns of their seamier districts. Since the docks were nearby, as well, Skid Road became the center of entertainment for a rough, hard-working lot of men, most of them single, who were fueled by strong coffee and heaped plates during the week, liquor and women on weekends. Every form of vice thrived. An astonishing number of "seamstresses" registered as businesses and virtually supported the city government with their license fees. The city fathers simply looked the other way at the number of sewing customers, day and night, these buxom seamstresses enjoyed. Owners of taverns perched on stilts over the tidewaters sometimes made pacts with unsavory shipowners to put "Mickey Finns" in the drinks of sturdy-looking men, then drop them through trapdoors of the tavern into the waiting arms of agents for the shipowners. When the unfortunate fellows awakened with magnificent headaches, they were on ships standing out to sea, facing an enforced period of sailorhood. Or the dropees, wallet missing, simply wound up dead, fished out of the Sound by undertakers.

Almost all the original Skid Road section, plus the majority of the business district (sixty-six blocks) and all wharves from Union to King streets, expired spectacularly in 1889, through a fast-moving fire that erupted when a pot of glue overturned at a cabinet shop. When the unchecked fire burned itself out, businessmen and "seamstresses" reopened in canvas tents, while they hastened to rebuild. The more sagacious built of brick, and a goodly portion of the old town was completed within a year. A burgeoning population resulted in the construction during post-fire years of 3,500 new buildings, many in the gap left by the fire. Seattle had a population of 37,000 in 1890, a gain of 6,000 since the fire.

The townsite of Seattle was highly uneven, though, composed of haphazard landfills by merchants, so the underpinnings of buildings varied widely. Furthermore, some of the fill had been sawdust from Yesler's Mill, not the most stable material in the world. To get from one merchant's store to another, it was not uncommon to climb steps, sometimes a lot of steps. There was another critical problem to be addressed: in 1892 it was discovered that a sewer trench dug along Front Street or First Avenue ran uphill.

Then the city fathers intervened only a year or so after the fire with a plan to resculpt the town. The streets were to be raised as much as eight to thirty feet, the resultant cavities filled by regrading the hills above.

Regrading of Seattle townsite. Photo from the Special Collections Division, University of Washington Libraries, Negative Number: U.W. #6195

The regrades themselves were ambitious projects undertaken over the next three decades. Men using horse teams and wagons, shovels and picks moved the dirt. Then mining carts on short rail systems were installed to haul the dirt away. Borrowing further from the gold-mining industry, City Engineer R.H. Thomson took high-pressure hydraulic hoses and sluiced down parts of the promontories, sending mudslides downhill—effectively covering up entire portions of the old city. About ninety-five percent of the fill went to create Harbor Island. The amount of earth moved away by the regrades exceeded the amount of concrete poured to create Grand Coulee Dam.

As the regrades ensued, concrete or brick walls were installed at either side of a projected street crossing to hold the fill required. Some resultant holes adjacent to the new streets were filled; some were not. Owners of certain buildings found themselves operating thereafter from the second floor, since the first floor was buried by the new landfills. After the lowering of Denny Hill in the 1920s, the regrading ceased.

Until all this got straightened out, the crazy quilt of street levels worsened. Legends say that naughty lads would sit on a street above and spit tobacco juice on the hapless below. And gulls were not the only other hazards; horses faced the wrong way on a street above could surprise one.

To give Thomson due credit, though, he did achieve a workable grade that enabled the city to grow away from the beach. While he was rearranging downtown Seattle's terrain, Thomson foresightedly installed water mains and what was considered a ridiculously large sewer system all the way to Lake Union. Raising the level of the Pioneer Square area remedied a peculiar sanitary problem. At high tide, flushing a toilet sometimes worked in reverse, producing a fountain.

Possibly some of the tales are exaggerated, but the hidden facts remain. There is, indeed, a labyrinth of the old city beneath Pioneer Square. One of Seattle's most popular attractions is the Underground Tour from the square.

Guides take visitors through "Seattle Covered," where boarded-up windows of old storefronts verify that buildings once stood at lower street levels. A few of the ruins have been identified; those that are merely the inundated first floors of several-story buildings were easy to catalogue. Blocks of other subterranean passages are too dangerous to enter or have caved in. The tours through the safe portions of the underground area, some bolstered by modern beams, began in 1965, the brain-child of author Bill Spiedel, a Seattle historian and humorist who authored *Sons of the Profits*, a lively, anecdotal tale of Seattle. They are a pleasantly catacombic experience.

The Mercer Girls

Seattle was prospering in the early 1860s, but most settlers were single men. While some married the winsome Indian women, there were not enough to go around. Always practical in Seattle, the bachelors advertised for women. Actually, they were more subtle than that, stating their case as needing teachers, seamstresses and such. The bachelors took up a collection, appointed Asa Mercer (president of the territorial university) the leader of the campaign, and paid his fare to go East and persuade women to come. The old *Seattle Gazette* inferred he had "calico on the brain."

Mercer chose New England as a source of eager females, because industry there was in economic decline, and many young women had lost their fathers or husbands to the Civil War. Eleven proper and educated young women, ranging in age from sixteen to twenty years, accompanied Mercer back to Seattle, arriving May 16, 1864. Out came the boiled shirts, razors, and shoe polish. The bachelors flocked to the public reception to look over the Mercer Girls.

They were bashful and respectful, somewhat overcome by the reality of gazing on civilized young women. They gave Mercer a rousing cheer, there were prayers for the ladies' health and prosperity, and the eleven were assigned to the care of the few couples already established in homes. By fall all had paying positions, but the summer was marked by picnics, balls, and musical events. Within mere months most of the women also had been claimed by eager suitors, except for Lizzie Ordway who preferred her teaching career.

With such success Mercer again went East in April 1865, ambitiously seeking 500 women willing to take their chances in Seattle. He solicited the help of General Grant in Washington, D.C., who was sympathetic to the plight of lonely men, having once been stationed at Vancouver Barracks in Washington Territory. He offered a steamship and crew for the trip.

At first, all went well. The original Mercer Girls had sent positive letters about their experiences, and by July, Mercer had 300 women ready to go—many of them war orphans of the Civil War, most from New York and New England states. Mercer returned to Washington, D.C., to make final arrangements for the provisioning of the promised ship, only to be told by the quartermaster general that he would not honor General Grant's order unless Mercer paid $80,000 for the lease. Transportation leader Ben Holladay came forward with a proposal that cleared the way again, but now the *New York Herald* published an article highly critical of the trip, suggesting the worst possible future for the women. In the face of the inferences, most of the women withdrew their assent to go. Mercer was running out of money.

Finally, the ship sailed on January 6, 1866, not with 300 but only 100 passengers, of whom there were only forty-six marriageable women, the rest married couples, children, and a few single men. By the time Mercer got to San Francisco, he was completely broke and had to sell agricultural machinery that he was bringing to Seattle in order to pay the hotel bills and passages north for his charges on several small ships.

Upon their arrival in Seattle in May 1866, not only the single men, but the married couples greeted the new Mercer Girls, the wives eager to learn about social life and fashions in the East. The new group of women easily found positions and eventually husbands. Indeed, Asa Mercer was married July 15, 1866, to Annie E. Stephens of Baltimore, a lady from the trip.

Today's leaders of society are proud to claim a Mercer Girl in the family. As pioneer writer Clarence Bagley later observed, not one of the Mercer Girls ever went wrong.

Coal Under the Freeway

Rolling along freeway #405 toward the south end of Lake Washington, one frequently is driving over coal beds. In 1853 Dr. R.M. Bigelow discovered coal on Black River, near today's Tukwila. R.M. Bigelow, H.H. Tobin, O.M. Eaton, and Frank Fanjoy formed Duwamish Coal Co., recorded Oct. 20, 1853, but with no capital or development.

Ten years later, Lyman Andrews filed a claim near Squak Lake (Lake Sammamish) and mined it some. The Seattle *Gazette* got excited about it and published a diagram showing where the Northern Pacific Railroad would run in relation to the mine, but NPR never came near that area.

That same year, Edwin Richardson noted coal on Coal Creek while surveying the land. Two ministers, Rev. George

Whitworth of Olympia, an amateur geologist, and Rev. Daniel Bagley, organized the Lake Washington Coal Company in 1866 to develop it. Other incorporators besides the two ministers were: Josiah Settle, John Ross, P.H. Lewis, Selucius Garfielde. The latter was the surveyor-general at the time, living in Olympia.

Coal was discovered in 1873, right under what became the town of Renton, and the following year at the Talbot Mine a bit southwest. Owners of these two mines hoisted the coal from the mines and slid it by chute into cars on a short railroad to the Black River for loading onto barges.

The developers at Coal Creek built a wagon road to the lake, barged the coal across to Fleaburg (Leschi Park), then followed a path along today's Jackson Street to Elliott Bay. Later they tried hauling it by tug and barge on the Black and Duwamish rivers. The first rig grounded in Black River, managed to float free, but, when the shipment finally got to a Duwamish dock, customs officials seized the tug for not having a salt water license.

After straightening out these problems, the developers gave the first coal as a test to U.S. Revenue Cutter *Lincoln*. It created such heat that the iron of the smokestack almost melted. The captain said it was dangerous because it was too flammable. Of course, being flammable is what coal is all about. Nevertheless, there seemed to be no market for the coal, even in San Francisco.

In 1879 the group reorganized, with Bagley and Whitworth again the principals, and built a tram and bunkers. This resulted in handling the coal even more times. Coal was loaded onto cars at the mines and ran down the tramway to Lake Washington. Barges transported the coal to another tramway from Lake Washington to Lake Union. Then the material went by barge across Lake Union, where it was finally loaded onto another tram from the south end of the lake to the foot of Pike Street. There the coal was trundled out to waiting ships at the docks—docks that often were invaded by teredoes (ship worms) and fell down . . . literally.

When a new developer put a small locomotive called the "Bodie" on the last leg from Lake Union, it was considered a "big deal." A few years later, after coal producers abandoned the mines, the path of the Lake Union-Pike Street tramway became a popular place for lovers to stroll on a Sunday afternoon.

Meanwhile the Renton and Talbot mines continued to produce coal for about ten years or until 1886, when a struggle between union organizers and owners closed both mines. In 1895 a group of local men organized the Renton Cooperative Coal Company and reopened the mines. Miners earned their money by piecework; a miner usually could fill four mine cars of coal a day, enough to earn a living. In 1901 Seattle Electric Company bought the properties and got serious about mining, taking coal from eleven levels. Shafts ran east from today's Benson Road to the heights above Cedar River. Over 300 men were employed there by 1909, and reports indicated there was no end to the coal deposits. But around 1918 the mines closed, the owners blaming labor troubles. Yet as late as 1928, at least seventeen coal mines still operated in the vicinity of Renton. Descendants of many Italian workers relate today their fathers' stories of coal mining there.

According to Morda C. Slauson in her book *Renton from Coal to Jets*, during the construction of freeway #405 at its junction with Benson Road, excavators discovered a large iron gate and heavy timbers across the mouth of a tunnel. Walter Reed, a former electrician at the mine, came to inspect the site and said it was the main entrance to the old Renton Coal Company mine and that the tunnel went straight into the hill for a thousand feet and then down at a 15-degree pitch for about a mile. In her book on Renton,

Slauson maintains that large coal deposits in the Renton/ Tukwila area lie under all of the developments there.

Seattle Grabs Center Stage from San Francisco

The first ship carrying gold from the 1897 Yukon Gold Rush landed in San Francisco, not Seattle. Putting into San Francisco harbor on July 15, 1897, the *Excelsior* carried a half ton of gold, and nationwide newspaper headlines screamed the facts of discovery. Two days later on July 17, the ship *Portland* landed at Seattle, greeted by a hysterical crowd. Passage for the ship's return trip to Alaska was already sold out. Other steamers were booking passages as fast as possible. Men and women walked off their jobs to go north. Colonel W.D. Wood, elected mayor of Seattle just months earlier, bought a ticket for the Yukon in 1897 and abandoned Seattle to its fate. Within days every vessel even slightly seaworthy—and many were dangerously decrepit— was pressed into service. Seattle stores quickly sold out of shovels, picks, gold pans, food, and clothing. Merchants frantically sought to buy more stock. Any stray dogs were picked up to be trained as pack animals or sled dogs, wind- ing up in Alaska as beasts of burden for prospectors.

But what of San Francisco? It was eclipsed by Seattle as THE embarkation point by its greater distance from Alaska, of course. But the greatest weapon Seattle mounted was a Chamber of Commerce publicity campaign of modern-day intensity. Leading the charge was a jobless ex-newspaper editor, Erastus Brainerd. Brainerd had worked briefly for three prestigious Eastern newspapers, the *New York World*, the *Atlanta Constitution*, and the *Philadelphia Press*; in

Seattle he was editor after 1890 for the Seattle *Press-Times*—but not too long. In 1897 he was largely unemployed.

The Chamber of Commerce had faith in him, though, and gave him a tidy budget to spend on making sure prospectors came through Seattle en route to Alaska. From his past jobs, Brainerd had good connections in the East and understood the value of promotion. Without delay, he eclipsed his competitor ports with advertising in major magazines and newspapers, including the *New York Journal*, *Scribner's*, and others.

In his book *Skid Road*, Murray Morgan described Brainerd's media blitz. The promoter developed a series of letters telling of the glories of Seattle, passing them out to gold prospectors returning from Alaska to mail to hometown newspapers. "He wrote articles for Eastern papers and magazines, including *Harper's Weekly*, and then quoted his effusions in news dispatches datelined Seattle without mentioning that their author was Seattle's paid booster."

Under the masthead of the Chamber of Commerce, Brainerd sent letters to city governments, outlining the needs of those planning to travel to Alaska. He sent a pamphlet about how to exist in the Klondike and how to get there. The information found its way into official bulletins from the U.S. State Department sent to foreign governments. He sent photos of Alaska, the Klondike, and Seattle to kings, governors, and presidents and then reprinted in other publications their letters of thanks. There was more, and it worked. As far as most prospectors knew, the only practical way to get to the gold fields was through Seattle.

Of course, in the process, the merchants thrived, for they intercepted the prospectors coming and going, and the real gold of the Yukon Gold Rush was left in Seattle.

By 1903 it was reported that $197,132,897 of gold dust and nuggets had been processed by the U.S. Government assay office since it opened on July 15, 1898. It was estimated that merchants had realized $18 million in sales of goods to Alaska and received almost $19 million from Alaska and the Yukon in gold, fish, and other products.

Erastus Brainerd's success led to his being named editor-in-chief of the *Seattle Post-Intelligencer* on January 1, 1904. He also helped bring about the election of Albert E. Mead as governor of Washington in 1905.

The Cross-Mountain Railroad That Wasn't

The Seattle fathers such as Arthur Denny, the Terrys, Bells, and Rentons were utterly dismayed in 1873 when the Northern Pacific Railroad chose Tacoma as its terminus. They had pledged lands and money toward the NPR with the understanding that the tracks would end in Seattle. Of course, the NPR had not yet been built across Stampede Pass.

Overnight Arthur Denny influenced many of the investors to switch their support to building the Seattle and Walla Walla Railroad, instead. The railroad was to go through Snoqualmie Pass, north of NPR's proposed route, and terminate in Seattle. The promoters said that, since NPR was associated with the Oregon Steam Navigation Company and its boats and rails along the Columbia River, it was doubtful they would ever build west to Tacoma, anyway.

Snorting defiance at being left in the lurch, the Seattle contingent consulted with Walla Walla businessmen and investors. Walla Walla and Yakima were concerned with the tons of grain produced, which must be shipped to ocean ports, and businessmen agreed to invest some money in the SWWR; however, hedging their bets, they said the money would go first toward tracks to Wallula on the Columbia River.

While Seattleites were very excited about the matter, lukewarm Walla Walla supporters soon switched their allegiance to Union Pacific Railroad, hoping to become a main line stop. The financing for SWWR was not forthcoming from either side, as the Seattle-based stockholders were more diligent about talking than paying.

When it looked as if the railroad would only be a paper one, the investors persuaded James M. Colman to become the head of the construction project. Colman had racked up an impressive record of taking Northwest mill businesses that lost money and turning them around. With a public bond issue, stockholders' pledges, and some money of his own, Colman agreed to take the helm. He proceeded to buy up land along a proposed right-of-way that led to the Newcastle coal fields, recognizing the immediate value of the coal and the dubious possibility that the railroad ever would go to Walla Walla.

In addition, Colman obtained title to the lands in his own name—not fully believing that the promised money would be paid in. And he was correct; it wasn't. Colman made certain deals with coal investors, started the Cedar Mountain Coal Mine, Inc., with J.J. McKinnon of the Renton and Newcastle operations, and proceeded to lay track across the tideflats toward Renton.

The investors and newspapermen roared their enthusiasm as the tracks moved along, believing the SWWR actually was going to be built. Only Colman knew in his heart that it probably would end at the coal mines, and twenty-two miles distant. He achieved his goal of tapping the coal mines; many men gained profitable wages by building the railroad and mining coal. But the Seattle and Walla Walla Railroad should have been named Seattle and Newcastle, for that was its terminus.

20

The Wonderful World of the Locks

Seattle is half surrounded by water, but it is salt water on the west, fresh water on the east. To merge the two without destroying lakes Washington and Union, the Army Corps of Engineers completed a complex lock-through system in 1917, a six-year project, although parts of the excavation from salt water into Salmon Bay (Ballard area) were completed between 1901-03.

At least two earlier efforts were made to access salt water from fresh. Harvey Pike, who filed a Union City plat in 1869 between lakes Union and Washington, tried to dig single-handedly a ditch between the two lakes but gave it up. He had been given part of the land as payment for painting the territorial university building. In 1871 Pike and others organized the Lake Washington Canal Association to further the joining. Little happened until 1883, when the Lake Washington Improvement Company was incorporated by David T. Denny, J.W. George, C.P. Stone, Thomas Burke, F.H. Whitworth, H.B. Bagley, and other entrepreneurs to construct a canal with locks. They hired Wah Chong, a local contractor, who put twenty-five Chinese laborers to work straightening and widening the existing small stream between Lake Union and Salmon Bay, and to build a log channel between lakes Union and Washington. Wah Chong's men also built a small wooden lock at the exit of Lake Union for lowering logs into the flume that led to Salmon Bay. For a time, logs indeed traveled from Lake Washington into the Sound in this fashion.

From the beginning of Seattle's settlement, residents eyed numerous possibilities for linking the lakes with the ocean. If a canal were built, they reasoned, ships could enter Lake Union and go on into Lake Washington. For one thing, this would eliminate the complex problems of loading coal that were inhibiting the development of the Newcastle and Renton coal mines. Furthermore, the teredos would fall off in fresh water. The Black River, outlet of Lake Washington, was considered as a possible maritime exit from Lake Washington, since it merged into the Duwamish River and on out to salt water. Eugene Semple, a former Washington territorial governor, proposed a canal through Beacon Hill to the Rainier valley and waterways at the mouth of the Duwamish River. These options were discarded after some work was actually performed on the Duwamish and portions sluiced off Beacon Hill.

Surveyors and planners focused on a route more or less that of the present, although Smith Cove was a possible alternative termination point instead of Shilshole Bay. The point that killed Smith Cove as an outlet was that the Great Northern Railway had already built its lines into Seattle from Ballard along Smith Cove. Company officials objected strenuously to moving the GNR tracks and threatened to abandon Seattle entirely. The city fathers hastened to adopt Shilshole.

Seattle developer James A. Moore came on the scene in 1906 with a contract from King County to build a half million dollar wooden lock at the head of Salmon Bay and lower the level of Lake Washington somewhat to permit its operation. One can imagine the concern this caused among lake residents, but, more important, Major Hiram M. Chittenden was assigned to Seattle that year and asserted that such a wooden lock would surely fail one day and drain lakes Union and Washington out into the Sound. He prevailed and Moore transferred his rights to the Lake Washington Canal Association, which raised enough money from an assessment district to begin a proper canal and lock system.

First the Army Corps of Engineers, spearheaded by Chittenden, had to wade through a thicket of controversies about the site for the locks, since waterside mills and other businesses lobbied for protection of their properties. Finally it was agreed that the locks would be placed in the narrows between Shilshole Bay, an inlet of Puget Sound, and Salmon Bay, where they are today.

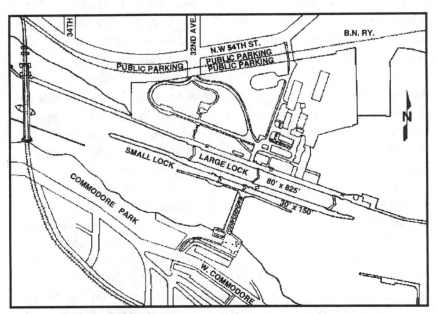

Courtesy of the U.S. Army Corps of Engineers

Work began in 1911 and proceeded thereafter in a methodical fashion. A crew site was in place by the middle of 1912 and much of the excavation was completed. The concrete lock walls and floors were done by mid-1914 and the steel gates in place a year later. The gates remained open so that boats could continue to access Ballard. In July 1916 the adjacent dam was finished and the gates closed forever. Salmon Bay was raised to an elevation of twenty-one feet above low water in Puget Sound, and a month later the small coffer dam holding back Lake Washington was removed to gradually mingle the waters of lakes Union and Washington over a three-month period. This resulted in a lowering of Lake Washington by seven to nine feet, depending on the natural seasonal level. A benefit to Lake Washington shoreline residents was cessation of serious flooding, for the water level in the lake in the past had risen as much as seven feet at times—unable to drain fast enough through the Black River exit. In turn, the deltas from the Black, White, and Cedar rivers where they headed for the Duwamish River and the Sound were less prone to flooding, too.

The needs of salmon struggling into Lake Washington and the streams beyond to spawn were included in the locks' designs. A ten-step fish ladder was built south of the spillway dam, and in 1976 a more modern one was built to enhance passage with twenty-one steps, or weirs, which allow the fish to leap from one weir to another and emerge in Salmon Bay to continue their journey. Attraction water (a swiftly flowing stream toward an incoming salmon) leads the salmon to the right spot. In the 1980s and '90s sea lions found the entrance to the fish ladder a dandy banquet table. At first, the story about "Herschel" the seal vs. wildlife experts who tried every means to discourage him from eating the returning salmon and steelhead was an amusing saga for residents. However, more "Herschels" joined the gang mugging the fish. Protected from destruction, the sea lions became a serious problem, and wildlife personnel tried transporting them way down into California waters— only to find them back in a few days at the Chittenden Locks. Special sanctions may be necessary to destroy certain of the predatory seals in the interests of protecting spawning fish.

The actual completion of the Lake Washington Ship Canal (the whole waterway including locks) was celebrated on July 4, 1917, by speeches and a parade of gaily bedecked boats making the trip through the locks. Work on dredging and increasing the width of the channels continued until

1934 and beyond. The locks were General Hiram M. Chittenden's last feat, for he died that same year of 1917 at age fifty-nine.

During construction the only serious problem incurred was the failure on March 13, 1914, of a temporary dam near the Fremont Bridge that retained Lake Union's waters. The lake dropped three to four feet below high-tide level, and salt water flowed into and out of Lake Union for ten days until the dam was repaired.

Two locks serve the traffic. The large lock for major ships and barges (and used for recreational traffic, too, when space permits) is 825 feet long, 80 feet wide, and enables lifts from 6 to 26 feet (depending on the tides and lake level). The smaller lock used for recreational boaters and small workboats is 150 feet long, 30 feet wide, and has the same lift capability. Rigs like a tow boat plus a raft of logs need every bit of the 825-foot length to make the trip through the big lock.

The locks immediately became one of Seattle's most popular visitor attractions, and, as time went on, facilities for visitors were added including six lighted windows in an underwater fish viewing room. Carl S. English Jr., a Corps employee, spent forty-three years transforming the muddy plain on the north side of the locks into a seven-acre showpiece garden. The location is very protected from winds and chill, and English planted exotic species that normally would not grow in the Northwest. The main feeling, though, is—appropriately—that of an English garden. It was a pleasant place for lock superintendents to live, as the Cavanaugh House, built on the hill overlooking the locks in 1913, is the official residence of the Seattle District Engineer.

The Metropolitan Tract

Due to the foresight of Arthur Denny and others, the University of Washington was located in Seattle in 1861 on land donated by Arthur Denny to Washington Territory, when the city was barely recognizable as such. The city fathers were eager to project a degree of sophistication that would attract new businesses and settlers. The plot consisted of ten acres way out in the country then, but now that site, still the property of the University of Washington, lies in the heart of the city—Metropolitan Center from Third to Fifth Avenue, Seneca to Union and including Four Seasons Olympic Hotel and Rainier Square.

Even in 1894, thirty-three years later, it was obvious that the property was inadequate for the growth of a university since it was located in the new center of Seattle after the business district began moving north from Pioneer Square. The campus was moved to a heavily forested 355-acre plot adjacent to Lake Washington and the portage route between Lake Washington and Lake Union. How fortunate for the financially strapped institution to be chosen as part of the site of the Alaska-Yukon-Pacific Exposition of 1909, since at least three buildings would be donated to the university after closure of AYP and much of the campus lands were cleared of timber.

As the city grew, the downtown property became fabulously valuable and continues to this day to supply a hefty sum for the university's use.

It was a gradual process. First the university tried to sell the site unsuccessfully. It was most unattractive at the time since the regrading from First Avenue to Third and Fourth left the original U/W building standing on a thirty-five-foot cliff. The regents leased the property for development, first to J. C. Levold, and in 1902 to James A. Moore for thirty years, extended in 1904 to fifty years. Moore embarked on the construction of a four-story building for the newspaper *Post-Intelligencer*. He also built some temporary buildings to use as rentals to acquire income while he was building the *P.I.* structure, but, after some disputes with the regents and financial problems, Moore sold his lease in 1907 to a group of capitalists led by John F. Douglas organized as Metropolitan Building Company. This group of professional developers not only completed the first building but went on to add several—the White Building, office space rented mostly by lumber-related firms; the Cobb Building, largely medical and dental; the Stuart Building, and the Metropolitan Theater which opened September 30, 1911. The Olympic Hotel, now the Four Seasons Olympic, was wrapped around the Metropolitan Theater when it was built in 1924.

In 1915 the White, Henry, and Stuart buildings joined to form a solid block abutting Fourth Avenue between University and Union. Tenants of the offices of Metropolitan Tract included many of the Northwest's most powerful companies. Other upscale private clubs thus tended to locate on the Metropolitan properties, too: Seattle Athletic Club, Rainier Club, Metropolitan Club, College Club, Lumbermen's Club. Douglas chose directors of the Metropolitan Building Company from his illustrious tenants.

The buildings reverted to the University of Washington's ownership in 1954, under the terms of Moore's original fifty-year lease. A management entity became known as the Metropolitan Tract. Due to the sale of a small portion of the tract, 9.4 acres then remained. The tract was expanded in 1958 through an exchange of property with the federal post office and, in 1962, with the purchase of land for the Olympic Hotel garage, making a total of 9.7 acres.

The magnificent Rainier Tower arose on the tract in 1978, after contractors demolished the White, Henry, and Stuart buildings. A part of the Cobb Building survives on

27

the corner of University Plaza and Fourth, adjacent to the Puget Sound Plaza, formerly the Washington Building site. The Skinner Building at Fifth and Union also remains. The IBM Building arose on the site of an ice skating arena, home to a team called the "Metropolitans." The buildings of the Metropolitan Tract are under the management of Unico Properties organized in 1953 by Roger L. Stevens, with James R. Ryan as the first president. Today the president and CEO is David Cortelyou.

Due to the foresight of Arthur Denny and other pioneer financiers, the Metropolitan Tract has borne great fruit for the benefit of the University of Washington. Few other state universities have such a stable and ongoing source of income.

The Mosquito Fleet

The Mosquito Fleet had nothing to do with insects. It was the name given to the myriads of small steamers that linked frontier towns adjacent to Puget Sound, the Hood Canal, and the Strait of Juan de Fuca. The residents of remote towns like Port Crescent and Gettysburg on the Strait, San de Fuca and Coupeville on Whidbey Island, and even larger towns like Bellingham relied on the steamers for groceries, washing machines, and business and pleasure appointments in other towns. One author said they were waterborne "Sears catalogs" for pioneers. There were few roads, so almost everything moved by the Mosquito Fleet buzzing back and forth.

One of the most venerable, still operating as a tourist boat, is the *Virginia V*. Built in Seattle in 1898 by Heffernan Ironworks, she is believed to be the very last authentic

Mosquito Fleet steamer. Her original owners were the West Pass Transport Company, so named because its craft plied the waters from Seattle to Tacoma via West Pass of Vashon Island. The *Virginia V* is 125 feet long with a 24-foot beam, narrow in appearance, but still a handsome vessel with extensive windows and woodwork. A modern Mosquito Fleet began operation in 1989, offering a variety of ferry, tourist excursion, and charter services throughout North Puget Sound. In particular, the *Spirit of Saratoga Passage* is used for sightseeing trips to the San Juan Islands and elsewhere, touting orca (whale) searches and bird-watching.

King of the Mosquito Fleet was Joshua Green, an enterprising young man from Mississippi who entered the steamboat world as a teenager in 1887. He and three other seaman working on the *Henry Bailey* went out on a plank and borrowed money to buy the old sternwheeler *Fanny Lake*. The new owners put her to work hauling freight all over the Sound and, by working long hours and loading speedily, earned enough to pay off the bank loan. This boat was only the beginning for Green, who acquired more and more Puget Sound boats, incorporating as Puget Sound Navigation Company. His boats continued to work Puget Sound until replaced by automobiles and trucks; some became early ferries thereafter. Green went on to become one of Seattle's prominent businessmen, owning and expanding the People's National Bank of Washington. In 1917 he also was the sole proprietor of the Port Townsend Southern Railroad, which soon connected with the Puget Sound Navigation steamers to provide better transportation for Olympic Peninsula patrons.

The original fleet was a necessity, not a pleasure. Unlike the side-wheelers and stern-wheelers that plied the Sound before steamboats, the little steamers had the amenities of waterborne buses and rolled like tennis balls during a big blow, but they were dear to the hearts of the outlying residents.

His actual newspaper source lost in time, a reporter was quoted as saying, "At five o'clock in Seattle, the little commuter steamers scurry off to their destinations like a swarm of mosquitos."

Typical of the early fleet was the ninety-nine-foot *Dode*, constructed in 1898 from the leftovers of a schooner. She left Pier 3, home to most of the small fleet, one day with passengers and freight for places like Kingston, Port Gamble, Seabeck, Brinnon, Holly, Dewatto, Lilliwaup Falls, Hoodsport, and Union City, retracing her route to Seattle the following day. The *Islander* served the San Juan Islands, largely populated with farmers and fishermen in the early part of the century, taking their produce, eggs, fish products, live chickens and ducks, and passengers to markets— some to the Farmers Market or the Pike Place Market in Seattle after establishment of the latter. Jim Faber, author of *Steamer's Wake*, captured the essence of the small steamer traffic, saying, "To the islanders, the steamer was a truck, an ambulance, a school bus, a hearse and a bearer of mail and visitors. Best of all it was a social hall where, in the warmth of a cabin, coffee could be shared and loneliness melted as the blue-black shores of the islands flowed by."

A typical Mosquito Fleet steamer somewhat resembled an overgrown fisherman's dory, with pointed bow and stern. The main deck was for passengers, facilities ranging from benches to comfortable chairs. Ships on longer runs to the north Sound might have cramped but adequate staterooms, as well, with one porthole apiece, bunks for two or three, and some sort of toilet facilities "down the hall." Below was the working deck with crew's quarters, more day-boat passenger benches, the noisy engine that gulped up cordwood like paper (later oil), and freight storage. A steamer running near top speed could consume as much as twenty-four cords of wood daily, requiring shore crews at scheduled stops to provide replenishment. Above the main deck was the pilot-house, from which the captain could see obstacles in the water and take note of his position for navigational purposes. There were lifeboats up there, too, fortunately seldom required.

The bustling fleet indeed spread out. As mentioned earlier, the *Dode* headed over to the Olympic Peninsula shores. The *Rosalie* served Bellingham, the San Juan Islands, and Port Townsend—a rather circuitous route. Others like the *Flyer, City of Everett, Hyak, Monticello, Sophia,* and *Bellingham,* served Tacoma, the area around Port Ludlow, the hamlets along the Strait of Juan de Fuca all the way to Neah Bay, Coupeville, and other stops on Whidbey Island, and one ran up into the Snohomish River as far as possible—for a time to Sultan.

Navigation aids were primitive or nonexistent, and—like the captains on the Mississippi River—Puget Sounders became familiar with every rock and cove along their route. At night, they navigated by timing the echo from shore, reef, or bank, each with a special sound to the trained ear. Calculations could be made based on the fact that sound travels through salt air at roughly 1,000 feet per second. The system was a sort of primitive, personalized radar and worked surprisingly well.

Home base for most of the Mosquito Fleet was Pier 3, Colman Dock, where Ivar's Acres of Clams restaurant stands. After enduring cold sheds, passengers delighted in James Colman's new 705-foot terminal of 1908, securely enclosed, topped with a clock tower, and boasting fourteen slips for the fleet. At their destinations in small towns, passengers were lucky to have any kind of terminal. Along the Strait of Juan de Fuca passengers often were met offshore by rowboats that delivered them to land.

When the Mosquito Fleet was phased out in the 1930s, supplanted by roads and rails, it had racked up a perfect safety record, not one life lost at sea. There were several good wetting-downs, however. And on shore, at Colman Dock, the cog system on a mechanically controlled gangplank malfunctioned, dumping twenty passengers into the cold water and drowning two.

Perhaps the most spectacular accident, but without harm to passengers, occurred in 1903, when the *Dode* towing the disabled *Bellingham* collided in the fog with the *Flyer*, which then ricocheted off into a German freighter—all not far from Colman Dock in Elliott Bay.

After most of the popular little steamers were retired, a few were used as excursion boats, and the most venerable of all, as mentioned earlier, is the handsome old *Virginia V.*

For more details on the Mosquito Fleet, read:

Faber, Jim. *Steamer's Wake.* Seattle: Enetai Press, 1985.

Newell, Gordon. *The Green Years.* Seattle: Superior Publishing Company, 1969.

The Fraternal Order of Eagles

On February 6, 1898, six men connected with Seattle's theaters met on a pleasant day on the docks. They sat in the sun on a pile of the Yesler Mill logs and compared notes. Because they were actors and bartenders and theatrical men, they had been excluded from some organizations. They were full of good will that day and decided to form their own, a workingman's lodge, one that anyone of good will could join. Then and there they shook hands and called the new society, "The Seattle Order of Good Things." (Some historical records say it was "The Brotherhood of Good Things.")

The six men were: John W. Considine, John Cort, Thomas J. Considine, Harry Leavitt, Mose Goldsmith, and Arthur Williams. Other friends enthusiastically embraced the idea and met later at the Bella Union Theater. The group adopted a constitution, changed the name to "Fraternal Order of Eagles," and, in effect, constituted the first Grand Aerie (a designation that still exists for the headquarters group).

Over a year later, the first local lodge, Seattle Aerie No. 1, was organized. The charter was signed on May 9, 1899, by the following: John Cort, John W. Considine, Eduard P. Edsen, George M. Holloway, Fred Lincoln, Thomas J. Considine, Dr. Horace E. Merkel, Chester Edwards, James Townsend, M.S. Winestocke, L.C. Brown, H. L. Leaver, and R.C. Corey. Since the theatrical people traveled considerably, they sought new chapters in other cities. Cort went to Spokane and Aerie No. 2 was born, to Tacoma No. 3, Portland No. 4, and San Francisco No. 5. By 1995 there were nine lodges in Seattle and over four thousand nationwide.

The lodge was founded on a four-pronged creed of Liberty, Truth, Justice, Equality. Soon after organization the groups assumed social responsibility for implementing such principles. In 1900 F.O.E. sponsored America's first Workmen's Compensation law. Another of the early philanthropic efforts of the Eagles, initiated in 1923, was to promote the awarding of old age pensions to destitute elderly. It was intended that such pensions would enable the elders to stay in their own homes and not be relegated to poorhouses. The effort resulted in the passage of such bills in twenty-eight states and two territories. A Washington Old Age Pension bill was signed February 22, 1933, by Governor Clarence D. Martin. The Eagles campaigned for the national Social Security act, and when Franklin D. Roosevelt signed it into law in 1935, he presented the signing pen to a delegation of Eagles invited to the ceremony.

Walter Winchell saluted the Eagles as the greatest contributor to philanthropic organizations in America. They are active worldwide, with projects such as: 1960, establishment of the Eagles Max Baer Heart Fund; 1967, Jimmy Durante Children's Fund; 1971, the Max Schroeder Eagle House in South Korea; 1983, Eagles to the Rescue in Poland; 1984, Feed the Hungry in Africa, and countless other projects.

The original Eagles have had several homes. Seattle Aerie No. 1 met wherever it could and soon had its own building at Seventh and Pine Street. On February 22, 1925, 12,000 people lined the streets of Seattle to see local and visiting Eagles marching in the rain to celebrate the laying of the cornerstone for a new, $1 million headquarters of Seattle Aerie No. 1 at Seventh and Union, expected to be the finest fraternal group building in America. Eight bands played the "Star Spangled Banner" and fireworks burst in the sky above as Otto P. Deluse of Indianapolis, then the grand worthy president of the order, and Frank Dowd, local secretary, placed the order's special memorabilia in a stone case and mortared it in. A parade followed the ceremonies.

The Eagles building warranted its exterior sign proclaiming it to be the "Eagles Temple" above an entry marquee. Etched copper topped the brick structure. The foyer had gray and white marble walls and wainscoting, and four huge paintings lined the walls, one of an eagle with one foot on a Bible to carry out the tenet of respecting God. All hallways and two ramps leading to the ballroom via a reception area were richly carpeted in red. The magnificent and spacious ballroom had a balcony and stage. The white plaster and terra cotta walls were ornately decorated with etched or embossed arches and other artworks. The ballroom had a hardwood floor suitable for dancing. Big bands were booked into the place; one could only attend as the guest of a member (which certainly tended to attract new members). Columns separated the ballroom on either side from two wings that were set up with tables and chairs for dining. The ballroom was the site of numerous traveling exhibitions, plays, and movies, at which time the balcony was outfitted with theater seats and the ballroom with chairs for the spectators.

The lodge's meeting room downstairs was almost as large and ornate. It was especially equipped for lodge rituals. Meetings were held weekly.

When the Washington State Convention and Trade Center was conceived, the Eagles building was sold. It is on the National Register of Historic Places and was leased by ACT I (American Contemporary Theater) to be converted into a theater for the presentation of dramas.

In 1995 Seattle Aerie No. 1 was located at 6205 Corson Avenue South, not far from Boeing Field.

Mummies on the Waterfront

Since he was a boy, Joe Standley was fascinated by curios, Indian artifacts, and odd objects. When he opened Ye Olde Curiosity Shop in 1899 near Pioneer Square, later on the Colman Dock, Alaskan prospectors, adventurers, and sailors from around the world gravitated to his shop to buy and sell objects—and to swap stories. Maybe it was not so weird, then, that "Daddy" Standley would be approached by a widow, whose husband's estate included "Sylvester," the Desert Mummy. About 1895, two cowboys riding through the Gila Bend Desert of Arizona found the mummified body of the man, half-buried in the hot sand. They carried him to a nearby town for possible identification, but he remained anonymous. He was about forty-five years old, five feet eleven inches tall, and weighed about 225 pounds originally.

He had been shot in the stomach and left there in the desert, where he dehydrated naturally through the hot sands and possible chemicals inherent to the terrain. He had hair, traces of a mustache, and intact teeth and nails. The seller said Sylvester had been in circus sideshows but did not know the circumstances of her husband's acquisition of him.

Of course, Standley added it to his collection, which included such items as dressed fleas, Ripley's name on one human hair, shrunken heads from Ecuador, a nine-foot blow gun, and preserved Siamese twin calves. A Tacoma die maker produced a die to stamp the Lord's Prayer on a pinhead. Another person painted a scene on a pinhead using one human hair as a brush. The Curiosity Shop was featured in Ripley's "Believe It Or Not."

But Standley and his heirs, who still operate the shop, were and are serious artifact merchants, too. Since the beginning, they have had splendid, authentic Alaskan artifact collections—masks and totem poles, all sizes, artworks, baskets, ivory and other carvings, tools, and weapons.

Standley entered selected items in the Alaska-Yukon-Pacific Exhibition of 1909, winning a gold medal. The exhibited collection was sold to the curator of the Museum of the American Indian for $5,000, a considerable sum in 1909.

Standley's own home in West Seattle became a showplace on the tourist bus circuit, where visitors gawked at the beautifully landscaped acre of lawn, decorated with totem poles, shell mounds, bird baths, whale jaw bones, sundials, a miniature log cabin playhouse, and a full-size Japanese teahouse.

Standley died in 1940, but his son, then his grandson and great-grandson have carried on the tradition. The present father/son team, Joe and Andy James, are just as intrigued as their ancestor with the curious and the artistic. Ye Olde Curiosity Shop is a living museum—some objects strictly for show, others for sale, including both expensive and rare works and tourist souvenir stocks.

In the early 1970s a visitor to the shop saw Sylvester and said, "Gee, would you like a female mummy, too?" Before long, "Sylvia" became a resident of the shop. She was found in the highlands of Central America, where she must have been buried in a shallow grave that became uncovered in time. A white female about five feet tall, her body is well preserved and she even has a full head of hair. She is believed by scientists to have been a Spanish immigrant to the New World fatally afflicted with tuberculosis. Again natural dehydration prevented decomposition. It is not clear how she came to be in the possession of the seller.

Still another, less complete mummy is "Gloria," who was identified as a cliff dweller from Arizona by the Smithsonian Institute. She was found in the back of a cave, it is said, where dehydration took place, and was of a species of human averaging only forty-two inches in height that became extinct 500 years ago or more.

Over the years the Curiosity Shop has supplied museums around the world with artifacts, especially Alaskan and Native American art, and retains an important collection itself. Among the museums with which the shop has worked are: the Royal Ontario Museum in Toronto, the Museum of the American Indian in New York, the National Museum of Stockholm, the Smithsonian Institute, and many others. Because of its finding and providing such objects to museums throughout the world, a professor of art from Arizona State University researched and wrote about the shop's impact on collections in 1994-95. The nearly hundred-year-old business has as offbeat a collection of works as when Dad Standley owned it.

The Strike of 1919

Seattle has the dubious distinction of being the first American city to endure a general strike. It did not last long, only five days, and caused little hardship, but it involved 60,000 workers.

The strike took place at a time when there was a nationwide dread of Communists and a fear that Russia and the Communists were going to take over the United States by working through labor organizations. The fuse that lit the spreading unrest was the strike by shipyard workers on January 22, 1919, challenging the validity of the Macy wage scale. To forestall any delays in manufacturing during World War I, a Macy Board was created in August 1917, composed of the Emergency Fleet Corporation (representing the Navy, U.S. Shipping Board, shipyards, etc.) and the American Federation of Labor (representing the shipyard workers). The Board's findings were to be binding upon both.

Seattle's waterfront teemed with shipbuilding, answering the demand by the United States Government for ships, ships, ships for World War I. Existing labor forces were insufficient; the call went out for workers to come to Seattle. When the war ended, the need for ships declined and there was a glut of shipyard workers. Workers who had lived in Seattle prior to the war vied with newcomers for the jobs, causing intra-union strife. Workers were laid off or their wages reduced, leading to a strike for wages at least equivalent to that paid in Eastern shipyards. The Emergency Fleet Corporation's leadership pointed out that they had a contract with AFL, but local workers defied the Macy Board as not having authority in peacetime.

In Seattle by early February there was growing resolve from other unions to stage a general sympathy strike. One by one, members of 99 of 101 unions voted to walk out. After a mass meeting of representatives of almost every union affiliated with the Central Labor Council on February 3, the spokesman announced that a general strike was called for 10:00 A.M., Thursday, February 6, 1919. Charles Doyle, secretary of the convention, added that "The unions certainly intend to spread the strike to other localities, if it becomes necessary, to win." On February 5, Leon Green, business agent of Electrical Workers, Local No. 77, stated that there would be no electric lights anywhere in the city. When a *Post-Intelligencer* reporter asked if exemptions would be made for hospitals, Green replied that there would be no exemptions whatever. Later this declaration was rescinded and the Council said that hospitals and special interests would not suffer. The culinary craft unions made plans to feed people on a large-scale basis, as required. Wholesalers were warned about perishables, because there would be an embargo against items like meat, vegetables, and milk coming into the city.

Heated rhetoric abounded in the city, both by union representatives and those representing business and organizations. Dr. Anna Louise Strong, a humanitarian whose opposition to war led to her recall from the Seattle School Board, had become a labor activist. She wrote in the *Union Record* on February 4, "We need the iron march of labor . . . Labor will preserve order . . . not the withdrawal of labor power, but the power of the strikers to manage will win this strike . . . Labor will not only SHUT down the industries, but Labor will REOPEN, under the management of the appropriate trades, such activities as are needed to preserve public health and public peace . . . we are starting on a road that leads—NO ONE KNOWS WHERE!"

On February 5, thirty-six organizations of "civic, fraternal, business and patriotic character" signed the following resolution:

Resolve, That we stand at all times for a government of law and order administered by the duly constituted authorities, city, county, state and national, and deprecate any agitation or action which would seek to ignore or override those authorities.

That in making this declaration we know that we express the sentiments of the vast majority of the people of Seattle.

That we urge all patriotic and loyal citizens, regardless of affiliations of any character, to discountenance and prevent, as far as lies in their power, any course of action which would plunge Seattle into disorder or bring irretrievable reproach upon her fair name.

An editor of the *P-I* heatedly berated the strikers, saying:

Seattle will not be terrorized; Seattle will not submit to any dictatorship, either in the name of organized labor or the soviets controlled by native or imported Bolsheviki . . . The hair-brained radicals who think they are starting a revolution . . . No organized society will win this strike, which is a revolt against not only 'society,' but against the American Federation of Labor . . ."

On February 5, the *Star* declared under a banner headline such views as: ". . . a test of YOUR Americanism . . . defying the government . . . acid test of American citizenship—an acid test of all those . . . who fought and died. The challenge is right up to you—men and women of Seattle. Under which flag do you stand?"

A statement issued by the Central Labor Council declared:

We hasten to assure the draft-slacking publisher of the *Star*, all the employers who hate labor, and all those who love to lick their boots, that we know exactly what they mean by "reds," . . . "bolsheviki," . . . "cleaning house"; that organized labor in Seattle was never so proud of itself, that it appreciates the reds more for the enemies they have made, that it has no intention of cleaning house to please its opponents, and that the general strike is permanently in the arsenal of labor's peaceful weapons.

As promised, the city came to a standstill on February 6 with a general strike. Streetcars stopped on their tracks, the lights went out, shipyards stood idle. Residents depending on public transportation were marooned in their homes.

Mayor Ole Hanson, who held a union card and was considered a friend of labor, was affronted by the strike and considered it unpatriotic (although some writers say that he was politicking for the upcoming 1920 election). Other officials blamed the strike on Communists or Bolsheviks within the ranks; indeed, there were a few such agitators among labor's ranks; however, the vast majority were patriotic Americans. Hanson threatened to declare martial law on February 8 unless the strike was called off.

Although leaders of the general strike denounced the mayor and Charles Piez, leader of the Emergency Fleet Corporation, they asked their union members to return to work after midnight. The strikers refused to do so. By Monday, February 11, the situation was confusing. Some workers had returned to their jobs but were asked to walk off again until Tuesday morning. Teamsters left their wagons standing in the street to flock to the Labor Temple during the afternoon to discuss the matter. Street and Electric Railway Employees Union members had provided limited service on Sunday and Monday and passed a resolution that further strike action was of no additional benefit to organized labor. Barbers finished their haircuts. By Tuesday morning the strike was over.

Although they were only a part of the striking force, the I.W.W. (Industrial Workers of the World) were later blamed for the strike. Dave Beck, who later unionized most of Seattle's labor force, was adamantly opposed to the strike, declaring it to be pointless and to have done more harm than good to the labor movement, and refused to have anything to do with the I.W.W.

Even though the sympathy strike was over, the shipyard workers stayed out, since they had not gained anything to date. Blaming the strike for its actions, the Emergency Fleet Corporation shut down many of Seattle's shipyards thereafter. Observers said the Corporation had planned to sharply reduce their interests in shipbuilding, anyway, and that this was a convenient excuse to close the shipyards.

The Market, the Heart and Soul of Seattle

The Pike Place Market has a firm place in the affections of Seattleites. It epitomizes enterprise and a free spirit, with 100 farmers, 200 craftspeople, and 250 commercial businesses exhibiting their wares daily to eager browsers. To locals it is simply referred to as "The Market."

They have learned never to go there while hungry, because the fresh fruits, vegetables, seafoods, and baked goods are sure to result in overbuying or eating one's way through the market and ruining any weight-loss diet.

Only about a dozen vendors came the day the Pike Place Market opened, August 17, 1907. The city of Seattle advertised that on that day farmers were welcome to come to Pike Place and to sell their produce directly to consumers. The rules were simple. Parking sites were first-come, first-served. Wagons were to be five feet apart and backed uniformly to the curb. The farmer was responsible for providing a garbage can. There was to be no shouting of wares. A policeman would be present to enforce the rules.

Fresh local seafood, farm produce, arts & crafts, restaurants, cafes, and street musicians are all part of the Pike Place Market scene. Courtesy of Seattle-King County News Bureau.

The first vendor to arrive, Renton farmer H.O. Blanchard, was mobbed by eager housewives, even as his sturdy team trudged toward the Market. His path was blocked, the produce sold within minutes. Despite the presence of a policeman, the Market was chaotic that day with shoppers disappointed at not finding more vendors.

The concept had grown out of a dissatisfaction with commission houses along Western Avenue, who largely controlled and set prices for the farmers' produce deliveries. It was suspected that too much money lined the commission merchants' pockets and too little the actual producers. An activist council member, Thomas P. Revelle, conceived the idea of a public market such as those found in Europe. With the aid of Colonel Alden J. Blethen, publisher of the *Seattle Times*, he managed to spearhead an ordinance allowing such a site. It was located on a level bluff overlooking Western Avenue, adjacent to the Leland Hotel, just where it is today.

The following Saturday seventy wagons came and still they sold out. At first, more than half the vendors were of Italian or Japanese descent, their verdant farms dotting the Duwamish and Renton valleys. Soon the farmers were agitating for some kind of shelter for rainy days and for storage of products until they could be sold. An eccentric ex-gold miner, Frank Goodwin, saw the possibilities of the proposal, purchased land around the site, and built a seventy-six-stall shed by November 1907, renting every one. At the grand opening, Goodwin furnished a dandy marching band and made a speech.

As the popularity of the market grew and grew, Goodwin and his fellow investors built down not up, carving out lower floors that could be entered from the bay side, Western Avenue. Eventually there were four levels to the Market and a bridge to the waterfront. Goodwin kept a watchful eye on the integrity of merchants, and those that loaded a bag with overripe fruit or made dishonest weights would soon find themselves out on the street. He reasoned, quite correctly, that the success or failure of the Market depended on the consumer's perception of honesty.

In their book *The Pike Place Market*, Alice Shorett and Murray Morgan captured the essence of a day at the Market—a flavor still evident today:

> "Pike Place was a hive of activity, where Horse-radish Jerry ground roots into pungent, self-advertising relish; where Robert Maddox told tales of his days in the Klondike as he twisted twine and wove nets which became sturdy shopping bags . . .

You could find almost anything at the Market, from violets to mastodon tusks, sometimes truffles, and always salmon . . ."

On Saturdays an orphanage band gave concerts. A popular attraction was the automatic doughnut machine of the Three Girls Bakery. A big white tomcat, Lightning, belonging to a nearby theater owner, stood guard over the market against mice, small dogs, and pigeons, but he reserved the right to check out unattended shopping bags for potential delights.

Storett and Morgan said that the Market soon became a gathering place for off-duty youths, much like the Mexican plaza serves as a promenade. Competition led to more imaginative presentations of their products by vendors—roses from radishes, an American eagle carved from a beet, price tags created by Japanese in broad brush strokes.

Even during World War I years, vendors from different ethnic backgrounds got along well. Truly the Market was a microcosm of the world. The Great Depression of the 1930s only caused the diverse nationalities to cling together in the common cause of squeaking by in a hostile economic situation. The Market had always been intended as a place for low income people to be able to buy good food, and during the Depression, the poorest became scavengers tolerated by the vendors.

The bombing of Pearl Harbor devastated the Market more than any one event, for a hefty percentage of the vendors were of Japanese descent. Following the orders of President Roosevelt, foreign-born Japanese, some with offspring that were American citizens, had to divest themselves of their property and subject themselves to incarceration away from the coast. Some returned to the Market after the war and were welcomed by their old comrades, but many went elsewhere or took up other trades.

45

Within city government and the business community opponents of the Market threatened to close it down at least twice, and dissension between vendors and the Market owners or city officials erupted occasionally. In the early 1920s there was an uproar when the city wanted to clear away the stalls largely covering the sidewalks of the Market streets. Another argument dealt with the encroachment of middlemen as vendors, instead of restricting the sellers (as was specified by the original city ordinance) to those who grew the produce personally.

From the 1920s to the early 1970s controversy raged over suggested plans to modernize the Market, to raze it entirely, to move it, to make it part of an Urban Renewal Plan with the addition of high-rise apartments, gardens, and the like. Each time the Market shoppers arose to defend the Market and express their wishes to keep it the way it was—an open-air farmers' market.

The matter culminated in 1971 with the successful passage of an initiative that created a seven-acre historical district and a Market Historical Commission to oversee it. Key figures in the long battle between those who wanted to change the character of the Market and build an ambitious plaza district (Pike Plaza), and those who tenaciously felt the Pike Place Market was an integral and important part of Seattle's ambience were Vic Steinbrueck, an architect, and Mark Tobey, an internationally renowned artist who loved to paint his impressions of the Market. They were part of a group of volunteers organized as Friends of the Market, a still operating group. The Friends collected thousands of signatures for the petition required to get the initiative on a ballot, publicized the merits of retaining the Market as is, and buttonholed politicians to vote their way. Instead of Pike Plaza, the Pike Place Market still stood after the voting was over. After the smoke cleared, the managing Commission was made up of representatives of the Friends, the city, and the Market property owners, with the city working amicably to achieve improvements (now that they had lost the Plaza) for safety, traffic flow, and such without actually drastically changing the appearance or character of the Market.

There were new faces at the market over the years. Old faces disappeared, too, notably Nellie Curtis, sleek owner of a high-class brothel that operated out of the LaSalle Hotel across the street from the produce market.

The Goodwins, Frank and nephew Arthur, had sold the Market property to Giuseppe (Joe) Desimone, who ran it— as only an old world Italian could—with charm, total authority, and kindliness. He died in 1946, but his family continued with the Market until bought out by the Preservation and Development Authority, a body created in 1973 to acquire, manage, and development properties in the Market, the seven acres placed on the National Register of Historic Places.

Although buildings have been improved in and around the Market and refrigerated cases have been added to maintain health standards as needed, the basic ambience of the Market has changed little. Residents and tourists still gravitate to the "Heart and Soul" of the city to browse through artistic displays of everything from whole salmon and bunches of dewy radishes to individually crafted jewelry and artworks. Adjacent to the Market derelicts doze on park benches side by side with well-dressed visitors munching on fresh bagels and absorbing the splendid view of Puget Sound and the Olympic Mountains. Musicians entertain, farmers joke with their counterparts in adjacent booths, and small children point at the displays. The free spirit of Seattle is alive and well.

The Floating Homes

You've heard of selling land to unsuspecting buyers, only to have them find the land under water. This happened in Seattle on Lake Union, but subsequent rulings about these lands proved to be the salvation of the lake itself.

Seattle may be exceptional among American cities in having an officially designated houseboat area within its central core. Lake Union is surrounded by commercial and multi-family complexes, but the lakeshore is restricted to businesses directly dealing with marine activities, with allowance at the south end for restaurants and such, plus a section of moorages for floating homes. Houseboats or floating homes have deep roots in Seattle's history.

With housing at a premium during the Yukon Gold Rush and after, those who had fishing boats or work boats tended to live aboard and tied up along Elliott Bay's waterfront. Later the city outlawed these informal moorages, and many boat dwellers moved to the mouth of the Duwamish (Harbor Island). A few impoverished men acquired hulks of boats, barges, or log rafts and built shacks on them, conveniently located to downtown and devoid of rental expense.

At the other end of the economic scale, prosperous businessmen began to build luxurious houseboats in the early part of the twentieth century, outfitted with small engines that permitted one to be a floating gypsy during nice weather. Such boats often were moored at Madison Park on Lake Washington. Madison Park and Leschi Park were the center of summer fun, with dance pavilions, campgrounds, sports fields—a carnival atmosphere. Seattle's neighborhoods had not reached to Lake Washington yet, and the parks were a cable car ride distant. The houseboats or floating homes were a natural amenity for those who could afford them. The first motor-propelled dwelling belonged to

H. A. Chadwick, editor of the *Argus* newspaper; he and his family roamed the entire lake during good weather. By 1905 there were thirty houseboats on Lake Washington, mostly used for weekend fun. Some owners began to occupy their floating homes full-time, and the interior decors became luxurious with polished ebony or cedar accents, comfortable upholstered furniture, electricity, and self-contained sanitary systems. As the century wore on, though, permanent homeowners along Lake Washington used their influence to drive houseboat moorages from the lake.

Lake Union did not begin as the mecca for houseboats; it seemed destined to become overwhelmed with factories and sawmills at first. With the reaming out of a ship canal and locks between the two lakes and salt water, the U.S. Navy even contemplated using Lake Union as a storage basin for mothballed ships. Fortunately for aesthetics, the Navy changed its mind after considering the possibility that an enemy attack could wipe out the ship canal and maroon all the ships.

Curiously, the houseboat community that came along later was the salvation of the lake, or today this gem might have been choked off from public use by walls of apartment high-rises and smoking factories. Houseboats came because of the sales of underwater land.

Some of the early industries included a huge sawmill toward the Aurora Bridge, the Lake Union Brick Company, Barber's Asphalt plant, the gasworks, now a park, and a seaplane hangar/factory where William E. Boeing built his first planes. The tangled legal mess governing property rights along the lakeshore came to a head with the passage of a bill by the Washington State Senate that the costs of staging the Alaska-Yukon-Pacific Exposition were to be partly amortized by selling Lake Union's shorelands. Commercial property owners already had built piers into the lake and, in some instances, filled lands adjacent to shore that they considered their own. Now they found they must purchase the lands under water adjacent to their shore properties. To gain some return on their unforeseen investments, the owners built moorages for houseboats which were beginning to appear on Lake Union—especially since they had become unwanted on Lake Washington (and forbidden there after 1938). They intended to build other, more profitable buildings and docks later on, but by the time the economy suggested such expansion, the houseboat colonies were well established and had become a political entity in themselves.

The early houseboat colonies were unquestionably picturesque. Although afloat, the homes tended to be stationary until it became necessary to have a tug move them to a new location. Some were attractive and maintained with petunias growing in window boxes. Others were mere shacks. Most were the permanent homes of blue collar workers trying to save money on housing. In fact, during World War I and the boom in population due to shipbuilding, the houseboats became an answer to scarce housing. During the 1920s, when shipbuilding had declined, bootlegging in the houseboat colony became a dandy source of income. Innocuous boat repair shops often shored up the bullet-damaged craft of runners like Roy Olmsted, discussed in Chapter 2.

Houseboats proliferated even more as cheap housing during the Great Depression—some as floating "Hoovervilles," or shacks built by the homeless, although more of these were on the Duwamish waterway.

Seattle residents were beginning to complain about the appearance of their central-core lake. Although there were many upright families on houseboats, there also were derelicts, alcoholics, and some prostitutes. During World War II and the increased competition for housing, the situation began to change as families with deep pockets filled with wartime wages were attracted to the houseboat colonies. By postwar years the houseboat colony was more circumspect and attractive, but moorage space became scarce as maritime industries proliferated, pleasure boating boomed, and marinas were built for them.

According to Howard Droker in his book on Seattle houseboats, Washington's restrictive liquor laws led to continuing illegal operations long after the repeal of the Volstead Act. On Lake Union a bootlegger, Russian John, served whiskey by the glass from his kitchen and by the bottle after closing hours for liquor stores. Another fellow set up business on his houseboat offshore, which could be approached only by a narrow, winding pier easily observed from the houseboat. George Wier made home brew on his boat moored near the Aurora Bridge, selling most of it to other boat dwellers. In the 1950s, while carrying two cases of his brew down the railroad tracks near his moorage, he fell and broke both legs, effectively terminating his operation.

Upland city dwellers and the city authorities began to look askance at the pollution and sprawl on Lake Union. The houseboaters were blamed for dumping raw sewage into the lake, although more pollution came from upland residences, for the city sewers emptied into the lake. Newspapers wrote articles about the future of Lake Union, and few were friendly to the houseboating communities—except perhaps those who espoused tourism, for the tourists thought the houseboats a charming aspect of Seattle life. The noose began to tighten when authorities demanded that boats be connected to sewers (although sewers around the lake were not yet built in 1958), or provide holding tanks and pumping systems until sewers were available.

The houseboat colony organized as the Floating Homes Association and battled the city for the next thirty years for its very survival, claiming harassment from city officials.

In 1969 the City Council created the Lake Union Advisory Committee to establish an overall plan for the lake's future, but the resultant plan was not adopted. Two years thereafter, an apartment complex was built out over the water through a loophole in zoning controls, bringing an outcry from both uplanders and water-dwellers. Should this continue, the lake would soon be ringed as a solid wall of such structures. Old rulings about underwater ownerships were reviewed and argued.

After the installation of sewers and other basic amenities, houseboats took on a new demeanor—one enjoyed today, that of attractively designed floating homes largely with upscale owners, a romantic way to live and still of tourist interest. The ongoing arguments of the legal status of the houseboats continued: whether they were taxable, whether they had rights to a shoreline moorage, should they be permitted.

Curiously enough, it was the Shoreline Management Act that helped to bring matters to a head with favorable results for the houseboating colony. Under Mayor Wesley Uhlman, a master plan for the lake was drawn up—one that permitted some moorages for houseboats as being consistent with a protection plan that opposed high-rise developments on the lake and encouraged expansion of public access, maritime emphasis, small businesses and such. Today houseboat living is a coveted microcosm of Seattle's lifestyle.

For the whole story, read *Seattle's Unsinkable Houseboats* by Howard Droker (Seattle: Howard A. Droker, 1977).

Steaming up Seattle

Hissing away under Seattle's downtown streets are nineteen miles of piping to bring steam heat to more than two hundred thirty buildings in one square mile. One would imagine that steam heat was abandoned decades ago, but not so. Architects of modern buildings such as the Washington State Trade and Convention Center and the new Seattle Art Museum chose to tap into the hundred-year-old steam system.

Two plants loom near the waterfront like hulks of the past or—equally possible—weird space age structures. The older one is at Post Street and Yesler Way. It is a fortress-like, reddish-brown, brick building with boarded-up windows and few doors, an assortment of stacks protruding, large and small, just off the teeming Pioneer Square retail area. Tucked away on alley-like Post Street, few visitors and residents notice it until they look up. Mostly it is used today as an auxiliary plant.

The other, more utilized plant is adjacent to and below the Pike Place Market. Painted sky blue with murals, it gleans attention for its color, but few observers can imagine what the building would house.

The steam heat system was born in 1893. The Seattle Heat and Power Company had a franchise to generate electricity with steam-driven generators and to supply water to operate hydraulic elevators. The by-product of excess steam was sold to heat buildings within a radius of two blocks. In 1900 the Seattle Electric Company was formed through acquisition of the former company plus several other small generating systems. The New Post Street Station was constructed to house a 4,000-horsepower steam generating plant and the piping system enlarged to cover most of the business district south of Madison Street.

Meantime, a similar enterprise, the Mutual Light and Heat Company, a subsidiary of the Diamond Ice Company, supplied excess steam from its power and ice making equipment to customers north of Madison Street. Over time, a series of mergers ensued that resulted in formation of

Post Street Power Station, Seattle Electric Company

Seattle Steam Corporation in 1951 and, later, the Seattle Steam Company, privately owned, in 1972. One of the prior corporate owners was Puget Sound Power and Light Company 1912-51.

The maze of piping underlying the city efficiently provided steam for space heat and water heating inexpensively. The plants were built so they could be converted from one fuel source to another quickly and without disrupting service. Oil, natural gas, or electricity (and, in the beginning, coal) were and are utilized, depending on which is the least costly at any given time.

The Post Street Station still has the original eight 500-horsepower boilers in place, but they are retired and have been replaced with a modern, large, single package boiler. The Western Avenue Station has four gas/oil fired boilers of varying capacities and one electric boiler. The original Western Avenue boilers were almost two stories high. In the basement below them, early day laborers shoveled coal as fuel for the boilers, while others shoveled the hot ash residue into rail cars. The whole operation required forty-five men.

Today the modern plant only needs two people, a fireman and an engineer. In addition, maintenance personnel, many of them pipe fitters, constantly check and maintain the vast system. The principle of the heating system is basic: fuel heats water in the boilers to create steam, and the steam is sent through the pipes at 140 pounds of pressure, 361 degrees F. The steam gradually condenses into water as it wends its way through the system and cools. It is trapped, cooled, and discharged to sewers. Various types of heat exchangers within the buildings tap into the system for space heat, domestic hot water, and other uses. That is all there is to it, a pretty simple operation. The operation includes modern air scrubbers and other environmental protection equipment to meet or exceed today's requirements.

A means of measuring how much steam any given building uses is provided, for which the owner pays the Seattle
Steam Plant.

Among the newer buildings using steam from the Plant
is the Washington Mutual Tower. The steam runs through
a heat exchanger to warm an air-delivery system to the
building. At fifty-five stories, it is the system's tallest
building serviced, heating all public areas and used as a
supplemental heat source for the upper floors. The advantage of using the piped-in steam is that a building design
need not include its own boiler system, saving not only
money but providing more rentable space. Also unneces-
sary are unsightly boilers and other equipment atop
buildings.

One would think that other steam companies would
leap into the business. The answer is fairly obvious. The
steam piping system has grown along with the city's
manifold increase in size since 1893. For another company
to try to install all that piping beneath the city would be
a mind and purse-boggling project. A sample of the chaos
such installation would create was already experienced
briefly by Seattle Steam Company. During the construction
of the Metro tunnel that leads into the lower levels of
Westlake Center downtown, Seattle Steam Company had to
reroute or replace many, many of its pipes, a real headache
for them.

As the city continues to grow, Seattle Steam can support
new developments and retrofit existing buildings within the
central business district.

Draft Horses on the P.I. Roof

On May 19, 1950, high-rise residents near the *Post-Intelligencer* building were astonished to see an eight-horse team of draft horses pulling a wagon around the rooftop of the newspaper's building. As a publicity stunt, the Budweiser hitch traveled to the block-square (and hopefully reinforced) rooftop on a freight elevator. It was said that the night maintenance man came to work that evening, took one look at the rooftop, and burst into tears.

Bobo the Gorilla

Some cities boast that President X or Movie Star Y was raised there. Seattle boasts of Bobo the Gorilla, one of the most popular icons of the 1950s-60s. It is possible that Bobo did not realize he WAS a gorilla, for he was raised after the age of two weeks by humans.

It all began in French Equatorial Africa in early 1951, when a professional gorilla hunter who caught and sold gorillas to zoos took the four-pound baby gorilla home to Columbus, Ohio. The hunter's mother cared for Bobo until the summer of 1951, when he was sold for $4,000 to an Alaskan fisherman, Bill Lowman, as a gift for his parents, Raymond and Jean Lowman of Anacortes, Washington. As a boy, Raymond had a pet chimp and always wanted another primate pet.

For Jean Lowman it was mother love at first sight. She cradled the baby in her arms, and for the next two years, she treated Bobo as a human child. She dressed him in T-shirts and jeans or slacks and a sweater; he ate in a high chair and sat in her lap while watching television. He loved to bang on the piano keys and raise havoc around the house, like a human two-year-old (and was thought to have the intelligence of a human of that age).

The Lowmans were conscientious in their gorilla raising and consulted with primate specialists as to diet, etc. When Bobo became too rambunctious and large to live in the house, they built him his own house complete with some furniture, a gym, and toys. In the small town of Anacortes, frequented by summer tourists headed for the ferry to Victoria, he attracted unwanted attention—visitors on the street staring at the home trying to get a glimpse of Bobo.

In an article for *The Weekly*, author David Humphries quoted from Jean Lowman's diary about a typical day in the life of Bobo in July 1953—a relation of events that makes it clear that Bobo had outgrown his human quarters:

1. Breaks dishes or cups almost every day. (But he loved to wash dishes, squatting on the edge of the sink.)

2. Gets into the cupboard where cocoa is stored, takes it and runs out to the backyard. He likes foods better when they're snitched.

3. Rips books and hides boots. He throws tennis shoes into the toilet.

4. He has a blue velvet pillow that he carries around everywhere.

5. He likes to eat the heads off of tiny matches.

6. Bobo is learning to kiss; he makes a pretty good smack.

7. He drags everything he can find outside. Tonight he sailed out the door with a sheet.

And so on, behavior any mother of a toddler would recognize. When a four-year-old girl came into the yard, he took her by the hand to see his toys.

Humphries added that, while Bobo was two, he had the strength of a Seahawks offensive lineman. Jean and Raymond Lowman realized that they had to relinquish him. Even though other zoos had offered up to $9,000, the Lowmans had promised him to Seattle's Woodland Park Zoo and sold him for the modest price of $5,500.

To ease the transition, Jean Lowman spent a few nights in the zoo's cage cuddling her baby Bobo, then gradually reduced the time she spent with him.

Bobo did not seem to mind the separation too much; he had discovered "show business." He became a hopeless ham, clowning around for his considerable and constant audiences. Bobo became a major attraction for the zoo, and management built him the "Great Ape House" at a cost of $200,000—a sum easily recovered from the additional entrance fees he brought into the coffers. A gentle beast, he posed with celebrities, dignitaries, and children on their birthdays. Children brought birthday cakes into his cage, which he gleefully mangled. He loved to pretend hostility by beating his chest and charging at the viewing window at the front of his cage, then seemed to laugh at the reaction of the children. The media loved him and wrote endlessly of his antics.

When he was a mature 520 pounds, the zoo decided he should have a mate and brought in Fifi. Although the two apes became good buddies, Bobo expressed no interest in mating with her. As the darling of Seattle, Bobo was not blamed for the situation; wags insisted that Fifi was too ugly and lacked personality—especially after Fifi was removed to another zoo and two other males were totally uninterested in her, as well.

Before Bobo could procreate, he stunned his fans by becoming ill in 1968 at only age sixteen and dying of a pulmonary embolism. Saddened children cried.

Bobo's remains were given to the Burke Museum at the University of Washington after he was first sent to a taxidermist for his hide to be stuffed for exhibit at the Museum of History and Industry (where it still is). A primate-anatomy student reduced his remains to a skeleton and, in the process, discovered that his skull was missing. *The Weekly*'s reporter, David Humphries, became fascinated with the bizarre incident and eventually traced the skull to a local collector of animal skulls, who admitted he had the skull but refused to divulge how he had obtained it. He successfully maintained his right to keep it.

Meantime, Bobo's pleasant primate face still thrills viewers at his post at MOHAI, the Museum of History and Industry.

Lake View Cemetery

Repository for Distinguished Pioneers and One Horse

Some of Seattle's most revered leaders are buried in Lake View Cemetery on Fifteenth Avenue East, where markers go back to 1850. The likes of Thomas Mercer, John Denny (father of Arthur), other Dennys and Borens, Princess Angeline, daughter of Chief Seattle, were laid to rest there lovingly . . . and one horse named Buck, the favorite cattle horse of W. Irving Wadleigh.

Wadleigh is more well known in Eastern Washington history for his partnership of Phelps & Wadleigh (actually W.S. Ladd, E.D. Phelps, and Wadleigh), who had vast cattle holdings on the eastern slope of the North Cascades. Ladd was originally from Portland, the latter two from Seattle. Wadleigh purchased Buck in Portland in 1871. He was a handsome sorrel Thoroughbred with the stamina required for cattle handling, even in the bleak, windy, snow-filled winters. Wadleigh and his horse were constant companions, sleeping side by side, fording the swift Columbia River, and always moving cattle. Then came the awful winter of 1880-81, when it snowed, then thawed and froze to make an impenetrable crust, not once but several times. The ranchers had not believed such a winter would occur and had put up no hay, so the cattle began to die. Powerless to do anything but wait, Wadleigh rode out on Buck to count his losses in the spring. Carcasses lay everywhere; out of 10,500 cattle only 2,000 remained.

Sick at heart, Wadleigh sold the remaining cattle after they were fattened up on spring grass and retired to Seattle, bringing Buck with him. But Buck was unaccustomed to the damp winter air of Seattle and contracted pneumonia and died.

On one of the highest spots in Lake View Cemetery Wadleigh erected a tall granite shaft. On the south side it was engraved:

BUCK
My Favorite Cattle Horse
Died September 20th, 1884
Aged
18 Years and 6 Months

On the eastern side was the inscription:

"For 13 years my trusty companion in blackness
of night, in storm, sunshine and danger."

On the north the words:

Corraled
In Adversity Faithful

Wadleigh went to work at the First National Bank in Seattle, where he was the target of hostility from many pioneer descendants who objected to sharing their cemetery with a horse, any horse.

About 1918, the monument was torn down. Citizens believed that Buck was disinterred, too, but Irving Wadleigh was evasive in a joking way about the matter. According to relatives, it is quite probable that Buck's remains still remain unidentified in the cemetery.

Longacres Racetrack

Longacres Park was sold in 1990 to the Boeing Company to be replaced by a corporate business park and flight training center. Under a temporary racing association, racing continued until September 21, 1992. It was the area's only major Thoroughbred racetrack.

From 1902-09 the Meadows racetrack thrived on the site of today's Boeing Field runways. The track was touted as a genteel place; management pointed to the special areas for women. Among the added attractions at Longacres were airplane exhibitions; Bill Boeing was a racing enthusiast, and it is said that his interest in producing better airplanes was whetted at the Meadows. There was no pari-mutuel betting, only bookies, about 150 of them by 1908. The following year Mayor Ole Hanson attacked gambling and helped to initiate a bill outlawing the sport of horse racing for money. The legislature passed it, the Meadows closed, and it would be twenty-five years before horses raced for money in Seattle again.

Photo courtesy of the Washington Thoroughbred Breeders Association

Meyer Gottstein and his son Joe, horse owners and enthusiasts at the Meadows, had to content themselves with making a fortune in real estate. Joe Gottstein became interested in live theater and in owning theaters and hired B. Marcus Priteca to design the Coliseum Theater at Fifth and Pike for him. Then in 1929 the stock market crashed, followed by deepening unemployment and financial instability for all. The state government was hurting for money, too, and the possible taxes to be realized from liquor sales and horse racing seemed attractive again. Prohibition was overthrown, and horse racing including pari-mutuel betting was approved by the legislature March 3, 1933. Some of its proponents thought the income realized would fund an old age pension for the state. Moral watchdogs were furious and, with the support of the *Seattle Post-Intelligencer*, tried to get enough signatures for a referendum against racing but came up 1,600 signatures short.

Joe Gottstein was elated. He had never lost his love for racing and Thoroughbred horses. He organized the Washington Jockey Club, secured Seattle's racing permit, bought a site and built Longacres—all before August 1933.

With his partner Bill Edris, Gottstein persuaded his good friend, architect Priteca, to design the race course in one month. A swarm of workers, grateful for a job, went to work and constructed the racetrack, clubhouse, grandstand, and thirty-seven barns in twenty-eight days on a 106-acre farm formerly owned by Jim Nelson. The partners planted poplars and weeping willow trees that grew to become a gentle backdrop for the exciting sport of horse racing.

The first day of racing was August 3, 1933. W.C. Swan was trainer #0001, Joe Hernandez the first caller. Ten thousand fans came to witness the races, and by the end of the thirty-nine-day meet, attendance doubled. The handle (amount bet) was modest, averaging $100,000 daily, but doubled by 1954. A big factor in growth was Gottstein's establishment of a $10,000 purse race in 1935 called the Longacres Mile. The popular race had fifty-seven runnings, 1935-92, was for three-year-olds and up, and the 1992 purse was $250,000 added. A horse named Coldwater, a 17-1 shot, won that first race, and Bolulight won the last Longacres Mile. The race won national interest. Jockeys like Eddie Arcaro, Johnny Longden, and Willie Shoemaker came to ride and win at least once. William "Willie" Shoemaker first rode at Longacres on August 28, 1949, bringing Irene's Angel in as runner-up in the $15,000-added Longacres Mile race. Local rider Gary Baze won four Longacres Miles.

Joe Gottstein was forced to sell his Coliseum Theater at one point in order to keep Longacres afloat. Incidentally, afloat was not always good—the track grounds were prone to serious flooding year after year until measures were taken to control it. Joe was a constant figure at the track and was known as a compassionate man toward the horsemen, pitching in some money if someone was really hurting.

The United States Army took over the track as a supply yard early in World War II and built an artillery barracks behind the tote board. Antiaircraft guns were installed on the track. When it was returned to Gottstein, he and his wife Luella remodeled the barracks into a cottage and often stayed right there at the track. A burst of anti-gambling fever by the "morals brigade" caused Longacres to close for the 1943 season, but it reopened in 1944.

Joe Gottstein followed the progress of horse racing right up to his death from cancer in 1971 at the age of seventy-nine. That same year the track racked up its first average half million dollar daily handle.

Gottstein's son-in-law Morris Alhadeff took over the reins and made the track even more prosperous. Gottstein had expanded the facilities over his thirty-eight-year ownership, including the addition in 1966 of a pavilion area with picnic tables and umbrellas. Alhadeff expanded the clubhouse area by almost 20,000 square feet in 1972 and was rewarded with the track's first million-dollar day on August 27. In 1973 Alhadeff added a new grandstand roof, and the following year the 5,200-square-foot Gazebo Terraces opened at the north end of the grandstand, which featured a unique gazebo with full concession and wagering facilities. Harry Henson turned the calling of races over to his son Gary in 1973, after thirty-five years at the microphone. In 1976 the Paddock Club opened at the south end of the grandstand. Two years later $2 million was bet on August 27, 1978, the day that Willie Shoemaker rode Bad 'N Big to victory in the Longacres Mile—Shoemaker's first appearance there for twenty-nine years.

Over the years, long-lasting or colorful events included:

The Fashion Handicap, 45 runnings, a 5½ furlong race for three and up fillies and mares.

Speed Handicap, 58 runnings, 1934-92, 6 furlongs for three and up.

Tacoma Handicap, 59 runnings—the entire history of the track, 6 furlongs for three-year-olds.

Seattle Slew Handicap, a mile for three-year-olds from 1977-92, honoring Seattle's namesake great. Slew never raced at Longacres, but after he won the Triple Crown, he came for an exhibition gallop around the track.

Gary Baze Tribute Stakes, 30 runnings of a mile race for three and older. Originally run as the Space Needle Handicap but, when popular local rider Gary Baze broke his leg early in the final 1992 season, Longacres Park Executive VP Lonny Powell honored him by renaming the race for him. Baze had won that stakes five times previously. Baze holds the all-time jockey's record at Longacres Park with 1,538 wins on 10,244 horses, followed by Lennie Knowles and Larry Pierce. Since women did not ride during the earlier days, it is fair to mention that Vicky Aragon still stood in fifth place overall with 754 wins on 4,924 mounts when the track closed. She also had earned top rider marks in 1986 and 1988. A local rider who won national honors was Gary Stevens, riding Winning Colors to win the 1988 Kentucky Derby and lead the 1990 purse earnings for jockeys in 1990. Jockey Hugh Wales was the only jockey at Longacres to ride and win races for seventeen consecutive seasons, ranking eighth in the all-time standings.

The Longacres Mile, 57 runnings, was for three and up. Among the illustrious winners was a locally bred horse, Trooper Seven, first to win two in a row 1980 and 1981. Track and barn personnel were so supportive in 1981 that they held banners like "Go Trooper Seven."

The Belle Roberts Handicap, 25 runnings, 1³⁄16 miles for three and up fillies and mares, honoring the wife of Hump Roberts, trainer with multiple championships and one of the founders of the Washington breeding industry. Belle died in 1991.

Warren Magnuson Handicap, Gottstein Futurity, Longacres Derby, Mercer Girls Stakes, Pepsi Independence Day Handicap, and so many others had special significance behind their titles.

Although a major track on the racing circuit, Longacres was known as a family track. Many extended families have been employed at diverse jobs there over several decades. They included the Leonards, Aliments, Roberts, Penneys, Gibsons, Bazes, Whitmires, and many others. The family members worked as starters, grooms, trainers, exercise riders, stall muckers, waiters, and whatever job was available. The track personnel became an extended family for many, no matter which name they bore.

Since there were few Thoroughbred tracks in the Northwest, as opposed to California or the East Coast, many local breeders tended to stay and run their racehorses at Longacres. Among them were: Dan Kenney Stables, Don Munger, Ted Nonamaker, the Vaden Ashby family, and the Dan Markle family.

Trainer Marion Smith, dubbed "Million Dollar" Smith, was one of the most renowned and successful trainers. Ben Harris was the only trainer to win four straight titles, 1989-92, seconded by Larry Ross who wound up his Longacres career in 1992 as the trainer of Military Hawk, winner of the Washington Handicap. Trainer Bud Klokstad aced the final 1992 season by winning fourteen separate stakes races, replacing the prior record of eight in one season. Racing Hall of Fame trainers winning at Longacres included Charlie Whittingham, Jack Van Berg, and Ron McAnally.

J.D. Taylor started as a jockey, then carved a niche for himself with thirty-eight years as a Longacres outrider—the person who "ponies" or leads the racehorses in the post parade, guides them into the starting gate, or captures horses that manage to get away from riders. Jim Worth was another talented outrider. Among the longtime jockeys were Basil James (1939 Rider of the Year nationally), Don and Basil Frazier, Joe Baze (prior to becoming a trainer), Gary Baze, Steve Goldsmith, Philip McGoldrick, and others.

Among the most popular horses at Longacres Park were:

Turbulator, known as "Tubby," who suffered an injured leg and did not start his racing career until he was four. At five, he won five stakes and set a track record. Fans were on their feet in the 1970 Longacres Mile when his jockey's stirrup became stuck in the starting gate and snapped. When he finally got out of the gate, his jockey Larry Pierce's other stirrup failed, yet Turbulator came in fifth. In his career he won twenty-one out of forty-seven starts.

Smogy Dew, a filly, the last to win the Longacres Derby in 1964, also won eight other stakes races, including six against male competitors. The Derby was a thrilling battle between Smogy Dew and George Royal.

Triplane, owned by Allen Drumheller, a pioneer Washington breeder, raced for eleven years, starting 204 times.

Belle of Rainier, a regal appearing gray filly, was a Washington-bred filly that won the 1981 Gottstein Futurity and several other stakes races in Washington, Canada, and California. She remains the leading Washington-bred filly or mare money earner.

Captain Condo, owned by Vaden Ashby, not only was one of the most popular horses with fans, but the big dappled gray also won seven of his thirty starts, plus sixteen seconds and seven thirds to win over a half million dollars.

Chinook Pass, owned by Ed Purvis, started only twenty-five times but won sixteen of them to win almost a half million dollars. He was the only Washington-bred horse ever to earn an Eclipse Award. He holds the world's record of .55-⅕ for 5½ furlongs set at Longacres September 17, 1982.

Peterhof's Patea, owned by Patti Strait and Roger Williams, is the top money winner for fillies or mares in Longacres races—$345,087.

Staff Rider, a two-year-old gelding in 1992, owned by the Jollie Four Stables, led in money won for a single season with $280,549, Longacres Park's last year.

The 1992 owner standings were topped by George Layman Jr., with a record of 64-40-29 out of 295 starts of his horses, winning $262,390.

In 1988 Morrie Alhadeff retired to leave the management to sons Mike and Ken. Under his sons' management in 1990, the track racked up a record daily handle of $1,320,919. Three days after the close of the 1990 meet, on September 27, 1990, the Alhadeffs accepted an offer for sale of the property to Boeing Company. Within hours the Emerald Racing Association was thrown together to preserve Thoroughbred racing in Washington. They cemented an agreement with Boeing to continue racing until the fall of 1992, giving track personnel a little more leeway and earning opportunity. On closing day September 21, 1992, a record 26,095 fans crowded in to bet $3,399,087. After that Longacres Park was silent—no more rhythmic pounding of galloping hooves, no more cheers of spectators, no more frenzied announcing as horses thundered neck and neck toward the wire. At this writing (1995) it appears that a new racetrack will rise at Auburn sometime in the near future.

The records do not tell the whole story of the track, of course. The people involved with the track *are* the history. Recommended reading for its striking photographs of the Longacres racetrack community: Best, David Grant. *Portrait of a Racetrack*. Redmond, Wash.: Best Editions, 1992. Or get the video, *The Miracle Strip*, produced by Stephen Sadis, 1993, at a video store or public library rental.

Potlatch, Prelude to Seafair

For Indians a potlatch ceremony was a celebration where, after one amassed as much wealth as possible, he gave it all away to friends and relatives at a big feast.

Today's wildly successful and exuberant marine festival Seafair, held in July, is rooted in an earlier non-Indian concoction, the Golden Potlatch and simply Potlatch. A Seattle schoolteacher, Pearl Dortt, won the prize for naming it, saying that Potlatch was suitable because Seattle planned to give a good time to everyone.

The first festival was held in 1911 at approximately the location of today's Seattle Center. Bands played, Indians exhibited a typical village, real cowboys and cowgirls twirled lassos from rearing horses.

Thousands flocked to the Colman Dock to watch Eugene Ely, pioneer aviator, take off from the mudflats of Harbor Island in a Curtiss biplane to swoop around overhead as a highlight of the Potlatch celebration. A water parade glided through Elliott Bay; among the vessels were the *H.B. Kennedy* and *Albion*. At 2:10 P.M. on that July 17, fourteen years after the steamship *Portland* docked from its Alaskan voyage carrying a ton of gold and cheering, newly rich miners, a stand-in steamer docked at Colman. The king and queen of the Golden Potlatch event stepped off to lead a parade through town, cheered by throngs of spectators. The king was outfitted as an Alaskan prospector in a flannel shirt, bedraggled coat, and heavy corduroy pants with socks pulled up around the cuffs, Alaska style. A heavily decorated flivver bore the Potlatch queen. There were log rolling contests, military and naval reviews, and motorboat races. A lapel pin resembling a totem pole face and called a "Potlatch Bug" was sold to help finance the affair.

By 1912 the parade entries included elaborate floats. One group paraded as living totem poles; a float pulled by local youths was a Potlatch Bug several feet high.

Behind the scenes in 1913, a riot enlivened the opening days. The *Seattle Times* had misunderstood an episode where a suffragette speaking on a soapbox near Pioneer Square had been hit by a man, who then was slugged by another man. A simple brawl, but the *Times* then was deeply embroiled in anti-Red railing and, since the event took place near the I.W.W. (Industrial Workers of the World or Wobblies) offices, jumped to the conclusion that the speaker was from I.W.W. dishonoring the USA in some way. The *Times* article inflamed Seattleites and sailors ashore for the Potlatch festivities. On Friday night, after a protest demonstration, the group of sailors and locals broke into I.W.W. offices, took papers and documents out into the street, and burned them. They ransacked Socialist offices and printing offices for "Red" literature. Apparently satisfied, the demonstrators simmered down and enjoyed the rest of Potlatch peaceably.

The five-day Potlatch event continued until 1914, after which World War I took precedence. Potlatch did not return until 1934 and 1935. The reincarnation of Potlatch was

timed to coincide with the visiting of the U.S. Fleet to
Seattle.

The Fleet added immeasurably to the Potlatch festivities. Nightly it used its searchlights to create a ballet of light
over the city. Its cutters entered the motorboat races. The
sailors flirted with girls.

Don Duncan of the *Times* described the 1934 affair in his
column of August 5, 1965:

"Paul Bunyan, Dan McGrew, The Lady Known as
Lou and Indians decked out as 'Chief Seattle and his
braves' were big in the parade. . . . Floats were
breathtakingly elaborate, and wasn't it wonderful
that those four-cylinder Model-A engines almost
never boiled?

"There was a junior pageant in Volunteer Park
called 'New Worlds,' and it traced the nation's ori-
gins and its westward movement. Horses ran for
Potlatch glory at Longacres. There were pistol shoots
and archery contests and American Legion junior
baseball play-offs and a sham battle staged by ma-
rines and naval reservists from Sand Point.

"Indians set up camp in Woodland Park, and
when night came they sat around campfires and
played the old 'shellal' game, and there was an
amusement center and fireworks in the Denny
Regrade, and a clipper ship, the *St. Paul* was
anchored in the Ballard Locks.

"Out in Green Lake, outboards sputtered and
little boats traveled up to 30 miles an hour—surely
about as fast as a man ought to go on water. . . ."

The Japanese sent over to Seattle a red *torii*, or gateway,
which was erected on University Avenue between Fourth
and Fifth. And the highlight of Potlatch 1934 was the presentation of Gilbert and Sullivan's *H.M.S. Pinafore*, the
admission one Potlatch Bug.

In 1935 crews from the *Seattle Times* and the U.S. Navy raced cutters on Lake Washington, with the Navy crew awarded the Times Cup. That year the dramatic presentation was "Men Over Mountains," about the history of the Northwest. Sixty-three naval craft arrived for the event and were open for visitation by the public.

Events were added during the decade such as a women's golf tournament, gallery exhibitions at the Seattle Art Museum, and the like.

The last Potlatch was held July 29-August 3, 1941. December 7, 1941 put an end to all the tomfoolery.

Potlatch was revived after World War II in 1950 with a new name, SEAFAIR. Agendas expanded to include jazz festivals, a torch light parade, hydroplane races, and the crazy antics of the Seafair Pirates, who come ashore from a ship or barge, "kidnap" girls or children, wave their swords around, and do a lot of yelling.

The biggest addition to Seafair was the merging of the hydroplane races into Seafair. It was 1951 when a crowd of half a million crowded the shores of Lake Washington to witness a new race called the Gold Cup, and admire Seattle's own entry, the *Slo Mo V*. A year earlier, in June 1950, the *Slo Mo IV*'s owner, Stan Sayres, and designer, Ted Jones, had roared out of Sayre's Hunt Point Dock, turned up the horsepower, and run a measured mile at 160.3225 mph to shatter the prior record held by the English craft *Bluebird*. Going back to Detroit a week later to go for the Gold Cup, long held by that city, the Seattle boat was not taken seriously until she stunned spectators and competitors by her speeds as much as 80 mph faster than anyone else! Her revolutionary design became the one to copy, and there the similarly designed hydros were in Seattle in 1951 to try to best the local boy. They didn't.

In 1962 Bill Muncey piloted *Miss Century 21* to rack up his fourth Gold Cup Championship.

Later popular hydroplanes included *Miss Bardahl, Miss Seattle Too*, and *Fascination*. Hydroplane races today on Lake Washington are so well attended that log booms are anchored along the course to accommodate pleasure boats and their spectator crews, as dense as schools of herring. The Potlatch turned Seafair still "gives a good time to everyone."

The Coffee Revolution

Boston had its tea party. Seattle heads the coffee revolution. And Starbucks Coffee Company unquestionably incited it. The revolution has spread across the nation and, to an extent, to foreign countries. In Seattle and around the Northwest, a grizzled,  muddy patron of a rural gas station doesn't order just coffee. He steps up to an espresso bar and asks for decaf coffee mocha with a dollop of cream or a latte, double milk . . . and does not give the matter a second thought.

While there have been gourmet coffee shops here and there for decades, Howard Schultz unquestionably started the widespread craze for fine coffees. Starbucks Coffee Company opened as a small store in 1971 at the Pike Place Market, a roaster and retailer of whole bean and ground coffees, and expanded to five stores and a wholesale business by 1982. Schultz became the director of retail operations then and, during a trip to Italy, the romance, the ambience, the importance of coffee in the lives of the Italians electrified his imagination. He noted there were over 200,000 espresso bars there and wondered if the approach might work in the United States. Starbucks at

Pike Place Market started brewing espressos, and patrons flocked there for coffee—the suit-and-tie group in early morning (along with a bagel or croissant), the market shopper, even the shoreside derelicts when they had the money.

Acquiring ownership of the company in 1987, Schultz had already pioneered the present-day coffee cafe idea by opening Il Giornale in the city's tallest business building, the Columbia Seafirst Center, soon adding stores in Vancouver and Seattle.

As Starbucks thereafter, shops were opened in town after town, and by 1995 there were well over 400 in North America and Japan. Starbucks is sold by mail order and on major airlines.

Coffee in Seattle has become a part of the Northwest culture. Possibly it is the result of decreased emphasis on drinking hard liquor, but perhaps it is the sociability of having a cup of coffee that fuels the interest. The variety of coffees available requires study, a sort of intellectual achievement when one knows the difference between Gold Coast and Guatemala Antigua or Ethiopia Harrar. Drinking coffee has become an ongoing experimentation, since vendors are willing to tailor the beverage to the imbiber's taste. Basic to the art of coffee drinking in Seattle is knowing the fine differences between espresso, cappuccino, caffe latte, caffe mocha, caffe Americano, espresso con panna, espresso macchiato, and plain old drip-brewed coffee. Before long, the list will include packaged cold coffee products, too.

Starbucks was named after the mate in Herman Melville's novel *Moby Dick* and continues to lead the coffee parade. New competitors are entering the market, though, including Seattle's Best, owned by an ex-Starbucks employee. After all, at a Seattle coffee outlet, the employees know the history of the coffees they sell as well as how to brew it.

Microbrews

Long considered a workingman's beverage, beer was an early favorite in Seattle. Commercial beers such as Olympia bragged about the clean, pure water as a factor of excellence. Teamsters' leader Dave Beck protected early Seattle breweries by refusing to let his men haul Eastern beers into Seattle. That changed, of course, but the small hometown brewer all but disappeared in the United States, and the products of major breweries became quite similar, most a pilsener. Especially absent were the hearty red or dark beers.

In later years the palates of beer drinkers in the United States began to change, as travelers discovered the varieties of beer brewed by small companies in Europe and elsewhere. Guiness, bass, and imported beers appeared on the East Coast, and soon Seattle brewers jumped into the breach. Washington's Yakima Valley is one of the best hop growing areas in the world, and superb malting facilities exist in Vancouver, Washington. Excellent water comes from the high mountain ranges that bisect the state of Washington.

Courtesy of Hart Brewing, Inc.

As a drink, beer dates back generations, especially in Germany and Great Britain. The local brewmaster made his product and supplied it fresh to the pubs or taverns. That's the thrust of microbreweries in Seattle: the product is served fresh. A fresh beer has no chemicals or preservatives to affect the taste. Brewed in small batches, the beer can be produced in a wide spectrum of flavors ranging from espresso stout like a Guiness black—highly hopped, dry roasty—on through the various ales to the pale lagers.

One Seattle company, Hart Brewing Company, known for Pyramid Ale, claims to make a wider variety of beers than any other brewery in the world. The products include stout, ale, lagers, plus fruit beers such as apricot ale, raspberry ale, blueberry lager, plus an anniversary ale, barleywine, with an alcohol content of eight percent. George Hancock, a partner of Hart Brewing, states that brewers regard the variety of beers as accompaniments to food— much as wines are considered.

Among other well-known local brands are Red Hook, Maritime Pacific, Pike Place, and Hale's. All tout their "live product," unpasteurized fresh beer. Factors such as aroma, flavor, aftertaste, and the head on the drawn product are keenly monitored in producing the beers. Microbrews are slanted somewhat to the European taste (they began in local villages, after all) and are not served as cold as the bottled beers to which Americans have become accustomed.

A brand new phenomenon even closer to the old European pub is appearing in the Northwest—the pub or tavern with the beer brewed on-site.

Jazz in Seattle

Seattle's jazz musicians have been greatly overlooked in the nation's histories of music. Three factors contributed to their obscurity even while many performers were outstanding: (1) the Pacific Northwest was considered the "end of the earth" in earlier days; (2) they did not often record their works; and (3) many Seattle jazz musicians were black, and black history was often ignored in early decades. The development of jazz artists in the international and central districts was a natural progression in Seattle.

Seattleites always had an inordinate interest in music and theatrical productions, beginning with the Yesler area box houses and theaters. Vaudeville became popular; indeed, early vaudeville players Nora and Ross Hendrix, grandparents of innovative rock guitarist Jimi, ran out of money in Seattle and stayed on as residents. The famous W.C. Handy played Seattle in the pre-'20s. Among the earliest fledgling stars to play Seattle was "Jelly Roll" Morton in 1920.

The police for years had a "tolerance" policy for illegal after-hour activities starting with such box houses—the days of John Cort and John Considine described in another chapter. Gambling and illegal booze were easy to find. Usually the police received relatively modest payoffs and made token raids on illegal houses, giving the owners advance notice. Seattle never was host to organized crime figures, either, and the free and easy underbelly of life endured until the 1950s when a cleanup occurred under Mayor Gordon Clinton. The legalization of liquor, controlled by the state, also led to the destruction of a wild and free section of Seattle's life.

An early figure in Seattle's entertainment world was E. Russell "Noodles" Smith, a gambler who arrived from Denver with a $17,000 stake won in Tonopah, Nevada, from two days and three nights of steady gambling. In 1917 he and Burr "Blackie" Williams opened the Dumas Club at 1040 Jackson, primarily a social club for blacks. In 1922 Williams and Smith renamed the existing Alhambra the "Black and Tan" at Twelfth and Jackson. The club became widely patronized by all of Seattle; "black and tan" was the term for a club that admitted both blacks and whites.

The action in that area sparked the opening of more entertainment spots—the Main Event, a gambling club,

Bowman's Joint, the Monarch Pool Hall, and the Hill Top Tavern. Among the gamblers of the '20s was George Horne, Lena's father.

As the prosperity of World War I's factory workers grew thin (black as well as white), the Depression loomed. Yet the flapper era had Seattle kicking up its heels. Increasingly it was music that enabled people of color to make real money. Locals learned to play in high school bands or military bands and went into the "dives," growing numbers of after-hours clubs, and jazz centers. Some of the Northwest musicians went on to national fame, and, in turn, Seattle was on the circuit for nationally recognized black and white jazz artists.

The clubs that catered to blacks usually were small, because there were still only 6,000 black Washington state residents in 1910 out of a total of 3 million people. Oddly enough, the failure of the musicians' unions to allow black members contributed to the popularity of Jackson Street, where the music was better, jazz was a real developing factor, and an easy, safe relationship existed between the races. A *de facto* line was drawn where black groups were not asked to play at downtown clubs nor white groups on Jackson Street. An amiable enough relationship existed if a white saxophonist wanted to sit in after hours at a black club—the only requirement was ability. Black musicians organized their own union, Local 493, and it was 1956 before the two unions merged.

Prohibition really sent after-hours clubs and roadhouses into orbit. Since much of the bootleg liquor came from Canada, roadhouses mushroomed along Highway 99 or the old Bothell-Everett Highway. Among them were the Green Mill, Parker's Highway Pavilion, Marino's the Jungle Temple, and the Ranch. In the south end of town there was the Snake Ranch, also known as Red Neck Kelly's. And, of course, two of the most prominent spots, the Black and Tan of Jackson Street, and Doc Hamilton's Barbecue Pit on

Twelfth. At Doc Hamilton's, Oscar Holden held forth on the piano, considered to be the father of Seattle jazz. He took pianist Palmer Johnson, formerly from Los Angeles, under his wing, and Johnson became one of the most important 1930s local stars. Johnson often joined forces with clarinetist Joseph Darensbourg after 1929 and, on occasion, with Gerald Wells (saxophone and flute).

Clubs like the 908 Club, Al's Lucky House, Washington Social Club, Rocking Chair Club, Congo Club, Two Pals, the 411, and Faurot's Hall (later known as the Encore Ballroom), all were popular in the central and international districts. The Congo Club operated as a good restaurant called the Congo Grill, but behind a swinging door was the equally swinging Congo Club, a circular bar and ballroom.

Important singers in Seattle included Edythe Turnham, Mildred Bailey (a white singer), and Evelyn Williamson, foster daughter of Noodles Smith.

There was a fundamental difference in those days between the black jazz bands and the downtown ones, the latter less free and toning down the riffs and rolls of an uninhibited jazzman. Among the white jazz groups were the Del Monte Blue Dogs, the J & V Syncopators, the Rainier Serenaders, Gene Paul and his Seattle Sax Band, Shorty Clough's Melody Boys, and Barney's Jazz Band, whose members mostly were from Sedro-Woolley and played Seattle's Parker's Pavilion. The white bands also played dances and gigs for the major hotels and theaters—Jackie Souders at the Olympic Hotel, George Lipschultz at the Fifth Avenue, etc. Vic Meyers worked the Rose Room of the Butler Hotel, Second and James, a colorful hotel that had figured in Pioneer Square's earlier history. Meyers became famous enough to be aired over national radio on Walter Winchell's show on NBC. Meyers was a true "character," an entertainer and showman at heart; on a dare he ran for governor in 1932 and actually came in second to become lieutenant governor. Citizens were horrified, but Meyers studied the legislative procedure and became a respectable if eccentric office holder.

Many of the white union bands played regularly at the Trianon Ballroom, a long-standing popular dance palace. Jackson Street's groups and black citizens were not welcome there then, which was frustrating to the bands who could not get such lucrative gigs. For a time, Monday nights at the Trianon were open to blacks only, and eventually the discrimination ceased of itself.

Among the most respected jazz pianists of the 1930s, Oscar Holden continued to hold his own, plus there was a new man, Julian Henson, and a lady sometimes portrayed as a Maori from New Zealand, Princess Belle.

A formidable promoter of musical events for years was Norman Bobrow. On February 4, 1940, he produced the first bona fide jazz concert on the west coast at Seattle's Metropolitan Theater, featuring, among others, the Palmer Johnson Sextet. The 1940s saw major stars play the Trianon, such as Duke Ellington, Jimmie Lunceford, Lionel Hampton, Dizzy Gillespie, and Fats Waller. Waller gave a concert at the Moore Theatre, too. Yet excellent local Jackson Street bands were not hired.

Big bands and swing music began to elbow out jazz, but after hours, after legitimate dance clubs closed, Jackson Street jumped until dawn. Race was no barrier to the after-hours crowd.

Among celebrities playing the Seattle scene in later years were greats like Ray Charles and Ernestine Anderson. Anderson was a favorite of promoter Bobrow, who did everything he could do to showcase her talent. In November 1946 he booked Anderson and the Ernie Lewis band at the Metropolitan Theater, as well as Gerald Wiggins soloing on piano, the Gay Jones combo, a trio fronted by Juanita Cruse, and a star list of Seattle supportive players. Anderson went on to big band lead singer with Johnny Otis and later with Lionel Hampton. White Seattle singer Janet Thurlow also was picked up by the Hampton band.

Duke Ellington not only played at the Trianon; earlier he had played concerts at the Palomar Theater in 1934 and 1937.

Midcentury performers who either came from Seattle or played it frequently were pianist Elmer Gill, alto saxophonist Pony Poinndexter, Floyd Standifer, and Chuck Metcalf. Other popular performers were Al Hickey and the Jive Bombers of 1944, Clarence Williams—one of the few guitar-playing blues singers (who still lives in Seattle), Ralph Stephens, Milton Walton, the Savoy Boys, and Dee Dee Hackett (female blues singer). . . . And Quincy Jones.

Jones grew up as a "Navy brat" in Bremerton, Washington, moving to Seattle as a teenager, where he played trumpet with the Garfield concert band and took lessons from Frank Waldron, a highly respected saxophonist and teacher who influenced many early Seattle musicians.

Jones played French horn, piano, drums, cymbals, violin, tuba, baritone and E-flat alto horn, too! His good friend was Charlie Taylor, son of Evelyn Bundy, who led the Garfield Ramblers in the 1920s. Taylor started his own band with Jones, saxophonist Oscar Holden Jr., his sister Grace, pianist (children of the pianist Oscar Holden), and others. Grace Holden soon quit, and new additions included Van Lear Douglas, Major Pigford, Harold Redman, Billy Johnson, Booker Martin, and Buddy Catlett (replacing Oscar Holden Jr.). Promoter Robert A. "Bumps" Blackwell financed them and helped to guide their career. They played senior proms, county fairs, resorts. The band got an opportunity with white musicians to form the integrated 41st Infantry Division Band, Washington National Guard, under Blackwell. After three summers of this, most of the band was mustered out before the Korean War.

Jones was increasingly interested in arranging and was tabbed by Gus Mankertz, a Seattle University music teacher, for a jazz workshop band. (Others were Buddy Catlett, Tommy Adams, Floyd Standifer, tenor saxophonist Rollo Strand, and trumpeter Don Smith.) While at the workshop, Jones wrote his first arrangement. He managed to find Lionel Hampton backstage at the Palomar Theater, played the "Four Winds Suite" for him, and Hampton invited Jones to join his band. However, Jones stayed in school and eventually went to Boston to the Berklee School of Music; he joined Hampton's band less than a year later. The two musicians became lifelong friends.

Jones' remarkable career is well known thereafter. He became one of Seattle's most famous sons, arranging movie scores, producing albums (including those with old friend Ray Charles), and a host of other successes.

Another Seattleite drawn to the Jackson Street scene was Patti Bown, who worked with another Seattle legend, Billy Tolles, and Ray Charles, Al Pierre and others. Quincy Jones helped her to break into the national scene. She eventually became musical director for Dinah Washington, toured with Sarah Vaughan, and in 1985 became a member of the New York Jazz Repertory Orchestra.

Truly Jackson Street's free and easy climate spawned some of the most celebrated jazz artists, many of whom are unsung heroes. From 1988 to 1993, author Paul de Barros conducted and supervised oral interviews of jazz musicians with Seattle roots, a task that has resulted in a splendid book with photos by Eduardo Calderon that finally uplifts Seattle's musicians to the rightful place in the history of jazz.

Recommended Reading:
Barros, Paul de. *Jackson Street After Hours*. Seattle: Sasquatch Books, 1993.

The Floating Bridges

Seattle's Lake Washington always has been a barrier to easterly expansion—a beautiful barrier but still a problem. Ferries in several places bridged the gap between downtown and settlements like Bellevue, Mercer Island, and Kirkland until July 2, 1940, when the Lacey V. Murrow Bridge was completed across the lake. The idea of using hollow concrete

Lacey V. Murrow Memorial Bridge (left) and Homer M. Hadley Memorial Floating Bridge (right) on Interstate 90 looking west from Mercer Island to Seattle. (Photo courtesy of the Washington State Department of Transportation.)

barges connected end to end to form a bridge was put forth by Homer Hadley, a Seattle engineer who had worked in Philadelphia designing concrete barges. In 1937 he proposed the idea to Lacey Murrow, then director of highways. Murrow embraced the idea and, despite derision from various people, managed to put through his decision. At the opening a few half-hearted disbelievers wore life jackets, more as a joke than a real doubt.

Lacey V. Murrow was a highly respected engineer and brother of the famous broadcaster Edward R. Murrow; the Murrow family came from the tiny town of Blanchard on Bellingham Bay. Both young men graduated from Washington State College, now a university. He became director of the State Highway Department at the astonishing age of only twenty-eight.

Locals customarily refer to the bridge as the "Mercer Island Bridge" or the "I-90 bridge." It had the distinction of being the world's first concrete floating bridge and, at one time, the world's largest floating structure of any kind.

The bridge was a daunting design problem for the engineers. Knowing that the long reach of open water could kick up formidable waves in gale force winds, the engineers anchored a barge in the lake, then dispatched a large tug to pass it as fast and close as possible, making the largest possible disturbance, to check wave forces.

When completed, the total length of the bridge was about 1.5 miles, 8,583 feet to be exact, including the floating and fixed portions. The over-water span is 7,700 feet.

The lake has a clay bottom, inhospitable to drilling bridge piers that would hold, so engineers designed an unusual anchoring system. One hundred thousand tons of steel and concrete rested upon twenty-five floating sections secured to the lake bottom by sixty-four massive anchors, each weighing sixty-five tons. The roadway was forty-five feet wide, two eastbound and two westbound lanes, plus four-foot sidewalks on either side. A fixed bridge completed the trip to the eastern shore of Lake Washington from Mercer Island. It was a toll bridge until July 2, 1949.

As Seattle grew and traffic increased on Interstate 90 across the floating bridge, the engineers began to plan for needed expansion. As early as 1960, highway planners designed changes in approaches to the bridge and also the passage across Mercer Island. Soon it was clear that the bridge itself must be expanded, necessitating complex changes to the approaches on the Seattle side. From planning to completion of the changes consumed about thirty years, with traffic turned into part of the system in 1989. To achieve the expansion, a new floating bridge was maneuvered into place beside the original Murrow segment, anchored, and connected to new tunnels and approaches. Traffic traveled over the new section for about four years, while renovation of parts of the original bridge transpired, new tunnels bored, etc. During the final stages of the work, gale force winds threatened to sink portions of the old bridge which had been undergoing renovation. As Seattleites followed the saga in the media, crews managed to save most of the pontoon structures, but some did go to the bottom of the lake. The old bridge pontoons were sold off, piece by piece, for use in other areas.

In late 1993 the whole new system was operational, and crews turned their attention to completing sections that would become carpool lanes, etc. The bridge system is also geared for possible rapid transit rail if that should evolve.

Farther north the Evergreen Point Floating Bridge took off from a point in the Montlake Cut between Lake Union and Lake Washington to span Lake Washington with its eastern terminus near Kirkland. Opening ceremonies took place on August 28, 1963. It was renamed the Gov. Albert D. Rosellini Evergreen Point Bridge in August 1988 (Governor Rosellini served 1957-65), but everyone still calls it the

Evergreen Point Bridge. The total length of the water span is 12,355 feet, and the floating part is 7,578 feet (exceeding that of the Murrow Bridge and making the Evergreen Point Bridge the longest floating bridge in the world). It has a draw span to permit tall ships to pass at a point where the lake is 200 feet deep.

The twenty-fifth anniversary of the bridge was marked by speeches (Governor Rosellini and others), music by the Mercer Island High School Dixieland Band, and a caravan across the bridge by vintage automobiles.

The Space Needle

Some said it was possible to build quickly because the structure was not covered, so that, after the World's Fair of 1962, the engineers could easily take it down, but the Space Needle became a permanent symbol of Seattle. A popular joke was that the Space Needle was a 607-foot building with two rooms.

World's Fair planners were groping for a "gimmick," an attraction that would be like no other. Edward E. Carlson, chairman of the World's Fair Committee, got the idea of a soaring tower while dining at the Stuttgart, Germany, Tower restaurant. Back home, he conferred with John Graham, then building a revolving restaurant in Honolulu, with Bagley Wright, Al Schweppe, and David E. "Ned" Skinner. All agreed that the idea was sound, but before doing further planning, the initiators had to find a plot of ground on which to build and obtain tentative financing.

Bagley Wright, Skinner, Clapp, Graham, and major contractor Howard H. Wright organized the Pentagram Corporation, asked Edward Carlson if his Western Hotels (later Westin) would put in the restaurant, and got promises of money from the Bank of California. Carlson was well aware of the interest in space then; even flying saucers were being scrutinized dubiously by scientists. But the popular conception of a flying saucer captured his imagination as a visual image for the top of the Needle. Architects John Ridley, Victor Steinbrueck, Arthur Edwards, and others are credited with contributing to the final design.

Seattle landmark 607-foot Space Needle dominates downtown skyline in this view looking south. Columbia Center (at left) is the tallest building on the West Coast; 14,411-foot Mt. Rainier appears on the horizon. (Photo credit Seattle-King County News Bureau—James Bell)

Howard H. Wright Company dropped the project in the lap of its project engineer, Al Bek (later to become a president of the company). Most building construction involves square corners, but here was a tower-like structure that curved and weaved in an art-form manner. Pacific Car Corporation tackled the job of warping the steel to shape, finally building templates as patterns for retempering the steel. The odd shapes did not come easily. Special hoisting machinery was designed to raise the steel to the proper level and fit it inside the core of the structure.

Bek credited the welding laboratory personnel as unsung heroes of the difficult construction job. Every weld had to be inspected, and to move the job along, the testing personnel came at night to test the welds. In winter and wind, snow and rain, the testers came in to walk the bare steel beams only one to three feet wide, inspecting every weld. Nothing was between them and eternity. Despite this dangerous task and others, no lives were lost in the building of the unusual structure.

The turntable for the restaurant was difficult to calibrate to exact speed, partly because steel expands and contracts ever so slightly during temperature changes. Portions installed and calibrated one day would be minutely "off" the next. Engineers abandoned the idea of scheduling a full rotation to occur in *exactly* one hour; the rotation does take place in *about* one hour, but don't set your watch's second hand by this factor. After completion of the restaurant, there was a fixed sill at about elbow-level of the diners. Ladies frequently panicked when they found their purses missing; they placed them on the sill, the restaurant rotated, and suddenly the purses were at different tables.

Because the World's Fair Committee was eager to get the featured building erected in time, labor and materials flowed easily to the job. There was considerable concern and negotiation between the builders and the Federal Aviation Administration, however, because of the Needle's height. The FAA had to reprogram its flight paths into Boeing Field and Seattle-Tacoma Airport to avoid the Needle. Before long, airline pilots came on their planes' intercoms to proudly point out to passengers the illuminated Space Needle.

The Needle was taken to the hearts of Seattle residents, a symbol of their soaring "Seattle Spirit," perhaps. "If no one else has done it before, a Seattle person can do it."

Among the people on the first elevator to ascend the Needle officially was a little boy who stepped out of the elevator and exclaimed, "Hello, God!" Two rival newspaper reporters were determined to be the first up the Needle; management solved the dilemma by choosing one to be the first by day, the other by night. Still another lady achieved a little-known "first." Gracie Hanson, who ran a discreet all-girl stage show near the Needle, was allowed to go up on a construction hoist.

The first opening party for the Space Needle was a fairly restrained affair attended by dignitaries, construction bosses, and politicians—an elegant dinner party. Then came the hordes of exuberant visitors that continue to the present day. Seattle's landmark was completed March 25, 1962, in plenty of time for the World's Fair.

CHAPTER 2

People

The Tapestry of Seattle

Seattleites come from the world's people. Most nationalities and religions are represented in the city. As one of the latest frontiers of America the city did not experience the massive foreign immigration of ethnic groups that settled into ghettos; rather, immigrants came as individuals or families. Many of the early immigrants to Seattle were already Americans from other parts of the United States, or Canadians, a mixture of nationalities, largely Northern European, dating back almost two hundred years. These and later arrivals in Seattle trickled in, responding to the possibility of jobs. If there is any single cohesive group in the city, it would be the workers. For many years, Seattle was known as a blue-collar town. The so-called Seattle Spirit is based on the theory that, if you want something enough, you can work to get it.

The Native People

The earliest residents were the local Indians. Chief Seattle's tribal descendants still are a part of the rich weave of Seattle's tapestry but are only a tiny fraction of the whole.

Most of the native people in Seattle have come from else-where, for the original tribes around Seattle were not populous. Certainly the most influential early Indian person was Chief Sealth or Seattle.

African-Americans

Few black people of any profession came to Seattle in the pioneer days. The city's earliest known black pioneer was William Gross or Grose, who worked on the railroad between Seattle and Tacoma, then established a combination hotel-restaurant called "Our House" in Seattle in 1858. In 1882 he purchased twelve acres of land around Twenty-fourth and Olive, gave a few lots to friends, and sold the rest. In 1900 only about 400 blacks lived in Seattle, most of them working in the nearby coal fields or on railroad crews. An exception was Horace R. Cayton who founded a rather conservative newspaper, the *Seattle Republican*, in 1894 and operated it until 1913.

Seattle blacks never endured the virulent race riots and discrimination of many eastern cities, and for the first decades moved through Seattle's life with little problem, little segregation in theaters or parks. Everyone went everywhere. A middle class, respectable, largely black neighborhood grew up around East Madison, where the church and family were central to life. World War I attracted blacks, as well as other groups, to Seattle for the plentiful jobs that were available. Following the war, though, the "war" jobs dried up, leaving many people at loose ends. Some blacks found the music business to be lucrative. (See section "Jazz in Seattle.") As the century wore on, the progress of blacks or African-Americans followed that in the rest of the nation. In 1995 they are found in every profession or trade; indeed, the mayor of Seattle is of African-American descent.

Seattle Mayor Norman Rice in 1995 (Photo courtesy of the City of Seattle)

The Chinese

The Chinese came to the West as railroad laborers. After the railroads were built, many moved into the cities to open laundries or small shops, to the mines, or to the country to work on farms. Because their culture was very different from their largely Caucasian neighbors, those early Seattle Chinese were regarded skeptically by the majority of residents. By 1885 there were isolated anti-Chinese incidents in the mines or hop fields. Before long there were complaints of Chinese taking the jobs of Caucasians and meetings about deportation following the Restriction Act of 1882 that denied permanent residence to non-citizen Chinese.

A few Seattleites like Thomas Burke called for moderation and recognition that the Chinese were just men trying to make a living like everyone else. Fearing violence, many Chinese left town voluntarily in the mid-1880s, even as a contract labor broker, Wah Chong, advertised that he could provide cheap labor—just the factor being used against the Chinese. On February 7, 1886, aggressive groups of men pressured individual Chinese to leave, actually carrying their possessions down to a waiting ship. However, there was insufficient room for all. The police came and, while they were escorting the remaining Chinese to their homes to await another ship, shots rang out and five people in the mob were wounded. The source of the shots was not determined. Federal troops arrived the next day to keep order, but a week later about seventy-five more Chinese left. Perhaps only a hundred stayed on. Because of this episode, the Chinese were not major threads in the early tapestry of Seattle. Much later, in a less hostile climate, Chinese and Chinese-Americans came to enrich the ethnic blend—so much so that the lively international district is sometimes called Chinatown, even though many ethnic groups thrive there. In 1994 people of Chinese descent were the largest ethnic group in Seattle.

The twentieth-century trickle of Chinese people with roots in the international district today include Hugh Chin, who came to Seattle in 1909 to open an open-air produce market. The enterprise became Wa Sang Company in 1928, a store still owned by members of the Chin family, Florence Eng and Ray Chin.

The Gee How Oak Tin Family Association Building at 513-19 Seventh Avenue South was built as a workingman's hotel in 1907 but became diversified later. Another building known as the Great Wall housed the Suey Sing Association upstairs, the Maynard Cafe on the main floor, and a Chinese gambling joint downstairs.

From 1927 to 1981 a Chinese community bulletin board stood at Seventh Avenue and South King Street to serve as a communications link with immigrant Chinese, many of whom could speak little English. The bilingual newspaper the *Seattle Chinese Post* took its place in 1981.

Two hotels were torn down to make way for Hing Hay Park on Maynard and King streets, built in 1975. The pavilion was donated by the city of Taipei. Another heart-warming memorial to the Chinese is the Danny Woo International District Community Garden, a strip of steep land adjacent to Interstate 5 that is open to low-income citizens who want to grow their own produce. Danny Woo was a local restaurateur.

One of Seattle's foremost Chinese-American leaders was Wing Luke who immigrated in 1931 from Kwantung Province. He attended the American University, served in the military services during World War II, and returned to study law. At the University of Washington he was the president of the Young Democrats and later became a member of the Seattle City Council. He died in a North Cascades plane crash on May 16, 1965, but was not found until October 5, 1968. The Wing Luke Museum honoring Oriental cultures is named for him.

Louie Gar Hip founded the Tsue Chong Company in 1917. The firm manufactured Rose Brand noodles and fortune cookies. Four generations of the family have operated it.

In the 1920s there were several Chinese restaurants, popular with Orientals and non-Orientals: Kiang Nam, Twin Dragons, King Fur. Some offered dancing as well as food.

The International District has added more ethnic groups: the Filipinos in relatively small numbers in early years, Vietnamese, Cambodians, and Thai in recent years.

An unusual amalgamation of Chinese, Japanese, African-Americans, and Filipinos organized the International Festival in 1951, still an important part of the Seafair festival.

❖ ❖ ❖

Among the heterogeneous mixture of adventurers, miners, sailors, and farmers who settled early Seattle, three recognizable ethnic groups were particularly visible in the city's life just before and after 1900—the Italians, Japanese, and Scandinavians. They and their descendants have been major players on the Seattle scene.

The Italians

The first Italian in Washington was Captain Giovanni Dominis, commander of the ship *Owyhee*, a China trader that entered the Columbia River in 1827 and again in 1829 to salt-cure salmon for transport to East Coast markets.

The majority of early Washington immigrants went to work on the railroads or mines between 1891 and 1914. They often were hired in groups through a labor "merchant," called a *padrone*, who dealt with the employers. The practice grew primarily from the immigrants' lack of language skills.

Newcastle (site of coal mines) and Renton had considerable Italian communities; in fact, about half of Renton's settlers were Italian, the other half Welsh-English. Alex Cugini came to Renton in 1922, typical in many ways of the Italian immigrant, except for his colorful past. Cugini had been an ambulance driver for Italy in World War I, fighting in the Dolomites at the location adopted later by Ernest Hemingway for his novel *Farewell to Arms*. Cugini (by then an American) received the Italian Medal of Honor in 1964, a half century after the war.

With little opportunity to prosper in Italy, Alex immigrated on borrowed money. He worked two shifts in the coal mines until he saved enough money to buy a horse. Then he worked one shift and cut support timbers until he saved enough money to buy a truck. He quit mining to cut timbers for the Cle Elum dam, then pilings for the approach to Lacey Murrow floating bridge.

Meanwhile, Josephine Belmondo—who would become Cugini's mother-in-law much later—came from Italy to join her husband (already in America), traveling alone in steerage with an infant and daughters two and four years of age. She landed somewhere along the St. Lawrence River and traveled by horse and sleigh to reach a terminal where she could board a train for Seattle. Josephine went to work in Renton at Black Manufacturing Company, a manufacturer of work clothes, and soon became the leader of two hundred workers.

One of Josephine's daughters became Alex Cugini's wife, and from such determined pioneer stock was born Alex Jr., who eventually took over his father's Barbee Mill still operating at Renton.

Many of the early Italian immigrants to Seattle came from related families around Florence. Peter De Laurenti bought out Mama Mustelo's grocery at the Pike Place Market and expanded it to a gourmet Italian grocery/delicatessen, adding another later in Bellevue. In his checkered early career, Alex Cugini had worked with Peter in selling bread for the Seattle French Bakery. The two youths picked up wonderfully aromatic fresh bread early each morning, boarded the train to Newcastle, and sold it door to door. Cugini veered off into lumber and De Laurenti stayed with groceries. . . . And so it was in the Italian community.

Italians also moved into an area around Rainier Avenue, a district of small homes often dubbed "Garlic Gulch," because homemakers grew verdant gardens of fresh vegetables, and tomatoes and garlic for their sauces. Families acquired more land and began to grow produce for sale, prospering when the Pike Place Market opened a stable outlet. Italian Joe Desimone was one of the first vendors to rent a stall and eventually became the Market's owner. (See page 45.) Key vendors in the Market were of Italian, Japanese, and the Sephardic Jewish communities. Desimone got along well with all of them, and, in his memory, the bridge from the Market over Western Avenue is named for Giuseppe "Joe." A plaque in the farmers' arcade honors Desimone, as well.

Hard-working entrepreneurs, the Italians moved into every phase of business. Today Ralph Vacca and Joe Leduca are key figures in the horse racing industry, the Washington Thoroughbred Breeders Association. The Centioli family bought Kentucky Fried Chicken franchises and Pagliacci Pizza outlets. P.F. Rosaia founded a floral business at Sixth and Pine Street; the Rosaias installed their own kitchen to feed their busy employees. With brothers Felix and Pete, P.F. opened the Hollywood Gardens on Second and Stewart. Jules Buffano was an orchestra leader at the Paramount Theater. Angelo Pellegrini became a professor at the University of Washington. A gourmet cook and wine connoisseur, Pellegrini also delighted Washingtonians with his humorous and useful books on food and wine.

And the Rosellini family wove a bright thread through the fabric of Seattle. (See page 117.)

The Japanese

With steamship service from Tokyo to Seattle available near the turn of the century, Japanese came to build railroads, including the extension of the Great Northern Railroad across Washington. They provided about twenty percent of the railroad labor by 1908. Japanese also found jobs in logging camps, mills like the Port Blakely facility, and fish canneries. To facilitate employment of workers, two firms organized as labor contractors and importers—the Tobo Company and the Furuya Company. Contrary to popular opinion, the Japanese worker did not accept lower than average wages, although there were exceptions.

The very earliest contacts (mid-1800s) between Japan and Washington had come in a peculiar manner during the still-existing Shogunate in Japan. Stern rules regulated the size of seagoing boats, aimed at keeping the Japanese citizens from going abroad to be "contaminated" by Western ways. Inevitably, coastal craft got dismasted by storms and drifted all the way across the Pacific Ocean to crash onto the coasts of Washington and Oregon. A few sailors survived such terrifying journeys and were either rescued by the British or taken prisoner by the coastal Indians, later liberated by the British, and taken to the Hudson's Bay post at Fort Vancouver, Washington.

Although he may never have met such fugitives, Ranald MacDonald, son of an HBC fur factor and a native American, was so intrigued with their saga that he pretended to be the only survivor of a shipwreck to enter Japan at Rishiri Island (Hokkaido). He became the first teacher of English to Japanese interpreters at Nagasaki.

In 1868 the Shogun was overthrown in favor of a more active rule by the Emperor and his supporters. The new government sought rapprochement with the West, and Japan opened its first consulate in Tacoma in 1895, moving it to Seattle in 1900. Japan's move toward an industrial society fueled greater and greater exports of lumber, machinery, silk, and foodstuffs from Washington through the port of Seattle, a prelude to Seattle's position today as the gateway to Japan.

In 1896 the first ship from Japan, the *Miike Maru*, entered Seattle, and before long, immigrants to America came to learn and to work. Most came to the Miike Maru Arrival Site that opened following the arrival of the ship.

Japanese families opened small businesses utilizing all members of the family. Others acquired inexpensive lands in the Renton valley and farmed. Before World War II, the Japanese made up a significant percentage of vendors in the Pike Place Market.

Boardinghouses and small hotels in the Jackson Street area catered to Japanese immigrants, and a Jackson Street Baptist church offered English lessons and a center for lonely Japanese, mostly men, to gather. At first there was no particular prejudice against the Japanese of the vicious type that had been directed against the Chinese; that came later.

The immigrants were a peaceful, quiet people, hard working and frugal, good citizens. However, unemployed Americans believed the Japanese were taking their jobs, and immigration was gradually curtailed. The "Gentlemen's Agreement" of 1908 restricted immigration of new laborers but permitted the wives and families of men already in the United States to join them. This led to the interesting "picture bride" period, where Japanese men arranged for women to join them in the United States from mere pictures of their prospective wives (since there were few marriageable Japanese women in the United States). Then in 1911 the Treaty of Commerce & Navigation allowed Japanese immigrants to own land only for nonagricultural purposes, followed by the 1913 Alien Land Law aimed at Japanese who tried to circumvent the land laws by registering the land in their Japanese-American offspring's names. Finally in 1921 the Alien Land Law prevented any noncitizens from owning land, and in 1924 the Oriental Exclusion Act restricted immigration completely. Japan itself was—to a small extent—a rather silent collaborator in these laws, for the government was increasingly disturbed at the numbers of its productive citizens leaving their country. Officially, though, Japan denounced the laws.

One of the earliest Japanese businesses still standing is the Higo Variety Store on Jackson Street, founded before 1913 by Sanzo Murikama. Today it is operated by two of his daughters, Aya and Masako. An unusual number of Japanese or Japanese-Americans owned drugstores, the druggist sometimes also dispensing medical advice. They included Main Drug, Gosho Drug, Izumi Drug, State Drug, Tokuda Drug, Bishop Drugs and Soda Fountain, and Arizumi Drug. Iku Arizumi and her sister Kuyo were the first women graduates of the University of Washington School of Pharmacy.

At least two interesting hotels were Japanese-owned. The Panama Hotel was a 1910 workingman's hotel which stored the possessions of many Japanese evacuated during World War II. The Northern Pacific Hotel, a six-story structure built in 1914 by Niroka "Frank" Shitamae, existed until the 1950s. For many years it was the only hotel with an elevator and a sink in each room. Three early Japanese-American restaurants were the Nikko Low, the Gyokko-ken, and Ma's Cafe. Another, the Puget Sound Cafe, was in the Puget Sound Hotel, demolished in December 1992.

By 1917 nearly six thousand Japanese called Seattle home, employed in extremely diverse industries from newspapers and banks to drugstores, although about a third were general laborers. The Japanese businessmen joined clubs and service organizations, but some were segregated. No Japanese were permitted to join the better private social clubs, so some businessmen decorated a room at the Olympic Hotel around 1930 to use as a club. Almost all doors were open to the immigrant businessman Masajiro Furuya, who prospered and also used his wealth to assist other immigrant businessmen and students. For the most part, despite some prejudice, the Japanese people blended into the tapestry of Seattle quite well.

A large number of Japanese were able to lease land, and prior to World War II, on Bainbridge Island alone, forty-three farms were operated by Japanese or Japanese-Americans. A big crop was rhubarb grown in greenhouses, one of only three places in the United States where this was done.

In response to the prejudice and misunderstandings about Japanese immigrants, whose failure to learn English and tendency to stay to themselves separated them from Americans, the Japan Society of Seattle (later renamed Japan-America Society) was formed in 1923 to foster understanding of the Japanese culture and trade with Japan. The initial members included such Seattle non-Japanese luminaries as Judge Thomas Burke and Reginald Parsons of the Dexter Horton National Bank. The organization still is a strong one, composed of business leaders, persons of Japanese descent, and a few Japanese nationals now working in the United States, including representatives of major companies such as Mitsubishi.

During the first three decades of this century, the native arts and crafts of the Japanese began to blossom in Seattle, partly as a means of reflecting Japanese life. There was a Rainier Ginsha, a haiku club still in existence. Dance flourished under the Sho Fu Kai (Pine Wind Club). Most important of all was the organization in 1923-24 of the Seattle Camera Club, all Japanese photographers. The first leader was Dr. Kyo Koike, who had plied his trade since 1916 in the Empire Hotel Building on Main Street.

An arts magazine declared that all the world was a picture to the Japanese. During only a five-year period the Japanese photographers produced a startling number of renowned photographers, including Frank Kunishige, Y. Morinaga, Dr. Koike, Y. Inagi, H. Onishi and others. Koike's work hung in the Frederick and Nelson salon during 1920, and he received awards in photographic magazine competition. In the 67th Royal Photographic Society of Great Britain salon, only twelve of the one hundred fifty-four photographs hung were from the United States, and three of those were by a Caucasian member of the Seattle

Camera Club, Ella McBride. In 1927 a survey showed twenty-one members of the club had made successful submission to salons and competitions of two hundred eighty-four prints. Despite the ability of the club members, the Seattle Camera Club disbanded in October 1929 because of the sharply declining economic conditions.

Three well-known Japanese painters of the era were Takuichi Fujii, Kenjiro Nomura, and Kamekichi Tokita. The latter two operated the No-To Sign Company near Sixth and Main and "moonlighted" as fine artists. The Northwest Annual show, which began in 1916 and was absorbed into the Seattle Art Museum in 1933, hung some of these artists' works. A contemporary artist and retired professor of art at the University of Washington, George Tsutakawa, is particularly respected for his development of wood and metal sculptures and fountain sculptures that are commissioned from abroad as well as the United States. Paul Horiuchi, a cohort of Mark Tobey, is famous for his unusual collages.

The friction resulting from the Alien Land Act and Exclusion Act not only was abrasive on Seattle community relationships but led to a reduction in exports from Seattle to Japan. The Exclusion Act was not rescinded until 1952, and the Alien Land Law was repealed in 1966. However, prior to the renewed bad feeling of World War II, the ice was thawing gradually. In March 1928 a Catholic bishop from Japan, Bishop Januarius Hayasaka, came to visit Seattle and read a mass at St. James Cathedral. There was considerable outreach by the Japanese community to explain their customs and history through social events. In January 1930 the Japanese Association of Seattle, representing 2,500 Japanese residents, planted 3,500 cherry trees at Seward Park. On April 7, 1934, Perry Day was celebrated in Seattle, the eightieth anniversary of the signing of Commodore Perry's Treaty of Kanagawa with the Japanese. Baroness Shizue Ishimoto was an interesting visitor to Seattle in

1937, speaking to the Japan Society on "Modern Women in Japan," commenting on the necessity of respecting the past but looking to the more modern role of women.

As citizens of a new land, some Japanese turned to Christianity instead of their usual Buddhism. One of the earliest Japanese churches was St. Peter's Episcopal founded in 1908 by Dr. Herbert Henry Gowen. Gowen gave sermons in Japanese there for a while, as he had learned the language while living in Hawaii. Gowen was an influential Seattle educator who founded the University of Washington School of International Studies and was a member of the Japan-America Society. In 1929 he received the Order of the Sacred Treasure, Third Class, from the Emperor of Japan.

Mary Jane Hashisaki of Bellingham, Washington, has lived through the pre-war and post-war periods in Seattle. The American-born daughter of 1908 immigrants, she lived in the international district. She talks of the old ones and their practice of both old and new ways. A traditional man was her father-in-law, Sueji Hashisaki, who worked on the railroad in Montana and, one day, walked into the Fujin Home for single women and asked if there was anyone from Sendai City, Japan. There was; he proposed on the spot, got married, and returned to Montana. They and their seven children lived happily ever after. Things were more American when Mary Jane was in school.

Most Japanese children went to Bailey Gatzert Elementary or Minor Elementary, and in high school to Garfield, Franklin, or Broadway. She remembers the formidable football-starring brothers Yanagimachi, four of them who played for Garfield High in the 1930s. She went to Mary Knoll, a private Catholic school, because Japanese language classes were part of the curriculum as well as English. Mary Knoll was a mission formed to work with the Japanese of Seattle. It was later torn down to make way for medical buildings near Providence Hospital.

GARFIELD.S PERFECT PLAY 1933 CHAMPIONSHIP GAME VS. LINCOLN

Harry Yanagimachi, pictured here as the lead blocker, was a stand-out on the 1933 Garfield High championship football team. The Yanagimachi brothers—Mako, Harry, Bill, and Frank—were star athletes, both in school and in Japanese community leagues. (Photo courtesy of Margaret Yanagimachi & Wing Luke Asian Museum)

Hashisaki's life revolved around the Catholic church; other Japanese children's lives revolved around the Buddhist temples and sports. Journalist James Sakamoto of the *North American Post*, a sports enthusiast who was almost blind from a boxing injury, made sure his firm sponsored the Pacific Basketball League and Pacific Baseball League for Japanese youths. Until Pearl Harbor Japanese family lives were much like that of other Americans.

All that changed drastically thereafter. Adult American citizens of Japanese descent were asked to move away from the coast, and many went to Spokane, Salt Lake City, or Denver. Aliens, often with American-born children, were warned that they would be evacuated to internment camps. Although a shocking situation for Seattle's Japanese, they received better treatment than the much-publicized incidents in California. They were given enough time to prepare, to put their cars on blocks in a garage, to sell their businesses or homes, to put possessions in storage. *Most* were able to make arrangements to live through this trying time; some were forced by unscrupulous officials into selling businesses or possessions at ridiculous prices. When they came back, the majority were able to resume their lives, but others found their possessions stolen or businesses taken or wrecked.

Most Seattle Japanese were sent to camps in Minidoka, Idaho, living in new army-style barracks, eating and doing laundry in centralized facilities. Some went to less favorable Tule Lake, California. The worst part of the evacuation period was that the camps were not yet ready to receive them, and Japanese from comfortable homes were forced to live for about five months at the Puyallup Fairgrounds, twenty miles from Seattle, in what had been horse stalls.

A Nisei or second-generation American Japanese, Gordon Hirabayashi, indignantly refused to obey the order to leave. He was a senior at the University of Washington, a vice president of the University YMCA, and a conscientious objector. He ignored the order requiring Japanese to register and the curfew. After most Japanese had left the city, he surrendered to the court, declaring that to comply with the army's orders for evacuation would be giving consent to wrong principles. He was tried and spent three months in prison. Although he appealed to the Ninth Circuit, then to the United States Supreme Court, he lost. The basis of the decision was that in wartime a government could suspend a citizen's rights if deemed necessary. Hirabayashi served another nine months' detention in the King County jail and continued his resistance to compliance, which eventually got him still another year, this time in federal prison. After the war he finished his B.A. degree at the University of Washington. Almost fifty years later he was able to obtain an order vacating his conviction. At least two others pursued a similar course of protest.

Fervently wanting to prove their loyalty to the United States, many young men volunteered to serve in the armed forces, and the prowess in Italy, especially, of the 442nd Division and 100th Battalion (Hawaii) is well known. Among those giving their lives during the Italian campaign was Mary Jane Hashisaki's brother.

Life was difficult for those returning to Seattle after World War II. The raw wounds of battle were still fresh, especially in the minds of returning soldiers from the Pacific. To them a Japanese face was an unsettling reminder of agonizing times. Yet a memorial was erected in honor of fifty-four Nisei War Dead at Lake View Cemetery. They served in Italy, the Aleutians, Guadalcanal, Leyte, India, Burma, and the Ryukus.

But time and new generations changed attitudes gradually. Indeed, by the 1960s and 1970s Seattleites had a keen interest in the Japanese culture. Trade was booming with Japan. Today discrimination has all but disappeared.

Among those from the Japanese-American community who have particularly contributed to the tapestry of Seattle are Dr. Bessie Inouye, a graduate of Pennsylvania Women's Medical School (which she attended during the war years), who came back to open a family practice in Seattle and has won awards for her contributions to the people of the city; Paul Horiuchi, an artist known nationally; Mary Jane Hashisaki, an American banished in her senior year of high school to be with her parents in an internment camp, who became a lecturer at Western Washington University; and C. Kimi Kondo, a judge of the Municipal Court of Seattle. Uwajimaya and Kinokuniya Book Stores are stores that include Oriental specialties and crafts. Tomio Moriguchi, who was president of Uwajimaya, is a member of the Federal Reserve Board. Aki Kurose of Laurelhurst school is a teacher who has been awarded numerous prestigious honors. Today doctors, dentists, architects, carpenters, and virtually every trade have their Japan-American members.

Seattle has a sister port relationship with Kobe, Japan. According to the 1990 census, Washingtonians of Japanese ancestry constitute about .7 percent of the population; perhaps half of them live in the Seattle area, or about 17,000 people.

The Scandinavians

Early Scandinavian immigrants came to Seattle in stages, most settling first in the Midwest before moving on to the Northwest after the railroads were built. In fact, Scandinavian immigrants helped to build the Northern Pacific and Great Northern, side by side with Italians and Japanese. James J. Hill of the Great Northern has been quoted as saying, "Give me enough Swedes and I'll build a railroad through hell."

The Pacific Northwest was very receptive to the skills of Scandinavians—loggers, fishermen, farmers, trades familiar to them. Most had left their homelands because of poor economic conditions for laborers, or because of the inheritance system which left all to the eldest son. Prior to the Civil War, Scandinavian immigrants were from landowning families or had some money; later ones, especially around the turn of the century, came in dire straits.

It wasn't easy to be Scandinavian. In Seattle before 1890 the majority of heavy work was performed by Scandinavians and Northern Europeans; later on it was Italians and Russians. Nonetheless, the Scandinavians delighted to get jobs at all. A housemaid might make three dollars a week plus board and room and considered herself lucky. Thursday and Sunday afternoons were maid's day off, and scores of young women went downtown to shop and socialize. Soon young men were "happening" to take those afternoons off, too, and many Scandinavian maids were married within three to four years of arrival.

Farmhands were treated almost as indentured servants, with a hovel for a room, poor food, and a conduct-book always with them in which employment and dismissal dates were recorded. No book, no job. Loggers of all nationalities were treated little better, with double-deck bunks in drafty shacks to call home. One had to make his way at his own expense from hiring hall to job and bring bedding. It was among loggers, many of them Scandinavian, that the initial organizers of the International Workers of the World found sympathy. Their demands did not seem unreasonable, basically (1) an eight-hour day with Sundays and holidays off, (2) a minimum wage of sixty dollars plus board, (3) wholesome food served in porcelain dishes, (4) sanitary sleeping quarters and warm blankets furnished by management, a dry room, laundry room, and showers, (5) free hospital care, (6) five dollars per day for river drivers, (7) two paydays per month with bank checks without discounts, (8) all men to be hired from the hiring hall and given free transportation to the job, (9) no discrimination. Nonetheless, in the early century the idea of workers' rights was considered revolutionary, and blood was shed during worker uprisings. By the second decade the labor union movement was infiltrated to an extent by truly subversive elements who disturbed the workers who were clamoring only for fair treatment, not revolution of the masses.

An early Danish immigrant, Ferdinand Hurop, was one of the most ardent advocates for workers' rights and unions. In 1893 he came to Seattle as a farmer and had been an editor of *The Social Democrat* in Chicago, a leader of a Danish settlement in Virginia, and author of articles for both Danish and Danish-American publications. Most Danes, however, were tradesmen or farmers, readily assimilated into the tapestry of Seattle. Notable businesses today that came from the Danish community are Molbak's Nursery of Woodinville, ScanDesign Furniture, and Larsen Brothers Bakery. Hans Marius Hansen, his wife, Anna, and children immigrated in 1907, and in 1913 started Sea View Greenhouse and Florists. Son Henry Hansen continued the business after his parents' death and during World War II managed two sets of greenhouses for Japanese owners who were interned, too. Hansen's Georgetown Florist still operates. Paul Mortenson came to the United States in 1888 and to Seattle in 1925. In 1943 he purchased property in Kirkland and operated Bonney Brook Nursery, specializing in begonias and rhododendrons.

The Danish Brotherhood lodge 29 was founded in 1888 to serve social needs and provide assistance for Danish people.

Although a small contingent in Seattle, in 1887 Indride Indridason and Bogie Bjornsson were the first Icelandic settlers in Seattle. They and about fifteen other Icelanders resided around Smith Cove.

The Finns tended to settle around Astoria and elsewhere, but in Seattle a small group of settlers is remembered by the naming of Finn Hill and Little Finn Hill on the east side of Lake Washington. Finn Oscar A. Wirkkala was credited with inventing many labor-saving devices for forest industries.

It was the Norwegians and Swedes who were woven into the fabric of Seattle in rather large numbers, particularly in Ballard, a separate town from its incorporation in 1890 until 1907, when it was annexed to Seattle. In 1900 there were 1,642 first-generation Norwegians in Seattle and another 2,577 of Norwegian parentage. By then, the Norwegians dominated certain trades, comprising about one-third of all fish and oystermen in Washington, a heavy percentage of the loggers, and soon fully 95 percent of schooner fleet sailors and 95 percent of the skippers. Indeed, the schooner fleet was referred to as the Scandinavian navy.

Conditions aboard ships were not always ideal, and in 1887 Andrew Furuseth became interested in the plight of sailors, becoming secretary of the Sailors Union of the Pacific Coast. He worked through Washington, D.C., sources to foster legislation to protect sailors and became well known in the seamen's unions.

Andrew F. Foss and wife Thea had no plans to engage in maritime activities when they first arrived in Seattle. After getting settled in 1889, Andrew left town for a construction job, and while he was away, Thea bought a rowboat and began to rent it out. She made money and bought more boats to be used as water taxis and for carrying supplies to ships. When Andrew returned, he found his wife Thea had made more money than he, so he joined her in building more launches and tugboats. Before long the Foss Maritime Company became and remains a major business, with its tugs named after various family members. Thea Foss was always very active in the operation, and the film *Tugboat Annie*, was based on her life.

One of Seattle's most beloved Norwegian-Americans was Ivar Haglund, founder of Ivar's restaurants. (See page 127.)

In 1892 Louis Foss, a Tacoma Democrat, was the first Norwegian to be elected to the state senate. Ole Hanson was elected mayor of Seattle in 1918 and had to deal with the General Strike of 1919. Arthur Langlie was governor of Washington from 1940-57, and more recent politicians of Norwegian descent were Henry M. Jackson and Warren Magnuson.

Sivert E. Sagstad came to Ballard in 1905 and opened a shipbuilding concern that provided at least 300 fishing vessels to the fleet.

The Norwegians were socializers. They organized the first Sons of Norway lodge in February 1910, and the Daughters of Norway, Valkyrien Lodge No. 1 in 1905. The Norwegians loved to ski, and the Seattle Ski Club was formed in 1928 by Norwegians, who held the first jumping tournament at Snoqualmie Pass in 1929.

They loved to sing, too, and started thirteen singing clubs in the Pacific Northwest as part of the Norwegian Singers Society of America. Annual festivals have been held, and in 1979 Mayor Charles Royer proclaimed May 17 as a permanent Norwegian Day in the city of Seattle, honoring Norwegian Constitution Day, first celebrated May 17, 1889.

Another colorful Norwegian immigrant was John "Klondike" Eriksen, who amassed $350,000 in gold during one mining season. Peter D. Wick came from Norway and after 1932 developed Wick Construction Company, one of the largest in Seattle.

In 1892 the Scandinavian-American Bank was organized in Seattle, the first of its kind west of Minneapolis.

Swedes followed many of the same paths as Norwegians, and non-Scandinavians tended to call all Scandinavians "Swedes." Some may have come to trap for Hudson's Bay Company before Seattle was even an idea. No one is sure just who were the first to arrive, but there was a Valhalla (Swedish secular society) chapter called Freja in Tacoma as early as 1884, so undoubtedly there were others in Seattle. On the Olympic Peninsula, a Swedish family named Olson settled among the Quinault Indians and had a team of trained elk instead of horses.

Axel Holman and Charles J. Johnson worked on the Cascade railroad tunnels. Alfred H. Anderson was a builder of railroads, sawmills, etc. He gave the state of Washington a large tract of land in Clallam County as a hunting reserve and donated the College of Forestry Building at the University of Washington.

John Anderson operated the Lake Washington Shipyards and was the owner of some of the Mosquito Fleet
boats. Karl J. Nordstrom was a naval architect who designed
early craft including the *North Coast, Skagit Belle, F.E.
Lovejoy*, and the USS *Harris*.

The area around Eighth Avenue and Howell in Seattle
was dubbed "Snoose Junction." There the Scandia Bakery
and Cafe was the hangout for Swedes; a few blocks away was
the Kaffe Stoa of Norwegians. The Scandia served pancakes
with lingonberries, waffles, soup, and for twenty cents one
could get a pot of coffee, a slice of wienerbrod, one of carda-
mom bread, and three cookies. Three take-out salt herrings
went for a quarter. Hard tack was popular, furnished by a
Mr. Johnson whose shop site is now under the Seattle
Center cement. The Scandia was started by Gust and Anna
Backman in 1908, and one illustrious later owner was
Emmett Watson. The whole restaurant was moved to the
Pike Place Market and some of the original fixtures have
been retained.

The Scandia ran a boarding house for single Swedes, as
did Peter and Helga Hilmo on Capitol Hill and Linnea Lien
on Melrose. To serve the needs of single, transient Swedish
loggers, sailors, and others, the Swedes organized the Good
Samaritan Society in about 1910. Transients stayed there
while in town and had their mail addressed to the Society.
In 1920 Otto R. Karlstrom founded the Lutheran Mission
and soon changed the name to the Compass Mission, now
the Lutheran Compass Center. In its first year of operation
it served 10,000 meals.

Another Swede founded the Millionair Club in 1921.
Martin Johanson had a real estate office at First and Yesler
and felt sorry for the homeless men milling around near his
office. He bought and donated a building at 98 Main Street
as the Millionair Club. It is now at 2515 Western Avenue and
still advocates work as a means of preserving self-respect.

Anyone who wants a job—moving furniture, digging ditches, whatever—merely stands ready to do so on any morning, and employers come along to offer whatever jobs they have.

The Swedes, too, had social and secular lodges. They organized Vasa Lodge chapters. Folk dancing has always been popular among Swedes, and in recent years, Gordon Tracie of Seattle has organized a Swedish Folk Dance Society to dance at a midsummer folk festival.

The Swedes have woven a large swath into the tapestry of Seattle. C.J. Erickson was a major contractor who built part of the sewer system of Seattle and the dry dock building at Bremerton. John Isaacson, a country blacksmith, eventually started the large Isaacson Iron Works, manufacturing anchors, logging gear, etc. Gus Sundberg of Ballard was such a wonderful tailor that his suits have graced the pages of *Fortune* and *Life* magazines. Most familiar to all were the founders of Seattle's major department stores, Frederick & Nelson and Nordstrom's.

Nels B. Nelson came from Colorado in the spring of 1891 at age thirty-seven, after making and losing a fortune there. A friend offered him a three-way partnership in a used furniture store, and before long, the store was thriving on Second Avenue. The men were innovative. They picked up and delivered and offered credit terms. It is said that the store's first credit customer was Princess Angeline, Chief Seattle's daughter, who bought a stove and paid for it over time by bringing in baskets and mats. Frederick & Nelson also brought meals to the old princess when she was infirm.

During the panic of 1893, Frederick & Nelson dealt with their customers' cash shortages by accepting bartered shingles, gold, firewood, and even laundry services. James Meecham and Mr. Siles were partners in the firm briefly, but by 1900 ownership was solely that of Donald E. Frederick and Nels Nelson. Nelson died at age fifty-three, but the store continued under Frederick's guidance.

In 1929 Frederick sold the store to Marshall Field Company of Chicago, which owned the business but leased the site on a hundred-year lease. Frederick died on July 6, 1937 at age seventy-seven.

For many years, Frederick & Nelson was a hallmark department store known for its quality and good merchandising practices. After World War II it established branch stores in Washington and Oregon. A British firm BATUS bought Marshall Field Company, a sale which naturally included Frederick & Nelson. Due to financial problems stemming from subsequent multiple changes in ownership, perhaps, the business closed in the spring of 1992.

John W. Nordstrom, Founder, circa 1925 Nordstrom, Inc. (Photo courtesy of Nordstrom Seattle)

Located very near to Frederick & Nelson was Nordstrom's. Swede John W. Nordstrom came to the United States at age sixteen, first working in Colorado and San Francisco. He came to Seattle and Tacoma to visit a cousin, Alfred Berlin, and worked briefly at jobs in Tacoma, Bellingham, Arlington, and Shelton before going off to the Yukon gold rush. Returning with a stake, he joined Carl Wallin in opening a shoe store downtown in 1901, with $5,000 total capital and twenty feet of store frontage. In his memoirs, Nordstrom says that Wallin had stepped out when their first customer entered the store, that he had no idea how to fit shoes but pulled a pair out of the window that seemed the right size and made a sale.

The stores prospered and soon there were branches in the University district, at Rhodes Department Store in Seattle, Lou Johnson's apparel store in Tacoma, and Adams, Inc., of Bellingham. In 1928 John Nordstrom retired, selling his share of the company to sons Everett and Elmer. In 1929 they bought out Wallin, and their brother Lloyd joined the company in 1933.

By 1950 Nordstrom's had opened stores in Northgate, Seattle, and at Portland. Deciding to diversify, Nordstrom acquired Best Apparel of Seattle and Portland and added clothing to their offerings. Soon they purchased a Portland fashion retailer, Nicholas Ungar, and merged its store with the one in downtown Portland. In August 1966, there was a new Nordstrom Best in Tacoma and one in Bellevue in 1967. The following year the brothers Nordstrom retired and turned operations over to their sons plus a family friend, Bob Bender. The company went public in 1971.

Today there are Nordstrom stores in fourteen states. Before 1997 the residents of six more states will be able to shop for shoes and clothes recognized for quality. In a survey compiled and published in *Consumer Reports*, November 1994, Nordstrom was tops for overall customer satisfaction. Not bad for a Seattle immigrant of vision, John W. Nordstrom.

Seattle residents who find themselves in Swedish Hospital owe their good care to the foresight of Dr. Nils August Johansen, who came from Lund, Sweden, in 1893 to study medicine at the University of Colorado. There he met and married Katherine Brown, and the two came to Seattle where it was hoped the climate would be beneficial to Katherine's asthma. Dr. Johansen saw that Seattle needed a hospital. He gathered a group of Swedish benefactors who held fund drives, raffles, and bazaars and operated a Swedish building at the Alaska-Yukon-Pacific Exposition of 1909. After 1909, with only $10,000, the group leased a two-story apartment building at 1733 Belmont Avenue and opened a hospital with twenty-five beds. Meanwhile, a Dr. E.M. Riniger had almost completed a new forty-bed facility at 803 Summit. In July 1912 Dr. Riniger became Seattle's first auto traffic casualty when his car was hit by a streetcar. His widow knew he wanted Seattle to have a good hospital and offered her husband's facility to Johansen's group for $90,723 plus another $4,200 for furnishings. Today Swedish Hospital has around seven hundred beds and a thousand staff members and is considered a first-class medical facility.

Today immigrants from the countries of the world continue to melt into the city's life. The very diversity of Seattle's tapestry makes it a fertile place for the international trade that is so much a part of the city's economy.

The Rosellini Family

It would be difficult to find an extended family that has contributed as much to Seattle as the Rosellinis. Most visible in public life have been Victor of Rosellini's Four-10, Rosellini's 610, and The Other Place; Albert, governor of Washington 1957-65, businessman and lawyer; Leo, a doctor and prime mover in the establishment of Seattle's blood bank; and Hugh, a judge who sat on the bench of the State Supreme Court in Olympia and formerly served as judge of the Superior Court of Pierce County.

Rosellini family: L to R. Victor, sister Amelia, husband "Bimbo," Albert, Hugh (not closely related but Chief Justice of the State of Washington Supreme Court). (Photo courtesy of the Rosellini family)

If ever one doubted the reality of opportunity in America, the Rosellinis are glowing examples. They came from humble, hard-working families who worked their way to the top. At the turn of the century in Italy, it was the custom when both parents were deceased that permission would have to be granted by the oldest member of the family to allow the younger brothers to relocate in America. Three Rosellini brothers, Checco (Frank), Giovanni (John), and Vittorio (Victor), were ordered to go to America. Frank and John were already in Tacoma when Vittorio came about 1905. The three brothers opened a wholesale grocery called Marconi's. Victor, fourth of Vittorio's five children, was born in 1915.

Vittorio's family returned to Italy in 1921 but came back within a couple of years. His mother declared that there would be more opportunity in America. With little progress in Tacoma, the family moved to San Francisco in 1928. Shortly after opening a restaurant at Seventeenth and Market Street, Vittorio died, leaving his wife with five children and "The Tunnel" restaurant to operate. The Rosellinis came four years later to Seattle, where Victor's mother married Louis "Fritz" Pettrofrizzo and the two operated the Roma Cafe.

Victor soon returned to San Francisco and, after fourteen years of learning the food and beverage trade, came again to Seattle in 1950 and opened Victor Rosellini's 610 restaurant at 610 Pine Street—the first San Francisco-style restaurant in town. Victor opened Rosellini's Four-10 right across the street from the Olympic Hotel in 1956. When the Rainier Tower was to be built there, the restaurant moved to Fourth and Wall. The Four-10 closed in 1989, and Rosellini and McHugh opened the "910" at 910 Second Avenue in 1991, where it attracts an upscale crowd.

A few weeks after he opened the Four-10, Victor was dubious about the restaurant's success. The restaurant was more elegant than other Italian restaurants and the menu more cosmopolitan; Seattleites were not sure what to make of it. The Four-10's institution of the "Happy Hour" is believed to be the first for the city, but promoting "all the martinis you can drink for one hour" was short-lived since too many imbibers had to be placed in taxis.

But eventually it became one of the city's most prestigious restaurants. Major social events were held at its second-floor dining room, and the world literally came to the Four-10. Presidents Kennedy and Reagan, Vice President Hubert Humphrey, Henry Kissinger, the moguls of Seattle, all came to the restaurant. On one occasion, a huge political rally hosted by Hubert Humphrey outgrew the Olympic

Hotel's facilities into the Four-10's dining room. Humphrey and most other dignitaries chose to book themselves into the Four-10 group. Dorothy Bullitt's ninetieth birthday was celebrated at the Four-10.

Like the martini promotion, public relations stunts sometimes were unusual. Piglets brought into the restaurant for an advertising campaign got loose and ran around the 610. One day patrons were astonished to find a small elephant contentedly downing plates of spaghetti in the restaurant.

Meanwhile, Victor and his Irish-Norwegian wife Marcia were serving Seattle. Marcia has been and still is a civic activist, having served on the Seattle Planning Commission and Seattle University's Women's Advisory Board. In 1995 she serves as a director of South Seattle Community College Foundation. Victor was vice-chairman of Century 21, the World's Fair Commission, working with Edward Carlson, Al Rochester, and others to make the dream come true. He served on the Chamber of Commerce, Boys Club, Visitors Bureau, and held at least fifteen positions in restaurant industry organizations, including the presidency of the National Restaurant Association. Since 1970 he served as general chairman of the Pacific Northwest Restaurant Convention & Exposition. He was named First Citizen of Seattle for 1984.

While Victor was becoming a respected restaurateur, his older brother Leo pursued a medical career by working at menial jobs, studying late, getting only a few hours sleep per night. He got his degree from Creighton University in Omaha, Nebraska, in 1937 and returned to intern at Harborview King County Hospital. In 1939 he was appointed junior resident surgeon at Harborview, an honor that all strive for and few attain. In 1940 he was appointed senior resident surgeon. He then went into private practice and was instrumental in organizing Seattle's medical clinic located on Broadway. He was one of the founders of the blood bank for Seattle, obtaining the funds through donations and fund-raising events. He served forty years as doctor for the Seattle Fire Department. In private practice he was instrumental in organizing the Seattle Medical Surgical Clinic located on Broadway. Among his philanthropies, he served on the Board of Regents of the University of Washington. He died on July 26, 1981.

Albert Rosellini, son of John, pursued a legal career. He was undecided about his career at first and worked, like his cousins, at simply making a living while going through college (College of Puget Sound and then the University of Washington). He intended to become a pharmacist but, in 1934, decided on law after meeting a man who served as chairman of a committee introducing a bill regarding Puget Sound ship regulation. He found politics interesting and decided to run for the position of state legislator but was narrowly defeated (only eighty votes) by the incumbent. After meeting Warren Magnuson, then running for the position of King County prosecutor, Albert was asked to assist with his campaign. Later Albert became chief criminal deputy prosecutor and went on to become a state senator for five terms. In 1957 Albert Rosellini became Washington's fourteenth governor and served two terms until 1965. He was the first Catholic or Italian in that office.

Among his accomplishments as governor, Rosellini implemented the creation of a medical school, dental school, and the University of Washington Hospital. As senator he had introduced a bill to create these additions. The state institutions for juvenile delinquency, adult corrections, mental illness, and others were in sad shape and had even lost their accreditations. Rosellini spurred action to restore them to proper condition and regain the accreditations. He created a Department of Commerce and Economic Development for the purpose of diversifying the economy so that the state would not be so dependent on just Boeing Aircraft for economic health. Included in the department was a tourist bureau and a division to promote international trade—through which the legislature appropriated the first $10 million to sponsor the Seattle World's Fair of 1962. Rosellini feels that the spin-off from that event has been profoundly advantageous to the state. Other achievements during Rosellini's four years were the building of the Hood Canal Bridge, the first floating bridge on tidal water in the world, the construction of the second bridge across Lake Washington—the Evergreen Point Bridge, later named the Albert D. Rosellini Bridge—and other projects.

His administration inevitably was criticized for the above improvements, financed partly by raising the state sales tax from 3⅓ percent to 4 percent. Opponents called him "Tax-ellini," an unfortunate dubbing that almost cost him re-election. He was accused of having only Italians or Catholics in his administration, but a survey requested by Rosellini found that, of twenty-eight directors of his administration, only four were Catholic and two Italian.

Governor Al, as he is often called, has been chairman of the U.S. Olympic Committee for the state of Washington, a member of Camp Brotherhood (Mt. Vernon) that builds shelters and structures for any religion to use for retreats or camping conferences, and is involved in other philanthropies.

Since leaving office, Governor Al returned to private law practice and for a time was the owner of the Premium Distributing Company. One of his more interesting consulting projects is for the MGM Development Co. which is developing a 1,200-acre industrial site near Beijing, China.

Frank had two sons who were very visible in Northwest life: Bruno, an investigator for the State Department of Labor, and Dean, a real estate broker.

Hugh Rosellini, son of immigrant Primo, is not a direct cousin, but the families came from the same village in Italy; Hugh was a close friend. The brothers and Hugh's parents all lived within four blocks of each other in Tacoma.

Hugh worked long, hard hours at a lumber mill to get his start. He said later that entering law would be cleaner and cooler than working at the mill. The careers of Hugh and Governor Al moved along parallel paths. Like Albert, Hugh entered the College of Puget Sound and University of Washington. After passing the bar examinations, Hugh practiced general law for several years and became a state legislator, working on the rules committee under Governor Mon Wallgren during the late 1940s. He was fascinated by the intricacies of law and served seven years as a Pierce County Superior Court judge. Later in the 1950s he ran for State Superior Court Judge and lost, but he ran a second time and was elected to remain until 1985. He died in 1986.

A third generation of Rosellinis is contributing to Seattle public life in law, teaching, nursing, and building. Their lives today are a far cry from the Florence-area Rosellinis who scrambled for sustenance on small farms.

William Boeing

To some, Boeing and Seattle are interchangeable words. Boeing—William E. Boeing—was a real human being, a curious, innovative, refreshing person. But he only actively headed the company from 1916 to 1934. After that, he was an intermittent consultant.

Courtesy of the Boeing Company Archives

Not so long after the Wright Brothers, Boeing, age twenty-two, and a friend wangled their first rides on a seaplane off Lake Washington. The friend was Conrad Westervelt, a fellow alumnus of the Sheffield Scientific School at Yale University, and the two young men decided they could build a better airplane than the one in which they had flown. Westervelt gathered all the information and designs he could get. Boeing learned to fly at Glenn Martin's Flying School in Los Angeles and bought a Martin seaplane.

Back in Seattle, Boeing and Westervelt hired a crew of twenty-one men and rented a hangar, where they manufactured two biplanes of a design they called the "B & W." They incorporated their firm on July 15, 1916, as Pacific Aero Products, soon changed to Boeing Airplane Company. In the articles were provisions for operating as a common carrier, as well. The two withstood the jeers of friends when they predicted that passenger airplanes would be commonplace one day, and, alarmed by the apparent inevitability of World War I, persuaded the U.S. Navy to give them a contract for fifty trainers.

Boeing was a man impatient with error. When he inspected spruce ribs that had been poorly sawn, he quietly threw them on the floor and crushed them under his foot. When he was on the East Coast at the inspection by the Navy of one of his World War I trainers, he was shown a frayed cable that had been improperly installed. He wired the factory that the worker responsible was to be fired immediately; there was no room for mistakes like that on airplanes.

After World War I and before common usage of aircraft for commercial purposes, times were tough. The Boeing Airplane Company was reduced to manufacturing wooden items like bedroom furniture and, it is said, was considering Ouija boards. Boeing himself juggled the management of the losing company and his considerable timber interests in Gray's Harbor, acquired prior to his aviation ventures.

Boeing stubbornly believed in aviation, though, and on March 3, 1919, he and a pilot, Eddie Hubbard, carried the first sack of international air mail from Vancouver, B.C. to Seattle. When the U.S. Postal Service asked for bids to fly a route from Chicago to San Francisco in 1927, Boeing entered and won with a bid substantially lower than any other. To carry the mail and a few passengers, too, the company proceeded to design and build twenty-five 40-A planes. William, or "Bill," Boeing formed the Boeing Air Transport Service, forerunner of United Air Lines.

In order to have a reliable source of components Boeing led the formation of the United Aircraft and Transport Corporation, composed of several companies including the Boeing Airplane Company, Pratt & Whitney (engines), Chance Vought, Hamilton Propeller Co., and Boeing Air Transport.

In 1934 Boeing was awarded the Daniel Guggenheim Medal for his pioneering of aviation and air transport, only the third American to receive the award. However, that same year, the United States government declared United Aircraft and Transport Corporation to be a monopoly and ordered the separation of its parts.

At this news, William E. Boeing was deeply angry and hurt. For eighteen years since 1916, he had invested large sums of his own money, mostly operating at a loss. Now when he had a "going concern," he was being accused of operating unfairly. His rage was such that he simply walked away from the aviation industry and sold his stock in Boeing Airplane Company and United Transport. He did return during World War II in an advisory capacity. The huge company that bears his name has, ever since, been operated and owned by others.

Where did he go thereafter? He had retained enough of his Minnesota family's fortune (and his lumber interests elsewhere) that he became a playboy, although a useful and creative one. He turned to raising winning racehorses, and later Hereford cattle, credited with improving the breed. He continued to fly a private plane, and from his yacht *Taconite* (taconite is a Mesabi iron ore) he became an expert fly fisherman. He died on his yacht September 28, 1956, at age seventy-four.

Ivar Haglund

Few called him Mr. Haglund. Ivar was one of Seattle's most loved characters, a philanthropist and astute businessman, too.

Courtesy of Ivar's Inc.

When he died January 30, 1985, after a colorful career in Seattle show business and restaurant ownership, the town mourned the loss of a genuine character, one who kept them laughing. His fish bars and fine restaurants still punctuate the city's business scene.

The only son of middle-aged parents, Ivar received a modest legacy of Alki property at age twenty-four, after the death of his father (his mother died when Ivar was three). On a pleasure trip to Seaside, Ivar the dilettante became interested in the aquarium operated by a cousin. In 1938, at age thirty-three, he launched into a lifelong business career by opening the Deep Sea Aquarium next to the Washington Fish & Oyster Company, Pier 54 (Pier 3 then). Typically original in his business methods, Ivar obtained his specimens by seining.

The problem was getting patrons to come and view the sealife. Ivar put on a nautical hat, got out his guitar and stood outside singing sea songs, then hired a truck to tour the city as he banged away at a bass drum in the truck bed. A sign on the drum proclaimed "AQUARIUM." Ivar's lifelong penchant for highly original advertising had begun.

So had his career in show biz. He managed to obtain credit for radio time and made his own commercials—very, very corny versions of sea ditties. When a regular program needed a replacement, the station hired Ivar who had acquired quite a following with his humorous commercials. Before long, Ivar had a paid show on CBS network station KJR, "Mister Wide Awake," where he coined such phrases as "Keep Clam" and "A Cheerful Clam Happy Hello," and wrote songs with outrageous lyrics that had the whole town (and beyond) laughing.

Of course, this was good for the aquarium business and, with the help of his wife Margaret and her step-father, an experienced restaurant operator of Westin Hotel facilities, the family opened Ivar's Acres of Clams as a prestige restaurant. This was one of his few mistakes. The top drawer clientele just was not there, so he reversed himself and went after the mom, pop, and kids business very successfully. One could hardly wade through the decor of hanging nets, life preservers, clam guns, and the like. Kids got diver's mask menus that they could put on with a rubber band. Now he was rolling.

His first crazy advertising stunt was at Christmas, 1940, when he stood in line with his pet seal Patsy in a baby buggy to see Santa Claus at Frederick & Nelson's department store. This netted him a news story in local papers. With the collaboration of Hank Minard of UPI and Jim McClean of *The Seattle Star* newspaper, more hilarious gimmicks followed.

Ivar originated a clam eating contest, the entrants stuffing down as many clams as possible during a ten-minute period. Before long, one Joe Silva from Massachusetts came to challenge first-time winner Richard Watson, who had downed 110 clams to win the original 1947 championship of the International Pacific Freestyle Amateur Clam Eating Contest Association. Before a rapt audience and delighted local and national news reporters the battle of the two was held in 1948 with Watson maintaining his title 131 to 127. The Acres of Clams prospered.

One year he staged a wrestling match in the aquarium tank between "Two Ton" Tony Galento and a seventy-five-pound octopus. The promotion got press as far away as Paris, and a complaint from the Humane Society. Ivar had to confess that the octopus was already dead and that Galento had kept the creature's eight arms moving around in the water so realistically that no one had detected the hoax.

Ivar started telling men to drink clam nectar as an encouragement toward greater virility, and he placed a sign outside his restaurant declaring he would not sell more than three cups of clam juice per man without the written permission of his wife.

Then came television in 1948. Within a decade there were enough sets in Seattle to make that medium attractive to showman Ivar. In 1957 KOMO-TV dreamed up a children's program with host Don McCune acting as "Captain Puget" and a stage set of his ship, the *Windward Four*. McCune was not well-known locally and suggested to Ivar Haglund that he should become Captain Puget's "First Mate Salty" on the show, a role Ivar relished. He had been doing children's programs for the schools, anyway, singing his homespun, corny yarns that the kids loved. As First Mate Salty he was a hit. He wrote and sang songs like "Hark, Hark the Shark," or "Run, Clam, Run." Children dragged their parents to Acres of Clams and Ivar enjoyed star status. The program won awards and ran until 1965.

The craziness never stopped, nor did the philanthropy. Many is the student or derelict or unemployed person who simply was handed money, no questions asked. Under the offbeat exterior Ivar Haglund was a deeply patriotic man. He footed the bill for the largest private 4th of July fireworks displays of the West, if not the nation (still staged today), emanating from Elliott Bay in front of Captain's Table. At the time of his death he was a Port Commissioner.

Ivar's business grew and became incorporated. Even the Wall Street scene became infected with Ivar's original "Fishcal Statements," parodies on the usual serious columns of assets and liabilities. Ivar opened a business in Vancouver, B.C., and began to expand into fish bars in other areas of Seattle and the Northwest. He was versatile; for nineteen years he operated an Ivar's on Broadway in the Capitol Hill district that served seafood, Chinese, and Mexican, and later added hamburgers. This was a departure, however, from later outlets, which mostly stuck to seafood.

If Ivar could be said to reach out to his public, surely his Lake Union restaurant, The Salmon House, was the keynote speaker. It is patterned after a Northwest Indian longhouse, as authentic as possible. At first, the restaurant was to be a sort of community restaurant with common tables, only salmon dinners served, and an open fire in the middle of the restaurant. Alder wood was used, of course, as it is the first choice for barbecuing salmon.

If Ivar himself had conjured up the opening night, it could not have been more unusual. The alder was too wet and began to smoke and smoke and smoke. Before long the full contingent of guests began to cough and choke and finally were forced to leave. Members of the private party, a Chamber of Commerce affair, were very understanding and left laughing—thinking this was a good joke on Ivar, who had pulled so many pranks over the years.

Ivar Haglund bought the historic Smith Tower, which is described elsewhere in this book. Typically he got into a brouhaha almost immediately thereafter by replacing the American flag atop the tower with a sixteen-foot-long windsock patterned after a Japanese carp but called "the salmon windsock." After a short period of laughing and pointing by the public, the city sent a subpoena demanding the Tower's owners come to court for violation of an ordinance forbidding the flying of pennants and such from buildings. At a city board meeting the discussion became a farce, with extensive news coverage and public attendance, all of the public speaking out in favor of Ivar's windsock. Taking a cue from Ivar, who was forever quoting terrible poetry, the hearing examiners and board members felt compelled to state their case, pro and con, in poetry, too. In the decision approving the variance, the examiner said:

High o'er the Smith Tower
Ivar's salmon-sock flies
"In the face of the law,"

Alfred J. Petty decries . . .
The Smith Tower is unique
No one showed any harm
Regarding the size,
The precedent, design or alarm . . .

The poetry was almost as bad as that of Ivar himself. The grand old man, the father all Seattleites wished were theirs, entertainer-philanthropist-restaurateur Ivar Haglund died of a massive heart attack January 30, 1985, at age 79. It would be difficult to find a Seattleite who has not heard Ivar's philosophy:

No longer the slave of ambition,
I laugh at the world and its shame,
As I think of my happy condition,
Surrounded by acres of clams.

As his final gift to his beloved state, he left almost his entire estate of several million dollars to the University of Washington and Washington State University.

Read more about him:
Stephens, Dave. *Ivar*. Seattle: Dave Stephens, 1988.

Labor Leader Dave Beck

Right in line with the Seattle Spirit, David (a name he never liked) Beck's life fit the axiom that hard work would bring profits. So well, indeed, that he wound up with a splendid home, fine cars, and an indictment from the IRS. Dave Beck was said to own Seattle for three decades as the leader of the Teamsters Union.

As the labor leader he operated more like a hardheaded businessman. Dave didn't favor messy strikes and damage to business, although sometimes the strong-arm tactics of overly enthusiastic cohorts turned out that way. Beck's avowed purpose was to make money, money for everybody, and if the employers from whom he extracted good wages did not prosper, neither would his union members. Before he was done organizing the city shortly after the end of World War II, an astonishing 95 percent of Seattle's workers were unionized.

After serving as a Navy machinist's mate in World War I, Beck started his labor career as a laundry driver, soon eclipsing his mates in the number of accounts he could serve. He became secretary of his local Teamsters in 1924 and became an organizer in 1925. His meteoric rise to power was partly due to his position as a moderate—moderate as compared to the left-leaning pronouncements of the likes of Harry Bridges, Pacific Coast Longshoremen's Union. The latter was part of the Committee for Industrial Organization or CIO, organized by John L. Lewis in 1935 within the American Federation of Labor but asked to leave by the AFL's leadership. Bridges took the tack that labor and management basically had nothing in common, where Beck believed that it was imperative that they work together or fail together. Since the Seattle labor scene of the 1930s was unquestionably influenced by the Communist Party, the latter tended to side with Bridges' approach and make employers more fearful of the possibility of a CIO takeover.

Beck was ruthless in his firm organizational tactics, where if a business refused to accept his union for its members, his Teamsters simply would not move the output. He espoused stability to employers, however, and—forced to choose between chaos and possible strikes on the one hand, or stability and paying higher wages on the other—they chose Beck. After all, he had expressed disapproval of the

1919 strike, maintaining that strikes only caused union members to lose more wages than they could ever recoup by winning a higher rate that way. He rejected the influence of the I.W.W., the so-called "Wobblies," and protected the fledgling beer business by stating that his Teamsters would not haul Eastern beer to Washington. Among the brands prohibited in the Pacific Northwest was Budweiser (Anheuser Busch), an odd situation because the company was the first brewery in the United States to organize its own workers. Beck usurped the power in his territory from William Green, then head of the AFL, who seemed powerless to control the Washingtonian.

With deep sighs of resignation, the businessmen of Seattle bowed to the muscle of the Teamsters. They even elected Beck a regent of the University of Washington, an honor that must have given him wry amusement since he never finished high school.

As the likes of Bridges joined the picket lines, Dave Beck joined the Elks Club. He wanted nothing to do with Communists and waved the American flag. But those who dared to challenge him might find their delivery trucks "accidentally" sideswiped or Teamster members ordered not to patronize them, too.

Beck rose to be president of the International Brotherhood of Teamsters in 1952. From a grand, new headquarters building in Washington, dedicated in 1955, he rubbed elbows with presidents and statesmen. Presidents Roosevelt, Eisenhower, and Truman asked him to be Secretary of Labor, which he refused. He also became an Exalted Ruler of the Elks.

Some said that Dave Beck became a willing victim to the old cliche of, "Power corrupts, and absolute power corrupts absolutely." The white marble Teamsters Union headquarters was reputed to have cost $5 million and included a rooftop sun deck, a modern theater, lavishly decorated reception rooms, a handmade heart-shaped conference table, and such. From his palatial home in Seattle, provided rent-free to him by the Teamsters, Beck spent money and gave expensive gifts. It was said that sometimes he paid for them out of Teamster funds, but in an interview later in life he sturdily denied this insinuation. He maintained that the union or others might have paid the bills temporarily, but that he always reimbursed them. His undoing was an investigating committee's discovery that he sold a union-owned automobile and the money was placed in his personal account. Considering that he handled vast sums of money, it seems likely that he truly forgot to reimburse the union for the $1,900; the sum seems paltry considering what he could have embezzled easily. Under the eagle eye of a Congressional committee investigating labor racketeering, he was convicted of embezzlement of that sum in 1958 and sentenced to up to fifteen years in jail, but the matter was appealed and the sentence reduced to five years.

In 1959 Dave Beck was indicted and scolded by Judge Boldt as he rejected Beck's appeal, a sad ending, really, to a remarkable career. Author Murray Morgan reported the judge's comments in his book, *Skid Road*:

". . . Did we not know what we now do know of Mr. Beck, his success story would be as thrilling and inspirational as almost any . . . The exposure of Mr. Beck's insatiable greed . . . is a sad and shocking story. . . . Mr. Beck plundered his union, his intimate associates, and in some instances personal friends, most of whom quite readily would have given him almost anything . . ."

Again Beck staunchly defended his honesty, claiming essentially that errors were possible, given the extent of the far-flung Teamsters Union operations, but that he had never been dishonest, ever. Beck also felt that Robert

Kennedy was "out to get him" in his energetic investigation of labor dealings in the United States.

The State Supreme Court upheld Beck's conviction for embezzlement in 1962, and he finally was marched off to McNeil Island prison.

Meanwhile, his affairs underwent further scrutiny. He was accused of milking thousands of dollars from union funds for construction of his home, but he did not own the home; he had sold it to the Teamsters and was living there free. When his meager records did not seem to add up to the income reported to the Internal Revenue Service, the discrepancies were hard to defend, although he asserted that the incorrect tax report was a simple error in calculations. He was charged, nonetheless, and the matter hung over his head as he languished in prison. He was paroled in December 1964, still noisily professing his innocence, and was pardoned by President Gerald Ford in 1976.

Free again, he became a well-paid guest speaker, and packed audiences greeted him on the talk show circuit. He was tried again for tax evasion in 1971 and was declared delinquent in $1 million of income taxes. Then and later he frequently pointed out that he never was convicted of *tax evasion*, merely that he was delinquent in payment of taxes—quite a different matter. Indeed, he sued certain media members for libel, since it had been printed that he was convicted of evasion.

In his retirement, he continued to profess his innocence of any wrongdoing, to make pronouncements about labor matters, and to enjoy considerable respect. During his heyday, he had been a generous giver to charitable causes and freely lent money to friends in trouble. During his reign, labor/management relations had been satisfactory, although Beck ruled with an iron hand. Just as certainly there had been thuggery and financial dealings in and out of the union that were questioned. Seattle never quite knew what to dub

Dave Beck—sinner or saint, perhaps a bit of both. His stormy and colorful life ended December 27, 1993; he died peacefully in his sleep.

Read more and decide: sinner or saint.

Morgan, Murray. *Skid Road*. Seattle: University of Washington Press, 1982.
Sale, Roger. *Seattle*. Seattle: University of Washington Press, 1976.
McCallum, John D. *Dave Beck*. Seattle: The Writing Works, Inc., 1978.

Dorothy Stimson Bullitt

She died in 1989 at the age of ninety-seven. Journalists and acquaintances spoke of her as "extraordinary," "the grande dame of broadcasting," "empire builder." She was all of these and more; she was the embodiment of the indomitable Seattle Spirit, except she was not from a working-class family.

Her early life was idyllic. Born into the affluent C.D. Stimson family, she had few cares. She had a horse, was a bit of a tomboy, and distinguished herself to her peers by climbing into the barn loft hand over hand on a rope. Like many children, she was required to take piano lessons only to find she loved music. After attending school in the East at the prestigious Briarcliff Manor, she studied voice for a while at Juilliard School in New York, then at the age of twenty-six, she married a handsome lawyer, Scott Bullitt of Louisville, Kentucky. Scott Bullitt became very active in the Washington State Democratic Party, and he and his wife had three children in five years. A continuation of Dorothy Bullitt's idyllic life? No! Scott Bullitt died in 1932 of cancer. Here it was that Dorothy exhibited that "we can do it" Seattle Spirit. She had no business experience, was trained to be a lady of culture, yet inherited some of her father's real estate, including a business, Stimson Realty Company.

Scott had been immersed in campaigning for the presidency of Franklin D. Roosevelt and had run for offices himself. It was typical of Dorothy's pluck that she took Scott's place the year of his death as a compromise official delegate to the National Democratic convention.

As she took stock of her situation, she realized she needed to act positively to preserve her business assets, some in jeopardy due to the Great Depression. Her father's estate included real estate holdings: an office building at 1411 Fourth Avenue; the Coliseum Theater; Firestone Building, Westlake Square Building; and insurance stock at a time when physical assets were almost liabilities. Tenants were moving out because they had become bankrupt; one building was mortgaged. Her father had died three years earlier, her brother a year before Scott Bullitt, and she, Dorothy, was "it."

But she learned fast and within a short time earned the respect of the downtown business community. By the end of the 1940s she had placed the family enterprises on sound footings and was ready for some interesting risk capital ventures.

In 1946 she bought a small AM radio station, KEVR, located in the Smith Tower. At first, the station covered local sports events with play-by-play commentary. With a natural-born promoter's savvy she was able to get new call letters from a merchant vessel that had the letters KING, giving the station an identity with King County, where Seattle is located. Yet it took some time to gain a loyal audience. An often-quoted anecdote relates that a ratings company returned KING's check with the comment that the station had no audience so had no rating.

Dorothy's love for classical music was a boon to listeners when, in 1948, her station KING-FM began classical programming, continuing to this day to serve an audience otherwise hard put to find the old masters on radio.

In 1948, at a time when there were only 6,000 television sets in Seattle, she bought station KRSC that had been on the air only eight months. She had faith that the medium would catch on. It was not a whim; characteristically, she read an article about television, had seen a television system demonstrated at the New York World's Fair, and investigated the practicability of it. Only then did she act decisively, elbowing out a competing buyer, Marshall Field of Chicago, and buying the station for $375,000, which her cohorts thought was completely outrageous.

Bullitt used her own copious common sense to foster programming for children, public information programs, and whatever entertaining features she could glean from networks. Ruth Prinz's program, "Wunda Wunda," became hugely popular, receiving the 1957 Peabody Award as the best children's program in the nation. Even though the station only had enough programming to operate from late afternoon to about 10:00 P.M., the number of TV sets grew sharply in Seattle and warranted program expansion. Instead of only pandering to the rich, as critics predicted, television was proving to be vastly popular with the middle class or working people. Folks who could not afford to travel widely and personally experience unusual events could vicariously enjoy them. Dorothy Bullitt's instincts were correct, and the television station acquired big-time ratings.

By now Seattle's business community no longer viewed Bullitt as an anomaly; she was firmly accepted as "one of the boys," for there were few women executives at mid-century. But for all her sturdy business ability, Dorothy Bullitt adhered to the era into which she was born. She always appeared immaculately dressed in well-cut suits or dresses and often wore a hat and gloves. Strangers to business conferences where Bullitt appeared soon learned to take seriously a womanly executive who first appeared as a "mere woman." Quietly but firmly she made sensible decisions and could outmaneuver the best of finaglers in a business deal.

Off duty she was ahead of her time, too, continuing a love of the sea to which her sailor father had introduced her. She herself could sail and enjoyed boats. She acquired an old Stimson Lumber Company tugboat that had sunk in Lake Union, fixed it up, and used it as a comfortable craft for putting around the Sound. In 1961 she left the presidency of KING in favor of her son, Stimson Bullitt, remaining chairman of the board until 1967 and a member until her death in 1989. Free to roam then, at age seventy in 1962, she, a friend of similar age, and a skipper traversed the United States solely by water. They set out in a power boat from Brownsville, Texas, went around Florida, up the East Coast and St. Lawrence River into the Great Lakes, down the Mississippi River to the Missouri, up that sluggish stream as far as possible, then a portage to the Snake and Columbia rivers at Pasco, out into the Pacific and back into Puget Sound—not without harrowing experiences.

Bullitt not only added to the King Broadcasting empire, but also was a power on charitable boards, carrying out a lifelong concern for the city of Seattle. Even during her fledgling business days during the Depression, she served on the state board that administered relief funds for the unemployed and, as such, signed the order to begin work on Grand Coulee Dam, one of many projects conceived by President Roosevelt to provide jobs. She was on the boards of directors of a bank and an insurance company. Out of respect for her husband's love of history, in 1979 Dorothy

Bullitt endowed a chair of American history in the Department of History of the University of Washington. She served on the library board, was the first woman vestryman of the Episcopal Cathedral of St. Mark, both contributed to and supported A Contemporary Theater's (ACT) productions, and became president in 1962 of the University of Washington Board of Regents.

Bullitt's keen commitment to the environment has been a factor in programming at KING-TV, as well as *Seattle*, a magazine once owned by the company. King Broadcasting Company was sold, however, in 1992 to the Providence Journal Company.

Bullitt's son Stimson and daughters Harriet and "Patsy" (Priscilla) still carry on their own businesses and philanthropies and are also active in the Bullitt Foundation.

When Dorothy Bullitt died in 1989 at the age of ninety-seven, her life had spanned the key years of Seattle's development, from three years after the great fire to the halcyon days of Boeing, Seafair, trade with the Orient, and imposing high-rise structures.

Bootlegger Roy Olmsted

National Prohibition was proclaimed January 16, 1920, an enforcement of the Eighteenth Amendment, but some cities of Western Washington already were officially dry. In 1910 Everett and Bellingham banned liquor sales, and Seattle began a prohibition program in 1916. The Roaring Twenties (and earlier) roared especially loud in Seattle, because Canada was relatively close, the high seas, too, and the tortuous waterways and remote mountain trails made bootlegging attractive.

But who would think of an upstanding Seattle police lieutenant, Roy Olmsted, as a major smuggler? He had been a shining light on the force for fourteen years. Since joining in 1906, he had advanced to the post of lieutenant. He was involved in the prosecution of members of two bootlegging gangs led, respectively, by Jack Marquett and Logan and Fred Billingsley. In the process, he learned volumes about their international connections and operations.

Only thirty-four years old, Olmsted fell victim to the dazzling financial rewards possible in rum-running (actually smuggling not rum, usually, but Scotch whiskey). Around 1919 he started quietly by accepting bribes from those being prosecuted and enjoyed the secret power, prestige, and money this gave him. He amassed sufficient capital, all the while maintaining an aura of integrity, to enable him to take the next step into active smuggling himself.

His first efforts only lasted a few weeks. Olmsted and Sgt. Thomas J. Clark were caught on March 22, 1920, unloading Canadian liquor from a fast boat at Meadowdale, about three miles north of Edmonds. Olmsted was convicted and expelled from the force, paying only a $500 fine. It was back to the drawing board for Olmsted, who had every intention of continuing his nefarious trade.

When Olmsted started to walk the other side of the line thereafter, he did it with the efficiency and imagination that had made him a good, if devious, cop. Organization, that's what it took. At the zenith of his illicit career, Olmsted employed ninety men, whose loyalty he incurred without having to threaten them physically, Mafia-style. In fact, he forbade his crews to carry guns, saying that no amount of money was worth someone's life.

At the time of Prohibition, the Canadian government assessed an export duty of twenty dollars a case on liquor moving into the United States but did not impose this fee on exports to other countries. Olmsted conceived the idea of putting his contraband on a freighter leaving Vancouver or Victoria for, say, Mexico, thus avoiding the duty. This gave him a huge price break in undercutting and driving out his bootleg competitors.

He first off-loaded the liquor out of Vancouver at D'Arcy Island in Haro Strait to await an auspicious time to run it into Puget Sound. There the booze—good bonded liquor, not rotgut—was loaded onto fast boats that hid in the maze of islands. The "feds" were out there waiting, but Olmsted chose dirty weather for his movements when other craft might be anchored securely in a protected cove. Even so, the pursuers often gave futile chase.

In scenarios that resembled Laurel and Hardy chases, the revenue men or law enforcement agents frequently lay waiting for one or another of Olmsted's fleet, but Olmsted had the best, most "souped-up" motorboats available. Knowing the intricate channels like their backyards, the runners in boats with names like *Comet*, *M222*, and *June*, left the government agents in their wakes. With a well-disguised system of payoffs to authorities in Seattle or elsewhere, most of Olmsted's movements went undetected.

As time went on, the government knew perfectly well who ran the operation but could not arrest Olmsted until it could prove its case. Olmsted had lined up several different ports at which the runners could make contact with trucks or cars. He maintained a fleet of paneled trucks displaying prominent signs like FRESH BAKERY GOODS, OCCIDENTAL BREAD, DAIRY PRODUCTS that moved freely about the city making deliveries. No one seemed to wonder why the signs did not include names, addresses, or phone numbers like most retail delivery trucks. At least not for a while. And Olmsted was grossing $200,000 a month from smuggling Canadian liquor—good Scotch, Glenlivet, Usher's Green Stripe, Old Smuggler. Among buyers he had an excellent reputation for not diluting the stuff, for providing quality liquor. Even though half of Seattle knew about his illegal activities, Olmsted rubbed elbows with the politicians and high society of town.

Along Bothell Highway near Seattle many speakeasies thrived, where liquor ran freely along with gambling with no limits. Many of the houseboats on Lake Union operated small-time outlets. Perhaps the most prestigious place that finally was raided was the Butler Hotel, said by some to have been Seattle's most palatial hostelry. Celebrities such as Presidents Grover Cleveland and Theodore Roosevelt slept there. Patrons of jazz clubs such as the Black and Tan at Twelfth and Jackson and Doc Hamilton's on Twelfth found booze easy to buy.

Olmsted communicated with his boats in codes only they understood as to drop sites, where the "feds" were, and so on. The most diabolic scheme attributed to him has been disproven. Olmsted and his wife owned Seattle's first radio station, the American Radio Telephone Company, which operated legitimately out of his home. One of the most popular programs broadcast was a children's story hour, with his wife the narrator. It was said that buried in the stories were key phrases that let captains and truckers know where to drop the contraband on a particular day . . . or where the government agents were known to be hiding in wait. Olmsted denied this to be true in an interview with author Norman Clark in the late 1950s. Nevertheless, the whole system worked splendidly for a time, with the government agents nearly driven to drink by the failure of their well-laid plans to catch the smugglers. Finally, through a phone tap, the agents learned some of Olmsted's secrets. Olmsted discovered the leak when the wire-tapper tried to blackmail him, offering to sell Olmsted the transcripts of conversations recorded to date. From his law enforcement background Olmsted merely laughed in his face, asserting that it was against the law to use wire taps and that the evidence could never be used against him. Thereafter he found the tap but figured the government agents would install others somewhere and used the knowledge to further lead agents astray with false broadcasts of drop sites and such. Then he would leave the house and use a public telephone to give his cronies the accurate directions.

But the government had its own spies at work and managed to sway one of Olmsted's chief henchmen to testify against him. The chief agent, William Whitney, was delighted when Canadian authorities apprehended one of Olmsted's crews on the boat *Eva B* on customs violations. There were 784 cases of booze aboard, and the crewmen talked. Soon it was time for law enforcement to make its move.

On November 17, 1924, police watched as fashionably dressed guests filed into Olmsted's home in Seattle's Mount Baker district, while officers quietly recorded the license plates of the cars in which they arrived. The sounds of merriment drifted out into the night air. Then the G-men moved in to arrest Olmsted and sixteen of his guests. During subsequent weeks ninety suspects were indicted on charges varying from possession to trafficking. Olmsted posted bail and returned to business as usual, although considerably curtailed. He did not come to trial until 1926. By then, some of those indicted with him had become nervous and offered to testify against him for leniency. The new mayor, Bertha Landes, was unforgiving about morals and liquor. Twenty-three of those indicted were convicted and sentenced. Roy Olmsted was sent to McNeil Island prison for four years and fined $5,000, but his wife Elsie was acquitted and remained free. Despite several appeals that tested the validity of wire taps, becoming landmark decisions, Olmsted remained in jail for almost three of his four years.

Olmsted mended his ways in later life, becoming a staunch advocate of the Christian Science religion.

◆ ◆ ◆

For the whole story of prohibition problems in Washington, read *The Dry Years* by Norman H. Clark. Seattle: University of Washington Press, 1965.

William "Bill" Gates and Microsoft

Certainly one of the most remarkable success sagas of the twentieth century is that of a Seattle man, William Gates. As the door to the computer age cracked open, Gates and his friend Paul Allen were there to rush through it. Gates was a student at Lakeside High School and, at age thirteen, was already intrigued by programming of computers.

In 1974-75, while undergraduate students at Harvard University, Gates and Allen realized the potential of the microcomputer, predicting that every home of the future might have one. Over much pizza and Pepsi, according to Gates, the two burned the midnight oil designing a computer language to operate a microcomputer—BASIC. In February 1975, the two completed the software and sold BASIC to their first customer, MITS of Albuquerque, New Mexico. Allen went to work for MITS the following month as Director of Software.

Microsoft, a partnership, was established April 4, 1975, in Albuquerque, with Allen working part-time at first, then full time after November 1976. Just entering his twenties, Bill (as everyone calls him) gained immediate respect and was asked to give the opening address at the First Annual World Altair Computer Convention. Microsoft began to acquire customers such as General Electric, National Cash Register, and Citibank.

Two new computer languages followed swiftly: Fortran in 1977, Cobol-80 in 1978 (responding to the development of more sophisticated microchips such as the 8080, Z-80, and 8085 microprocessors). On January 1, 1979, Microsoft moved to Seattle, actually Bellevue first with a factory at Redmond, where it remains today. At that time, they had thirty-eight employees. In 1994 they had 16,379. Gates was back in his hometown.

Gates and Allen were modest young entrepreneurs but obviously brilliant. On April 4, 1979, Paul Allen was presented with the ICP Million Dollar Award for the software operating the 8080 microprocessor. Microsoft began to branch out and license foreign companies to sell its products. The growth was nothing short of phenomenal, an over-used cliche really true this time.

Apple Computer was recognized as a formidable competitor with its Apple and "Mac" or Macintosh units. In August 1980 Microsoft released the SoftCard system, enabling Apple II users more sophisticated uses than before. As time passed, Microsoft continued to add products for Macintosh products, not just IBMs and Compaqs—those with DOS (Disk Operating System).

On June 25, 1981, Microsoft became a privately held corporation with Gates as President and Chairman of the Board, Allen as Executive Vice President. Allen resigned about two years later but remained on the board.

Despite his much-reported fame, Gates' life did not change dramatically. He continued to be very active in the life of Microsoft and to live in relative privacy. His youthful and distinctive appearance, though, made it impossible to be anonymous. He commented that people, especially young computer enthusiasts, frequently stopped him in airports to ask if it was still possible to get into the software industry and become wildly wealthy.

Microsoft introduced the first Windows operating system as early as November 1983, although the retail version came somewhat later and became popular in the early 1990s. The "mouse" became a household word, a hand-held pointing device that was considered more user-friendly than a keyboard. The company continued to lead the industry, introducing one new software program after another, including applications to run on Macintosh computers.

There even was a software package for flight simulation on a computer, very popular "just for fun."

The Software Publishers Association awarded Microsoft five awards of excellence for 1985. "Best Business Product" and "Best Productivity Product" went to Excel for Macintosh use. "Best Technical Achievement," "Best User Interface," and "Best Software Product" went to Windows.

An important date was June 1, 1989, when Microsoft announced the formation of the Multimedia Division, dedicated to developing and marketing multimedia systems software and consumer products. By 1990, 5,975 people worked for Microsoft, and Bill Gates was named No. 1 in *Computer Resellers News'* eighth annual rating of the twenty-five most influential executives in the personal computer industry, a rating he was to win several more times.

There seemed to be no end, and surely it is not yet in sight. In 1992 President Bush awarded William Gates the National Medal of Technology. On December 1, 1992, Microsoft registered its first wholly owned subsidiary, Microsoft AO, in Russia. Futuristic even for those in the multimedia field were products introduced in early March, 1993—five interactive multimedia titles: Dinosaurs; Multimedia Mozart; The Dissonant Quartet; Multimedia Stravinsky; and Bookshelf. Later that year came software products for children: Creative Writer and Fine Artist.

After years of tending mostly to business, as far as the media reported, anyway, Gates began to enjoy the fruits of his labor a bit. He acquired property and began the construction of an unusual home. He married Melinda French on January 1, 1994, a change in his life he says is great.

Gates receives so much mail and is asked so many questions by other computer people that he has gone on electronic mail with a column. Bill Gates' advice to would-be software entrepreneurs is: ". . . shoot for $2 million a year in sales by selling 10,000 of a $200 product. That's pretty good and it happens all the time."

And "create a product that helps people do something specific or gives practical information in areas such as medicine, insurance, accounting, architecture or government processes."

Today Bill Gates' Microsoft has international subsidiaries in forty-eight countries, products are developed in thirty languages, and the net revenue for the fiscal year ending June 1994 was over $4.6 billion. Not bad for a twenty-year existence.

Emmett Watson

For decades Seattleites have opened their newspapers first to Emmett Watson's column in the *Seattle Post-Intelligencer*. His slices of life gave them a sense of community, of the inside track of Seattle. In his later years he was seen as something of a jovial curmudgeon. He waged a tongue-in-cheek war for Lesser Seattle, not Greater Seattle, to keep population growth in check. His sarcastically funny remarks sometimes were abrasive to non-Washingtonians, who saw his views as those of the entire region, an anti-growth, anti-outsider sentiment. Whatever readers thought,

Emmett Watson was and is passionate about Washington, especially Seattle.

Emmett Watson is a native son. He grew up on Duwamish Head north of where Boeing Field now is located. In his book *Digressions of a Native Son* he tells of riding cable cars on Yesler, James, and Madison and of the early waterfront that was "crowded, smelly, tough, and altogether splendid," instead of a tourist destination. His early passion was to become a professional baseball player, and he haunted the old Civic Field and the later Sick's Stadium to watch the Rainiers play. He played four years of baseball for the University of Washington and picked up semipro games at night for $5 to $7.50 per game. For a brief period he was hired as a replacement catcher when the first-stringer was injured and traveled the circuit. This stint led to a job at the *Seattle Star* because the editor thought it would be good to have an ex-Rainier as a sports writer. He stayed there for two years, at the *Seattle Times* for four years, then became a fixture at the *Seattle Post-Intelligencer* for thirty-three years, then back to the *Times* until the present—now as a contract writer. He switched from sports reporting to writing a column for twenty-six years about happenings around Seattle. Since 1982 he has written several books. A fellow *P.I.* newsman turned author was Nard Jones, who wrote sixteen books and a stream of articles and essays.

Watson followed keenly the trials of Dave Beck, whom he came to know well, but found Charlie Burdell, Beck's lawyer, even more interesting—an unconventional, mild-looking man who liked difficult cases and won more than his share with somewhat unorthodox means. In his books Watson tells of Seattle people, great and humble, in a manner that makes you feel you knew them personally. Watson grows rhapsodic is his description of Seattle. From *Digressions* you read:

".. . whenever I leave it for any period of time, the glow is always there when I return. It is a beautiful city, unbelievably blessed by nature, . . ."

". . . how easy it is to live here, . . ."

How should a city be?

". . . above all else diverse. . . . A city should accommodate, willingly, all points of view, and not ever be suckered by incantations using the slippery catchword, 'progress,' spelled with a capital 'P'. . . . A city should be like the old stew pot bubbling on the stove in less prosperous times; a kettle of nourishment, host to variety, always simmering, subtly changing flavor with each new addition or subtraction."

Recommended reading:

Watson, Emmett. *Digressions of a Native Son*. Seattle: The Pacific Institute, Inc., 1982. And: *Once Upon a Time in Seattle*. Seattle: Lesser Seattle Publishing, 1992.

More People

PRINCESS ANGELINE was the daughter of Chief Seattle. Catherine (Mrs. Doc) Maynard gave her the Christian name Angeline because she was so pretty. In the ensuing years Catherine and Angeline were fast friends. When Angeline became infirm, her pioneer friends did not desert her and brought her food. When she died in 1896, her home was draped in black. She was taken to her tomb in Lake View Cemetery in a hearse drawn by a team of black horses, followed by many of her pioneer settler friends. A monument at Lake View honors her. Angeline's friend Catherine followed her in death in 1906 and was also buried at Lake View Cemetery.

ALDEN BLETHEN, sometimes called Colonel Blethen, was a career journalist and editor of the *Seattle Times*. He purchased the newspaper in 1896. At first the newspaper espoused Democratic positions but around 1904 tended to support Republican politics more. By the time World War I loomed, the *Times* reflected Blethen's extreme patriotism and, some said, an obsession against any political position he considered radical or in opposition to property rights.

HENRY BRODERICK chaired the committees managing both the Alaska-Yukon-Pacific Exposition of 1909 and the Seattle World's Fair of 1962. He was a major investor in Seattle real estate.

TED BUNDY was the infamous murderer executed in Florida in 1989. In Seattle he appeared to be an upstanding young man and worked as a volunteer at the Crisis Center. Ann Rule, a coworker and ex-policewoman, has written books about Bundy and several other serial killers.

THOMAS BURKE was associated with railroads at first—his own, the Seattle, Lakeshore and Eastern—and the Great Northern Railway. Burke settled in Seattle in 1875, soon setting up a law partnership with John J. McGilvra. He did much legal work for James J. Hill and was a visible figure in early Seattle politics and business.

EDWARD CARLSON was the capable head of the Seattle World's Fair Committee.

WAH CHONG was a major labor broker for the Chinese community in the 1880s.

JAMES COLMAN built the Seattle and Walla Walla Railroad to Renton. He constructed Colman Dock used by the Mosquito Fleet, steamships, state ferries, and the Alaska Marine Highway ferry until it moved to Bellingham in 1989. He had numerous business interests; the Colman Building is named after him.

NELLIE CORNISH was the founder of the Cornish School, still a fine arts school especially renowned for its interior design and music curricula, now known as Cornish College of the Arts.

JAMES ELLIS was the chief author of "Forward Thrust" in 1965, an urban renewal plan for Seattle that included the building of the Kingdome and Seattle's rapid transit system Metro.

JOSHUA GREEN was the head of Puget Sound Navigation Company and the founder of Peoples National Bank.

OLE HANSON was mayor of Seattle during the Strike of 1919. Some felt he was opportunistic in his handling of the situation.

JIMI HENDRIX was an innovative guitarist considered to have a great influence on the direction of 1970s music. He was born in Seattle in 1942 and attended Garfield High School. There he played with James Thomas and his Tomcats. He dropped out of school to join the U.S. 101st Airborne Division but was injured during his twenty-sixth jump. After playing with rhythm and blues bands in Memphis, Tennessee, he formed his own band, Jimmy James and the Blue Flames. The band was not successful but Hendrix himself was hired by John Hammond for his own band as a lead guitarist. He began to experiment with unusual sounds, distortion and feedback, partly made possible through advancing technology in electronic equipment. A producer, Charles Chandler, took over his promotion, and a show billed as the Jimi Hendrix Experience traveled throughout Europe and North America during 1968 and 1969 to sellout crowds. About this time, Jimi also adopted wild stage antics that revved up his audiences. He played a concert at Sick's Stadium in 1970 and, only a few months later, died on September 18, 1970. He is buried at Greenwood Memorial Park, Renton, where fans still come almost every day to see his gravestone, a simple slab with his name and a guitar etched into it. Because his approach to music is considered pivotal, supporters are raising money for a memorial museum for Jimi Hendrix and hope that it will be completed by 1997.

BERTHA LANDES cleaned up Seattle's graft and corruption after she was elected mayor in 1926. It was she that helped to put the finger on flagrant bootlegger Roy Olmsted and others of his cronies.

BRUCE LEE was born Lee Yuen Kam. He was not a native of Seattle but is buried, along with his son Brandon, in Lakeview Cemetery. Lee was considered the greatest martial artist of the century and became a movie cult figure. He died in Hong Kong in 1973.

GYPSY ROSE LEE was born Rose Louise Hovick in Seattle in 1914. Her mother-manager Madame Rose booked Lee and her sister June (later known as June Havoc) into programs for lodges and such. In 1929 Gypsy Rose Lee made her debut in burlesque, and within two years she was a headline attraction at Billy Minsky's Republic Theatre on Broadway, New York City. She went on to appear in the Ziegfeld Follies of 1936, *The Streets of Paris* at the New York World's Fair of 1940, the Broadway musical *Star and Garter* in 1942, and many cabarets and theatres. She wrote two published mystery novels: *The G-string Murders*, 1941, and *Mother Finds a Body*, 1942. She died in 1970.

ROBERT MORAN was the head of a large shipyard operating before 1900. The Moran Brothers built at least twelve boats used during the Yukon gold rush and Seattle's first steel and iron vessel in 1898. The Moran Brothers also won the contract to build the USS *Nebraska*, a battleship. Moran's vacation and retirement home is today's Rosario Resort on Orcas Island.

NORMAN RICE is the first man of African-American lineage to be elected mayor of Seattle. Prior to the election he was on the Seattle City Council. Rice was elected mayor in 1990 and was re-elected in 1994 for another four years.

BILL SPIEDEL was a clever promoter and writer who published humorous books about Pioneer Square, the underground areas, and characters of the city. He founded the Underground Tours.

VICTOR STEINBRUECK was an architect and a professor at the University of Washington. He was passionately devoted to preserving the Pike Place Market and was very active in the movement that resulted in the naming of the market as a Historic District.

C.D. STIMSON was one of the most important businessmen and philanthropists of Seattle. He was treasurer and partner of Stimson Land Company and treasurer and general manager of Stimson Mill Company of Ballard. He invested in Seattle enterprises such as the founding of the Coliseum Theatre (with Joe Gottstein), the Madison Street Railway Line, and the Plaza Hotel which stood on the site of today's Westlake Park. He was the father of Dorothy Stimson Bullitt of King Broadcasting Company.

ANNA LOUISE STRONG took a Ph.D. degree from the University of Chicago, one of the first women ever to do so. She was aptly named "Strong," for she was a fiery campaigner for social justice and leaned ever farther to the left in her politics. During the 1919 strike, her editorial for the newspaper *Union Record* frightened Seattle businessmen into believing a true labor revolution was at hand, led by the Communists.

TAMOTSU TAKIZAKI was a master of Kendo and a master of Zen teaching. He was a good friend of artist Paul Horiuchi and an inspiration to him. Takazaki operated an antique store in Seattle.

R. H. THOMSON was the unsung hero who developed parts of Seattle's water supply and sewage systems, and supervised the Denny regrade and modifications to Jackson and Dearborn streets.

MARK TOBEY was an artist who first taught at Cornish School, went to Europe to study and paint, then returned to paint in Seattle. He became recognized not only regionally, but internationally. Tobey particularly liked to paint the scenes and people at the Pike Place Market. Tobey left Seattle again in 1950, but the introduction to his book *The World of a Market* was used as a powerful endorsement for saving the market. Among his works is the mural at the Seattle Opera House, a collage of images from many parts of the world.

BAGLEY WRIGHT is an art collector and Seattle arts supporter, after whom the Bagley Wright Theatre is named.

CHAPTER 3

The Sports Page

Team Sports

Baseball

A team called the Alkis played in an ordinary field around 1877 against such teams as Victoria, B.C., but little more is known about them. The next stirrings of baseball fever came in 1890 when Seattle, Tacoma, Spokane, and Portland organized the Pacific Northwest League. The Seattle Reds won a pennant in 1892 but soon either became inactive or folded. In 1896 D.E. Dugdale secured a Seattle franchise with a team known as the "Braves" (some records say it was a new name for the Seattle Reds) and played at Athletic Park on Fourteenth and Yesler until 1904.

In 1903 the newly organized Pacific Coast League wanted to add a Seattle franchise, and, with more well-financed backers, a new PCL Seattle team racked up a winning streak of nineteen games straight. After the season ended the team absorbed Dugdale's Braves. In 1906 they had their best season ever sparked by Harry "Rube" Vickers, a 6'2", 225-pound righthanded pitcher who appeared in 64 games. He pitched 526 innings, which in 1994 remained the all-time record in organized baseball.

His pitching included 408 strikeouts. Unfortunately, Vickers' prowess attracted notice, and he was snatched away by the Philadelphia Athletics in 1907. "Sea Lion" Hall was a second prominent player for Seattle, which joined the Class B Northwestern League in 1907.

The Pacific Coast League had its ups and downs—up to six and even eight teams and down to four. When World War I broke out, it ceased altogether for a time.

Seattle returned to the Pacific Coast League as the Seattle Indians in 1919. After a long and checkered career the Indians won the Pacific Coast League championship in 1924, beating favorites Los Angeles and San Francisco. In part the win was due to the hitting of "Brick" Elred.

The Indians continued to play at Dugdale Park until the Fourth of July, 1932, when Dugdale Park's wooden bleachers caught fire from errant fireworks and burned to the ground, causing the Indians to move to the less than impressive Civic Field, a barren spot at Republican and Harrison mostly used by high school teams. The surface was terribly hard, and the fence had about five feet of boards and another five of chicken wire.

The inconvenient field was a blessing to hitters like Art (Mike) Hunt who, aided by a short left field, punched out thirty-nine home runs in 1937.

Looming bankruptcy was averted by the interest of an unexpected fan, Emil Sick, scion of a vast brewing empire that spanned western Canada and Washington. He bought the team in December 1937 and renamed it the SEATTLE RAINIERS in honor of the view of Mount Rainier.

A dynamo of management skills with positions on boards and associations, Emil Sick was president of the Sick Brewing Company on Rainier Avenue, which brewed Rheinlander beer. In 1938 he decided to do something about Seattle's dire need for a baseball stadium and announced he would build one. His daughter is quoted in a 1939 *Seattlife* magazine as asking, "Daddy, did you buy a baseball club or save the country from disaster?" Certainly this was the enthusiastic and much-publicized response from Seattle media.

So Sick's Seattle Stadium arose quickly, its name the target for punsters league-wide. It was a fine stadium of concrete and steel, one that equaled any in service in the PCL. Sick and his wife went on to rank among the major philanthropists of Seattle, not only in baseball activities but also literary arts.

Meanwhile, another minor league thrived briefly in the mid-forties. The SEATTLE STEELHEADS, with blacks-only players made a promising debut in early May, 1946, in a six-franchise circuit of Oakland, San Francisco, Fresno, Seattle, Portland, and Los Angeles. Unfortunately, it was mismanaged and underfinanced and folded in July.

Back to the Rainiers, Sick appointed as the new manager Jack Lelivelt, who had been the coach of the Los Angeles Angels for seven and one-half years. His secret weapon turned out to be the signing of local high school star Fred Hutchinson. In 1938, his one year with the Rainiers, he led the PCL in wins (25), winning percentage (.781), and ERA (2.48). Hutchinson moved to the Detroit Tigers in 1939, playing there until 1952, when he was appointed their manager.

Even without Hutchinson in the lineup the Rainiers went on to dominate the PCL, appearing in the playoffs six consecutive years, as champions three of those years 1939-41. Lelivelt died of a heart attack in 1941, an emotional as well as professional blow for the team. Nevertheless the Rainiers won the President's Cup three years straight from 1940-42, depending on four key players especially to accomplish the feat: pitchers Hal Turpin and Tracie "Kewpie Dick" Barrett, Dick Gyselman at third base, and center-fielder Jo Jo White. They won no more pennants in the forties but continued to attract good crowds. In 1951 the Rainiers were coached by a Hall of Fame man, Rogers Hornsby, and proceeded to win the pennant again. In 1955 Fred Hutchinson returned to his hometown to become the Rainiers' manager, and again the Rainiers won the pennant. He died of lung cancer in 1964; in December 1975 his brother, Dr. William Hutchinson, started The Fred Hutchinson Cancer Center and named it for his brother.

Toward the end of the 1950s the PCL teams lived through a tumultuous period of change and restructuring of the league itself. In 1960 an aging Sick sold the Rainiers to the Boston Red Sox. He died in 1964, remembered affectionately for his exemplary treatment of his Rainiers.

As the Boston Red Sox AAA affiliate, the Seattle team continued to operate as the Rainiers through 1964. Dewey Soriano prevailed upon the California Angels to move their franchise to Seattle, which then played as the Seattle Angels. The coaches were Bob Lemon, 1965-66; Chuck Tanner, 1967; and Joe Adcock, 1968.

The city of Seattle bought Sick's Stadium from the Rainier Brewing Company with which Sick's breweries had merged. Ths stadium became the home of the Angels. The Angels reached second place in 1965 and won the PCL pennant in 1966. A Seattle franchise in the American League was awarded in 1968 to Pacific Northwest Sports Inc., the chief investor being William Daley, which acquired the Angels in order to hold the Seattle territory open while negotiations ensued. Here's what transpired:

In August 1967, Charlie Finley of the Kansas City A's came to Seattle on a search for a new location for his team and was received enthusiastically by Mayor J.D. Braman, Dewey Soriano, president of the Pacific Coast League, and Bert West, the president of the Seattle Angels. Washington's Governor Dan Evans sent encouraging words. After looking at Sick's Stadium and probing the situation, Finley requested that King County commissioners should investigate getting a stadium bond issue on the agenda, and the media jumped on the bandwagon, believing that the A's were going to move to Seattle. Instead, Finley's team moved to Oakland.

The bubble seemed to have burst, but the American League officers soon designated that Seattle would enter play by 1970 as an expansion team, its owners to be Pacific Northwest Sports, Inc. In addition to Daley, the owners included Dewey Soriano, Alan Fritchey, and Greg Devine, the latter three from Cleveland, Ohio. The owners successfully lobbied to make the starting date 1969, a year earlier than first decreed.

After holding a public contest, the management announced the name of the all-new team to be the SEATTLE PILOTS. Their first games were April 8 and 9, 1969, against the California Angels at Anaheim. Because of Seattle's reputation for rain, the sports announcer played background music of "Singin' in the Rain" while giving the lineup. Seattle won this, their first game in the major leagues. They lost the second and, with a split, went home to the cheers of the hometown Seattleites. On April 11-13 Seattleites saw their first major league baseball game in Sick's Stadium against the Chicago White Sox. Over 17,150 hysterical fans cheered, first the special opening festivities, then the game. Seattle won that first game and the second, but lost the third of the series to Chicago.

So it went, a ball club's typical up and down season, but the fledgling Pilots stood in third place by August. Then one injury after another struck the team, and they finished the season in last place, not an unusual standing for a new expansion team. However, the real blow was to come. The crowds turning out at Sick's Stadium faded away as the season wore on, and attendance was considered insufficient to enable the owners to continue carrying the club. . . . And the long-awaited domed stadium was not yet built, factions vying for a downtown location vs. Seattle Center. The owners filed bankruptcy, and the Milwaukee Brewers purchased the team out of bankruptcy in 1970. But Seattle's brief claim to a major league team was over.

On February 6, 1976, the American League again agreed to let Seattle have a club. The owners of the new SEATTLE MARINERS, a name chosen in a public contest, were: Stanley Golub, Walter Schoenfeld, Lester Smith, James A. Walsh, James Stillwell Jr., and Danny Kaye, the movie star who was an avid baseball fan.

On March 1, 1977, the new Mariners began practice at the spring training camp in Tempe, Arizona. The roster included pitcher Glenn Abbott; infielders Juan Bernhardt, Julio Cruz, Dan Meyer, and Craig Reynolds; and outfielder Ruppert Jones. Pitchers Rick Honeycutt and Enrique Romo and outfielder Larry Milbourne were acquired later in the year.

Seattle finally completed its vast new Kingdome in March 1976 for baseball and football teams to use (see section on buildings). On April 6, 1977, the Mariners played the California Angels before a Kingdome crowd of 57,762. An ex-Seattle Pilots member, Diego Segui, was the Mariners starting pitcher.

Like any new team the Mariners had to lose some games until they began to act as a unit, but the fans were wildly enthusiastic, anyway. The most dedicated fan of all was Danny Kaye, who often clowned for the media.

The Mariners did okay for a new team, finishing their first year in sixth place in the Western Division of the American League. The first few years were wildly inconsistent, though, with wins or losses unpredictable. One of the early stars was Julio Cruz, who was fleet and an accomplished base thief. Another was hard-hitting Bruce Bochte beginning in 1978.

Bochte came to the club after batting a combined .301 for California and Cleveland in 1977. He started out well for the Mariners, then had trouble keeping up his hitting record for a while. He was increasingly frustrated and puzzled, but eventually in 1979 he regained his confidence and led the Mariners with a .316 average and in 1980 made .300. Tom Paciorek led the team in 1981, but Bochte hit 134 doubles, making him the team's all-time leader in that category until 1988. "Willie Horton Night" was declared on June 9, 1979, to honor the Mariner who belted his 300th career home run on June 6, the forty-third player to do so.

George Argyros became the new principal owner January 14, 1981, following which the team underwent a turbulent turnover of several players and the replacement of coach Maury Wills with Rene Lachemann, age thirty-six. It was a strange year with a massive slump followed by a powerful recovery that brought the Mariners to within six and a half games of the leaders of the league at playoff time (although they did not make the playoffs). In a deadlock with the Red Sox that year, a game stretched into an incredible twenty innings, with the Mariners finally triumphing 8-7.

Highlights of the 1982 season included the attainment of win number 300 for pitcher Gaylord Perry; only fourteen pitchers to that date had ever racked up that many. They finished the season in fourth place, thumbing their noses at those who predicted they would be last. The Mariners were an up-and-coming club to be reckoned with, and the Seattle fans were solidly and noisily behind them.

Surprisingly, in 1983 Argyros fired Rene Lachemann and replaced him with Del Crandall, a minor league manager who had previously managed the Milwaukee Brewers 1972-75. Argyros replaced Crandall in September 1984 with Chuck Cottier, salvaging a 59-76 record in September with a 15-12 rest of season to finish with their second best record ever, 74-88. Pitcher Mark Langston led the league for strikeouts. Alvin Davis was named American League Rookie of the Year and is the club's all-time leader in almost every important offensive category. In 1985 under the new manager, Chuck Cottier, the team finished again 74-88. During a losing 1986 season the Mariners set two interesting though dismal records. In a game against Oakland eighteen Mariners struck out; five days later against the same team sixteen players struck out again. That same year Red Sox pitcher Roger Clemens struck out every single Mariners starter at least once in a particular game. Perhaps these statistics added fuel to the move to chuck Chuck Cottier. He was replaced temporarily by Marty Martinez, then by Dick Williams, who had played thirteen seasons with five different major league clubs. He was one of only two managers to lead three different teams to pennants.

An immediate upswing in the Mariners' fortunes could be credited to Williams. After the 1986 season was over, general manager Dick Balderson (perhaps with input by Williams) made several trades hotly contested by the fans, but his judgment was sound. In 1987 the Mariners had their best early season to date, coming within two games of first place in late May, and finishing fourth for the season. For unknown reasons, at this point George Argyros announced the team was for sale but changed his mind a few days later. He did sell the team on October 5, 1989, to a partnership of Jeff Smulyan, Emmis Broadcasting, Michael Browning, and the Morgan Stanley Group, Inc.

Dick Williams continued as manager until June 6, 1988. He was fired and replaced by Jim Snyder on an interim basis. But from 1989 through 1991, Jim Lefebvre headed the Mariners, followed by Bill Plummer in 1992, and Lou Piniella in 1993.

For the first time in its history, the Mariners club won more than they lost in 1991 under Jim Lefebvre, 83-79 for the season, finishing in only fifth place, nonetheless.

In 1993 the Mariners rose to fourth under Piniella and again were over the .500 mark at 82-80. The 1994 season was cut short by a baseball strike, leaving the Mariners hanging in third place at the time with a 49-63 record.

Ken Griffey and Ken Griffey Jr. became the first father and son to play in the same major league lineup (after Ken Sr. signed with the Mariners on August 29, 1990) in a game against the Kansas City Royals on August 31. That was the same year Ken Jr. belted in 22 home runs and 80 RBIs (runs batted in). Ken Jr. continued to be a major hitter. In 1991 he batted .327 with 100 RBIs, in 1992 he hit 27 homers with 103 RBIs, in 1993 he batted .309 with a whopping 45 home runs and 109 RBIs. Despite the short season caused by the baseball strike of 1994, Griffey broke Babe Ruth's record of 30 HRs by June 30 by hitting 32 home runs.

Griffey Jr. also was voted the *Seattle Post-Intelligencer*'s Sports Star of the Year for 1989. He was named the team's Most Valuable Player from 1990-93, plus a host of other awards, a remarkable career for one so young—only twenty-four years old in 1994.

Other records were set in 1992: Randy Johnson tied a league record for left-handed pitchers by striking out eighteen batters at Texas; Edgar Martinez became the first Mariner ever to lead the league at hitting—a .343 average. In 1993 Chris Bosio threw the second no-hitter in club history against the Boston Red Sox, and Randy Johnson struck out 308 batters that same year.

On July 1, 1992, the Baseball Club of Seattle assumed control of the Mariners, and Chuck Armstrong was named president.

As if a baseball strike wasn't problem enough in 1994, the Mariners had to play some of their home games at their opponents' stadiums after acoustical ceiling tiles fell from the Kingdome's dome.

Football

The Seattle Seahawks

About the same time as construction began on the King-dome (November 1972), Seattleites started booming for a football team of their own. In 1974 came the news that the National Football League would allow Seattle to join the league in 1976, touching off a wild celebration capped by the surge to buy season tickets months and years in advance. When 58,000 season tickets had been sold, the management refused to market any more, in order to leave some room for one-time attendees. The primary owner of the team was Lloyd Nordstrom on behalf of the Nordstrom family, plus partners Herman Sarkowsky, D.E. Skinner, Howard S. Wright, M. Lamont Bean, and Lynn P. Himmelman. Jack Patera was named head coach.

A "Seahawk" is a bird of the gull family and was picked as the team's name from entries in a public contest. The Seattle Seahawks got their feet wet in a pre-season game against the San Francisco 49ers on August 1, 1976, losing by only one touchdown 20-27. Star of the show was Jim Zorn, Seahawks quarterback, who was both fleet and canny. He had rammed ahead in the final moments and was tackled on the 49ers two-yard line as the game ended.

That first year the Seahawks developed a formidable duo of Zorn passing and Steve Largent receiving, one that would continue to keep fans on their feet in future games. The season's tally was 2-12, but as a new team the Seahawks were considered lucky to win any at all.

The following year, despite their star Zorn being gimpy, the Seahawks won five games and hosted the Pro Bowl. They established a record for the most wins ever of a second year expansion team. In 1978, still with the Zorn-Largent menace in place, plus the rushing of big Sherman Smith, the Seahawks finished with 9-7, only a game behind Denver in the quest for the playoffs, pretty hot stuff for a rookie team.

The next few years were checkered ones. In 1979 the team again finished 9-7, with Largent and Zorn gaining acclaim. In 1980 things came apart and the Seahawks plummeted to last place in the five-team division with a 4-12 season. They stayed in the cellar in 1981, and the 1982 season was disrupted all over the nation by a players' strike.

Even in defeat there was no question about Zorn and Largent's stardom. Coaches said that, while Largent was not a super-fast runner, he was agile and quick, reacting with lightning reflexes to the moves of attackers. In his career with the Seahawks, lasting until 1990, Largent won every important pass receiving record in NFL history. He caught 819 passes for 13,089 yards and 100 touchdowns. Eight times during the fourteen years of being a Seahawk, Largent racked up more than 1,000 yards receiving in a season. Furthermore, he was the stuff heroes are made of—a genuinely nice guy, who performed many hours of charitable works on his own time.

Zorn made records, too, throwing for 3,661 yards in 1979, a club record. And while Largent received the most plaudits, it took an equally fine passer to put the ball into Largent's hands, after all.

Despite the passing game the Seahawks had poor records in 1980 and 1981, in last place both years. Coach Jack Patera was replaced by Chuck Knox, formerly with the Los Angeles Rams and Buffalo Bills. He made trades and changes, the greatest of which was the building of a rock-solid defense. An essential member of the team was Curt Warner, who racked up 1,449 yards rushing in 335 attempts. A surprising switch was the demotion of Zorn to backup quarterback under Dave Kreig, who had been second to Zorn previously. Zorn left the Seahawks the following year. Kreig was a lively and reliable passer and led the Seahawks into the 1983 championship game with the Los Angeles Raiders, but the latter were too strong. Nonetheless, in 1984 the Seahawks bounded back to come within two games (the last two at that) of winning the AFC West title. Kreig continued for a decade to be a key player.

The next three years saw the Seahawks showing winning ways but not enough to make the playoffs, except in 1987 when they then lost the first round. It was 1987, also, when the Seattle Seahawks signed a much-publicized college star, Brian Bosworth. "The Boz" became a big media star but was plagued by injuries so much that his talent was not fully realized. Knox was spoiling for a championship and a chance at the Super Bowl. To the strong combination of Kreig and Largent, Knox added a powerful running back, John L. Williams, in 1986 who started his career as a first-stringer. Opponents knew him for his stiff arm defense against tackles. For a 220-pounder he also could run like a deer. Williams' brilliant performance in 1988, racking up 877 yards rushing plus a surprising 58 pass catches, put the Seahawks into the winning circle at last—their first AFC West division title. Coach Knox had the distinction of taking three different teams to the playoffs.

The Nordstroms and partners sold the Seahawks on August 30, 1988, to Ken Behring and Ken Hofman. That same year Steve Largent became the all-time NFL leader in pass receiving yards with 12,167 yards at San Diego. Dave Kreig equaled his own record in November with five touchdown passes in a winning game against the Los Angeles Raiders. It was a good year at 9-7 in first place, but the Seahawks were eliminated from the playoffs by the Cincinnati Bengals. After the 1989 season with the Seahawks finishing at 7-9 in fourth place, Steve Largent retired from pro football with a handful of records and honors in hand. Before the last game (a loss to the Washington Redskins) Largent received special plaudits and his name was the first inducted into the Seahawks Ring of Honor. Jim Zorn was the second inducted in 1991.

In 1990 coach Chuck Knox racked up his 159th winning game, placing him in seventh place all-time. That year Derrick Fenner ended the season leading the AFC in total touchdowns and rushing touchdowns. The Seahawks finished 9-7 in third place.

The biggest excitement of 1991 came with a decisive win, 23-9, over the Los Angeles Rams in the Kingdome, the Seahawks' first victory over the Rams in five regular season games. After the season was over, by mutual agreement, Chuck Knox left the Seahawks after nine years as head coach. He compiled an overall record of 80-63-0 for regular season play and guided the Seahawks to four playoff appearances, with the AFC West title in 1988. Tom Flores was named head coach for 1992.

Dave Brown, a former Seahawks cornerback, returned on January 24, 1992 to act as defensive assistant and was the third inductee into the Seahawks Ring of Honor. In pregame ceremonies, broadcaster Pete Gross was the fourth person inducted into the Ring of Honor on November 30.

Special teams, 1993 Seattle Seahawks (Courtesy of Seattle Seahawks)

The 1992 and 1993 seasons were disappointing ones, despite individual brilliance by Cortez Kennedy, named NFL Defensive Player of the Year in 1992, and quarterback Rick Mirer, NFL Offensive Rookie of the Year in 1993. The Seahawks finished 6-10 and in fifth place for 1994 under coach Tom Flores. The team had an NFL-high seventeen players on injured reserve during the season, none returning in 1994 after injury, which undoubtedly affected their record. Running back Chris Warren led the American Football Conference in both rushing (1,545 yards) and total yards from scrimmage (1,868) and was second in the NFL in both categories to the Detroit Lions' Barry Sanders. Wide receiver Brian Blades caught 81 passes for 1,086 yards, his third year of more than 1,000. Only Blades and Steve Largent have racked up "over 1,000" records for the Seahawks. Two linebackers shone for the Seahawks. Rod Stephens finished the season with 128 tackles and Terry Wooden with 127.

Basketball

Around 1970 seemed to be the magic time for sports teams in Seattle. The Seattle SuperSonics joined the National Basketball Association in the 1967-68 expansion, competing in the Western Conference Division. The owner of the club was Sam Schulman; the first coach for two seasons was Al Bianchi. Like all new teams the Sonics, as they are popularly called, got off to a slow start.

In 1968-69 the picture changed when Lenny Wilkens came aboard from the St. Louis Hawks. Not only did Wilkens bring personal scoring ability to the team, but he was a dedicated player and set a fine example for the rest of the team. When Bianchi resigned partway through the season, Seattle SuperSonics manager Dick Vertlieb asked Wilkens to act as a player-manager temporarily. That "temporarily" turned out to be three years; after leading a drastically improved team to a winning record of 47-35 in 1971-72, Wilkens asked to be relieved of coaching and was stunned to find himself traded off as a player to Cleveland. On January 6, 1995, Wilkens as the coach of the Atlanta Hawks won his 939th game, taking the record for regular-season wins away from Red Auerbach set in 1966.

Schulman hired Bill Russell, formerly a coach for the Boston Celtics, for the 1973-74 season. Russell was an excellent technical coach, but his manner sometimes was abrasive. Nonetheless, with Spencer Haywood and Fred Brown leading the scoring, the Sonics turned a losing record into a winner at 43-39 in 1974-75. Sports fans like to nickname their players, and because of his reputation for long, looping shots, they named Brown "Downtown Freddy." Another fast and agile player, a real ball stealer, was rewarded with the name, "Slick" Watts (Donald Earl). Michael E. Goodman in a 1993 book about the SuperSonics quoted Schulman as saying, "I wish I had 12 Slick Watts on my team." He was an inspiration to the team and fans, on and off the court, where he frequently was involved in charitable works.

Until the 1977-78 season the Sonics were unimpressive. That year Schulman replaced Russell with his former assistant Bob Hopkins, but that was not working, either. Lenny Wilkens had returned to be the Sonics' manager, and Schulman asked him to be the coach. After rearranging the team, a move that cost him the affection of Slick Watts who requested a trade, Wilkens built his team around 7'2" Marvin Webster at center, Jack Sikma at forward, Gus Williams, and Dennis Johnson. The lineup worked so well that the Sonics made the playoffs and into the NBA finals where they lost to the Washington Bullets. With a different set of players—Webster had gone to the New York Knicks— that included newcomer Lonnie Shelton and John Johnson, Gus Williams, Dennis Johnson, Jack Sikma, "Downtown Freddy" Brown, and Paul Silas, the Sonics roared back the following year to capture the NBA championship. Fans called the above players the "Seattle Seven." A victory parade wound through Seattle's downtown area, showering the Sonics with confetti and cheers.

During the early 1980s the Seattle Seven became dispersed, however, and the team's record fell. It was not all their fault. Superstar Magic Johnson had entered the NBA picture for the Los Angeles Lakers and the Lakers swept the playoffs for several years.

The Sonics remained respectable, shooting their way into the playoffs, but there they could not maintain their steam. Meanwhile, communications magnate Barry Ackerly bought the franchise for the SuperSonics in 1983.

In 1985-86 Wilkens left and the Sonics had a new coach, Bernie Bickerstaff, formerly assistant coach to the Washington Bullets. Bickerstaff was an empathetic coach and soon had the Sonics welded into a team instead of a bunch of individuals. The team reached the playoffs and conference finals in 1986-87, and Bickerstaff was named Sporting News NBA Coach of the Year. Seattle hosted the NBA All-Star game February 8, 1987, and the Sonics' Tom Chambers was named the All-Star Game Most Valuable Player.

During the late 1980s key players included Xavier McDaniel (the "X-man"), Dale Ellis, Tom Chambers and Nate McMillan, Derrick McKey, Michael Cage, and Olden Polynice. The Sonics made the playoffs in 1987-88 and 1988-89 but their fortunes ended there each time. An interesting highlight of 1989 was a game against the Milwaukee Bucks, where the game lasted for five overtimes with the Sonics finally triumphing 155-154. The game tied a record for the longest game in NBA history.

In 1990-91 K.C. Jones, formerly the SuperSonics manager, was named head coach, but he lasted only until January 1993, when George Karl replaced him. Under both, the Sonics were remolded again and again through trades and rearranged starters. Gone were McDaniel, Ellis, and Polynice. Added were new stars like Shawn Kemp, Eddie Johnson, Benoit Benjamin, and Dana Barros. The great number of turnovers in personnel seem to have borne fruit, however. The Sonics finished second in the Pacific Division in 1992-93. In 1993-94 the Sonics made it to the top, winning the Pacific Division for only the second time in history. They also expanded on their prior year's record of games won (63). Better yet, their improving record caused a sellout for all forty-one home games.

Only three Sonics have been honored for their contributions to the teams by having their numbers retired: Fred Brown #32, Jack Sikma #43, and Lenny Wilkens #19.

Note: Although college sports are not included here, the prowess of its University of Washington teams is possibly of the keenest interest overall to Seattleites. Especially gripping are the annual football or basketball games between cross-state rivals, the University of Washington Huskies and the Washington State Cougars—the "dawgs" and the "cats."

Seattle Slew

Seattle gets credit for a star that never lived in Seattle—Seattle Slew, the winner of Thoroughbred racing's pearl, the Triple Crown, and the first to do so undefeated. The races constituting the Triple Crown are the Preakness, Kentucky Derby, and Belmont Stakes.

Seattle Slew's owners lived in White Swan on the eastern side of the North Cascade Mountains, a crossroads town in the foothills of Mount Adams, more than a hundred miles from Seattle. They were Mickey and Karen Taylor, and later silent partners from the East—New York veterinarian Dr. Jim Hill and wife Sally—incorporated as Wooden Horse Investments, Inc. Dr. Jim, as a track vet, could not own an interest in a racehorse and did not own stock until 1977. The group bought the unnamed colt, simply Hip Number 128, on July 19, 1975, for $17,500 at the Fasig-Tipton Kentucky yearling sale. The colt's handler called him Baby Huey, because he seemed so big, awkward, and a little coarse in conformation. But Jim Hill's practiced eye saw a runner.

He was very right.

Trainers and handlers continued to dub him Baby Huey or Hugo as the tall, undistinguished-looking colt went through his initial training. He was very amiable, though, and seemed to enjoy his working gallops. One day the trainer told the exercise rider to breeze the colt for three-eighths of a mile, no big deal. Was he in for a surprise! Permitted to really run for the first time, awkward Baby Huey became a greyhound, his long stride gobbling up the yards. When the rider pulled him up, everyone watching knew they had something special. The trick was to keep the big secret until he was ready to race, a secret that became badly kept.

Meanwhile, the Taylors applied to the Thoroughbred registry for the name "Seattle Slew," and it was granted. "Seattle" for the area, since the eastern racing circuit would never identify White Swan, and "Slew" for the marshy terrain of the Hills' Florida birthplace. The training staff still called him Huey.

In his maiden race at Belmont Park on September 20, 1976, the dark horse's potential speed had seeped out to betters somehow. Insiders who gleefully saw initial odds at 10:1 watched the tote board go to 5:2, their hoped-for returns melting away. Seattle Slew won the six-furlong race in

1 minute 10-1/5 seconds, leaving the nearest competitor behind by five lengths.

Slew's two-year-old season included only two more races, both of which he won—a seven-furlong claiming race and the Champagne Stakes at Belmont, where he romped home 9-3/4 lengths in front with the fastest mile ever run by a two-year-old.

Instead of using him up and risking injury, the owners quit for the year and turned the colt out to rest and let his big body mature for the more grueling three-year-old season.

Seattle Slew was embraced by all of Washington state as its hometown star. The Cinderella story of the Taylors as owners, racing for their fourth season only, was told and retold. Mickey was a logger who made good; Karen was an airline flight attendant. They were local thirty-ish kids who prospered in a tough game.

The unruffled bay colt did not disappoint them in his three-year-old season. After easily winning three more races, he slept quietly in his stall the day of the Kentucky Derby, the first Saturday in May. He gobbled up his feed enthusiastically and looked for more, but on race day breakfast was curtailed. As he came out onto the track, the crowd's excitement penetrated his usually calm attitude and he began to prance and sweat, worrying his trainers. In the gate Slew cocked his head to the side at the moment before the gates opened and came out crab-like, losing ground. Two lengths in the rear, jockey Jean Cruguet skillfully threaded through the field and pulled Slew in front to win easily by two lengths. The strong colt was still surging and could easily have gone farther. After only six races ever, Seattle Slew had won the Kentucky Derby handily. The next morning he was playful and exuberant, ready to go again.

In the Preakness, Seattle Slew would be asked to run a mile and three-sixteenths. This time Slew was entirely calm and self-possessed, as if he knew there would be no problem. He ran the first mile in the fastest time ever clocked to date in the Preakness; still fresh and in the lead, he ran the rest of the race without pressure, coming in a length and a half in front. The time was the second fastest ever, the same as that of Secretariat, 1 minute 54-2/5 seconds, even though jockey Jean Cruguet was not pressing the colt and was saving his strength for the final leg of the Triple Crown.

Now the Slew crew was tense. Could he do it? Could he win the Belmont Stakes and sweep the Triple Crown? And undefeated previously, as no other horse had done? Did he have any more left to give, to run the mile and a half? Of course, his jockey thought. He had breezed through the Preakness.

And so it was. Trainer Turner's agenda for readying the colt was a series of long, easy gallops instead of speed runs. Just building up even more endurance and wind and keeping the Slew, or Hugo, as the crew tended to call him, all relaxed.

The system worked. Seeming to be out for a morning gallop as he started into the Belmont Stakes, Seattle Slew covered the ground effortlessly—running as slow, his trainer said later, as he could be persuaded to run, yet keeping pace with the others. When the time came to win the race, Cruguet tapped him a couple of times and Slew surged ahead to win easily by four lengths on the muddy track.

He did it! He won the Triple Crown, catapulting Seattle Slew into racing legend—even if he wasn't from Seattle.

In 1978 he added more jewels to his crown by winning the Woodward Stakes and Stuyvesant Handicap. After that he was syndicated for $12 million. A match race between Affirmed and Seattle Slew in the 1978 Marlboro Cup was the first meeting ever between Triple Crown winners. Slew won that, too, with a time of 1:45 3/4, only a tiny fraction behind

Secretariat's record for 1-1/8 miles. Seattle Slew was turned out to stud after winning over $1.2 million in purses.

Read more about Slew:
Cady, Steve and Barton Silverman. *Seattle Slew*. New York: The Viking Press, 1977.

Buildings

The Kingdome

Obtaining a major league baseball franchise and the building of a major sports stadium were a "chicken-and-egg" situation in the 1960s and early 1970s. Sick's Stadium was obsolete, although it was used by Pacific Coast League Rainiers. The stadium project was placed on the ballot twice, 1960 and 1966, only to go down in defeat—partly because of adamant opposition led by Frank Ruano, Stephen Chadwick, and Donald Schmechel. The 1966 campaign also was injured by the simultaneous appeal in 1966 for school bonds.

The stadium committee rammed a bill (SB 205) through the state government in 1967 that authorized King County to use 2 percent of the existing 4½ percent hotel sales tax to retire stadium construction bonds. That enablement plus a multimillion dollar community improvement campaign called "Forward Thrust," and a public relations visit by Mickey Mantle resulted in a 62 percent voter approval of stadium bonds of $40 million in 1968.

While waiting for the stadium to be built, the American League team, Seattle Pilots, came and went. The bonds were approved but a virulent battle about the site for the stadium ensued, chiefly pro and con for its location at Seattle Center. At one time a committee had to evaluate the merits of 109 suggested other sites. It took John Spellman, elected King County Executive in April 1969, to get things off center. He wove his way through the political and legal pitfalls and on December 7, 1971, pulled the first iron spike from the old railway tracks that blocked the present 35.9-acre stadium site. By the end of the year the design team of architects, engineers, and planners—Naramore, Skilling, and Praeger—held a briefing on the plans.

Even then, opponent of the plan Frank Ruano collected signatures on a petition to place an anti-stadium proposal on the next ballot. The case was tried in court, and Kitsap County Superior Court Judge Oluf Johnsen declared the stadium program was not subject to referendum or initiative, invalidating the ballot proposal.

The county named Gerald Schlatter, head of its Division of Architecture, as overseer and then Project Director. The original prime contractor was the Donald M. Drake Company of Portland, Oregon. On November 2, 1972, ground was officially broken, pilings were driven, and construction on roof support columns began. By the spring of 1974, some were in place, despite delays from an ironworkers strike. Drake Company got into a dispute with the county and defied orders to return to work. The county declared the company in default of its contract and assigned Peter Kiewit Sons Construction Company to proceed with the work.

Kiewit was ahead of schedule when the forty-two roof support columns and domed roof were completed by June 1975. The Kingdome opened March 27, 1976. At the peak of construction 336 people were employed. Bob Sowder of Naramore, *et al.* and Jack Christiansen of Skilling *et al.*, both of Seattle, directed the design team, along with Praeger-Kavanagh-Waterbury of New York, architects and engineers. County officials advising John Spellman included

Ruby Chow, Bill Reams, Norman Maleng, stadium manager Ted Bowsfield, and stadium project manager Gerald Schlatter.

Courtesy of the Kingdome

The Kingdome is 660 feet in diameter and 250 feet high at its apex. It is anchored on its site by 1,822 concrete-filled steel pipes and forty-two wooden piles that extend down sixty feet into hardpan earth. Computers were used to create a model of the dome, then subjected to loads and stresses three and a half times greater than the maximum anticipated. Originally the stadium had 15,000 theater-type seats, and the balance were aluminum bench seats with backs. A federal grant of $765,000 subsequently was obtained to reinforce the flooring so it could support heavy equipment and displays and also provide for a utility grid under the floor for electrical and telephone circuits to be used by exhibitors.

Provision was made for parking 2,700 cars on site; officials estimated that 17,000 additional cars would find space on and off street within a nine-block perimeter.

A colorful porcelain bottle commemorating the King-dome went on sale in the fall of 1975 at Washington State Liquor stores as a collector's item. A "Stadium '75" pin sale began in the fall of 1973 in anticipation of a 1975 opening; funds were to underwrite the cost of opening ceremonies, which did not occur until March 27, 1976, tapping into the bicentennial year promotions. The first scheduled event in the Kingdome was on April 9, an exhibition soccer match between the Seattle Sounders and the New York Cosmos.

Since its opening, the Kingdome has hosted events such as a boat show, RV show, home show, auto show, rodeo, truck and tractor pull, concerts, paper airplane contests, motor-cycle (motocross) races, and conventions, as well as sports events. Surprisingly versatile conversion methods permit seating for sports events of 65,000 for football, 40,000 for basketball, and 60,000 for baseball. For concerts, speakers, and such, the Kingdome holds 75,000. The conversion times range from six to thirty hours by a crew of twenty.

Trade show exhibitors assemble their displays on the floor and add carpets themselves. Dirt is rented from a nearby excavating firm, trucked in, and spread on the floor for rodeo and motocross events. Bulldozers mold the dirt to form the motocross track and rodeo corrals. Afterward the dirt is trucked back to the excavators.

About half the Kingdome is utilized for basketball. The hardwood court is constructed of 240 rectangular pieces, bolted and latched together. Portable seats are then wheeled into position for the audience. Other sports events are on half-inch-thick Astroturf with a five-eighths-inch energy-absorbent foam pad underneath. The turf comes in fifteen-foot-wide sections, fastened together with zippers. For baseball a section of sideline bleachers is retracted by a hydraulic system and an infield wall inserted. Cutouts in the Astroturf provide an area of dirt for the bases and sliding.

The pitcher's mound is maintained on a removable platform, also with dirt added.

Although the stadium's construction cost overran the $40 million estimate by $20 million, the taxpayers actually paid for less than $13 million. An exceptional increase in the revenue received from the hotel tax paid for the bulk of construction.

The Kingdome has played host to numerous major events, including an NBA All-Star game, an NFL Pro Bowl, World Cup Soccer, and the 50th major league baseball All-Star game, with few problems. On July 19, 1994, four ceiling tiles, thirty-two inches by forty-eight inches, fell into the stadium, rendering it unsafe and closed for repairs until October 21, 1994. During the repairs two employees lost their lives in a fall; a plaque in their memory was installed on the exterior of the Kingdome at the entrance to Gate D.

All of the 40,000 acoustical tiles were removed and a new type of surfacing applied for greater safety. The stadium reopened November 4, 1994.

The Kingdome includes a sports museum, largely housing the collection of sports memorabilia of *Seattle Post-Intelligencer* reporter Royal Brougham. Tours of the museum and building are offered.

The Smith Tower

For several decades the Smith Tower on Second and Yesler, forty-two stories high, was the tallest building west of the Mississippi. Upon its completion in 1914, it was the fourth tallest building in the entire world. Dwarfed now by downtown skyscrapers, the Tower is on the National Register of Historic Places.

Most of Seattle in the early decades consisted of modest structures a few stories high. Yet the setting was spectacular, backed by the usually snow-covered Cascade Mountains, their "tower" 14,500-foot Mount Rainier. The steep slopes of the city afforded splendid views of Puget Sound, the Olympic Mountains, and the islands in between. Back in Syracuse, New York, seamstress Mary Slocum served and became a friend of the mother of Mrs. L.C. Smith. Mr. Smith already had done well at gunsmithing and was amassing a true fortune from using his technical experience to manufacture typewriters.

Smith Tower

Slocum moved to Seattle in the early 1880s, and eight years later, Mrs. Smith visited her there. She returned home to rave about Seattle's future and beauty to her husband, who soon made a visit to see if the rhetoric were true. Thus, he was in a receptive mood in the early nineties when J.W. Clise of Seattle went East to sell lands belonging to Watson C. Squire, then one of the largest individual property owners in Seattle. Smith proceeded to buy not only the Second and Yesler site, but the following, several with four- and five-story buildings on them: the Pacific Block, the northwest and southwest corners of Occidental and Main streets, the northeast corner of King and Occidental, the Marshall Building at the southeast corner and the Grand Central Hotel at the northeast corner of First and Main, and the northwest corner of First and King.

Almost two decades passed until Smith and a friendly competitor sparred about who would build the tallest structure in Seattle. The competitor, James Hoge, planned a building at Second and Cherry of about fourteen stories. When Smith discussed it with his family, his son Burns (who had been studying skyscraper design) convinced his father, with help from Mrs. Smith, that the building should be so tall that none would be likely to eclipse it. So it was that the building was designed for twenty-one full-width stories, plus a twenty-story tower and pyramid topping it off at forty-two stories. The architects, Gaggin & Gaggin of Syracuse, went to work in 1911 and the work was completed in 1914.

Smith spared no expense in making the building handsome and, unusual in that day, in assuring that it was highly resistant to fire or earthquake damage. The structure was anchored by 1,276 concrete pilings twenty-two feet long. A sway factor of twelve feet was incorporated into the building, a futuristic antiearthquake feature. The building suffered no damage from subsequent quakes, at least two of them severe. Framing was of steel. E.E. Davis Company, using a single crane, set a record by erecting eight floors of steelwork in one week.

One must touch the mouldings and doors to realize that these are not of wood but of metal. Eight coats of handpainted baked on enamel produce a convincing mahogany appearance. Smith was proud of his handiwork, and his initials L.C.S. appear on every brass doorknob and elevator front, and elsewhere in the building—about 2,000 times. Liberal use of solid bronze on window frames, and Alaskan marble and Mexican Pedara onyx in the interior added to the feeling of opulence. The Second Avenue lobby had a beamed ceiling that appeared to be supported by twenty-two Indian heads, hand carved and painted.

The 600-room building was topped by an electric lantern of solid bronze and heavy glass, eleven feet high, eight and a half feet in diameter beaming 6,000 candle power of light. Incoming ships used the lighted Smith Tower as a navigation beacon. At one time the ball or bubble atop the Tower flashed the hour and quarter-hour at night with red, white, and blue lights. An American flag flew from the tower.

Eight copper and brass elevators installed by Otis, sporting fancy grillwork fronts, are still at work—operated by persons, not automation.

L.C. Smith died before his building was completed, but his ideas were carried forward by his son Burns. On July 4, 1914, the business and social set attended an opening party. Smith gave a special tour to Admiral Teijiro Kuroi, commanding the Japanese training squadron then in the harbor. James Hoge, Smith's original competitor and owner of the second tallest building in Seattle, showed good sportsmanship by sending a big bouquet of flowers. A public relations employee startled media representatives by setting a fire on one of the floors to illustrate how fireproof the structure was.

L.C. Smith was a family man, as well as magnate. He dreamed of creating a setting worthy of a wedding for his daughter. On the forty-first floor of the Tower, he designed a Chinese Room, which has been used throughout the years for special parties and events. Spacious windows frame the matchless Northwest scenery. The paneling and ceiling are inscribed in Chinese characters telling of Washington's history. Furnishings are of very heavy imported blackwood, elaborately carved. One chair, the "Wishing Chair," was a gift from the Empress of China. According to legend, if a single woman sat in the chair, she would be married within the year.

Smith did not live to see his daughter married in the magnificent setting—but she was, indeed, married there within the year after she sat in the chair.

Publicity seekers could not resist the Tower. On opening day in 1914, some joker threw a dummy off the observation deck, sending a gasp of dismay through the crowds. A year later, a one-armed man declared he would parachute from the deck and, before police could stop him, did so—slamming against the fourth floor and landing stunned but safely. The observation deck subsequently was enclosed securely.

Still, a "cat" burglar in 1934 climbed to the twenty-first floor and pillaged offices as he went. Promptly caught, he surrendered his booty, a mere $362 in cash, jewelry, fountain pens, and stamps.

The pyramid-shaped portion of the tower, one flight above the Chinese Room, became the studio of artist Jack Corsaw in the late 1950s. In 1964 the building manager, Sanford Brandmarker, converted the space into a magnificent apartment for himself.

On the floor above the pyramid is a 15,000-gallon water tank. Between the 1920s and 1940s, sightseers were allowed on the floor and left their names scribbled on the walls and on the tank—graffiti from all over the world. However, today the public is not permitted above the thirty-fifth floor, where the Chinese Room is located.

In May 1976, quirky businessman Ivar Haglund purchased the Smith Tower and announced he would call it the "Ivary Tower." The city fathers and Seattle residents rose up in dismay and quashed the idea. Haglund did replace the American flag on the tower with his own insignia, a salmon windsock. (See Ivar, page 127.)

Pioneer Building

City father Henry Yesler was a fortunate man. At the time of the 1889 fire, only the foundation was under construction for his proposed Yesler Building on Pioneer Square, so it sustained minor damage. Today it stands intact as the Pioneer Building.

Handsome sandstone facade of 1889 Pioneer Building overlooks cobblestoned Pioneer Square, Seattle's historic district dating from the 1889 fire. Tours of pre-fire underground city depart from here year-round. (Photo courtesy of Seattle-King County News Bureau)

Prior to construction, the site was that of Yesler's residence. It was the scene of Seattle's last lynch party on January 18, 1882.

The city was tense, anyway, because of a series of armed robberies and the assassination of President Garfield. On January 17, a popular businessman, George Reynolds, was accosted by two men as he walked home from work. When the thugs called to him to hold up his hands, Reynolds reached for a revolver and the men shot him dead. The murderers were soon caught and dragged off to jail, with the police having a tough time restraining an angry mob. At a proper arraignment the following day, the judge said the men, James Sullivan and William Howard, should be held without bail, but this was insufficient for the spectators. They wrested the culprits from officers and hung them on maple trees in front of Yesler's residence.

There were those who would have approved such a disposition of hard-headed businessman Henry Yesler, too. However, in history he is hailed as an upstanding pioneer.

Whatever Yesler's character may have been, his building became the bulwark of Pioneer Square, then center of Seattle's business district. It was the datum point from which all elevations were measured by surveyors. It was hailed as the most beautiful building in the West, noted for its two dramatic, skylighted inner courts five stories high, its elegant African mahogany paneling, and Richardsonian architecture. The latter featured heavy stone masonry and varying window design from level to level. Elmer Fisher was the architect of the building and, reportedly, of fifty-four buildings rebuilt soon after the 1889 fire. Directing the project was J.D. Lowman.

The Pioneer Building had a checkered tenant history. The first tenant was Puget Sound National Bank, and other businesses followed. For a time there was a skybridge across the street to the Butler Hotel where some ladies of dubious professions lived. Apparently some Pioneer Building men took long lunch hours. The Butler Hotel, however, was advertised as the finest hotel west of Denver and north of San Francisco, with guests of the calibre of Grover Cleveland, Theodore Roosevelt, and General John J. Pershing—so who could say but what the gentlemen were entertaining luminaries from out of town at lunch. Three decades later, a speakeasy thrived on one of the upper floors of the Pioneer Building, where patrons were warned of trouble by a buzzer system.

A *Seattle Times* article of October 14, 1941, reported that the five top floors were being closed because of excessive maintenance costs and empty offices.

In 1951 part of the building was used as a migrant center. Five of the building's six floors stood unoccupied for over twenty years until 1974, when restoration began.

The sprucing up of the Pioneer Building headed the list as a keystone to the rescue of the historic district from squalor. The architect for the renovation was Ralph Anderson. After extensive renovation and cleaning, the major tenant was Seattle's Metro, the transportation and operations complex. Twenty years later, the building houses a clientele typical of any office building. Some major changes were made during restoration: the heating and air conditioning systems were concealed in the original elevator shaft, and new open cage elevators were installed elsewhere.

Nippon Kan

Tucked below the noisy ramparts of Interstate 5 on Washington Street in the international district is a performance hall, the Nippon Kan Theatre. It was built in 1909 by the Cascade Investment Company formed by Messrs. Taka-hashi, Hirade, and Tsukuno, with financial backing by Masajiro Furuya. Built on a steep hill, it is a two- to four-story wooden structure with a meeting hall/stage on the first floor and offices elsewhere.

During pre-war days the Nippon Kan was the center of social activities for the Japanese and Japanese-American community. The Japanese were keenly interested in current events and one entire 1910 program in the Nippon Kan archives lists twelve speakers with topics ranging from the election of the officers of the Japanese Association in Washington State to "My Opinion on Current Events." The discussions drew standing-room audiences, who sat on the hard benches or rented or brought cushions with them.

Japanese theatre productions were popular, and the endlessly long kabuki plays brought out whole families who brought their lunches (and cushions) with them for performances as long as six hours. Not only Japanese cultural events were held there, but Boy Scouts and Girl Scouts met there, "Roaring Twenties" dancers, and non-Japan-related events. Traveling evangelists thundered their messages in the hall, as there were several Christian, as well as Buddhist congregations with many Japanese members in Seattle—especially the Catholic Maryknoll organization, the Baptist Church, and others.

Sports clubs received instruction at the Nippon Kan and gave demonstrations of the martial arts. Metropolitan Opera singer Tamaki Miura and Tomi Kanazawa who had sung in the opera *Madame Butterfly* came to the Nippon Kan. Shisui Miyashita, composer and conductor, led the Seattle Symphony Orchestra in a performance featuring pianist Sachiko Ochi at the Nippon Kan in 1936.

Of course, all activities came to a halt after the relocation of many Seattle Japanese. The building fell into disrepair. Ed and Betty Burke purchased the building from the former owner, Abie Label. It was not much to look at, all but drowned by rampant blackberry bushes. The roof leaked, it needed paint, and fires had been lit on the second floor by transients, fortunately not resulting in destruction. The Burkes fixed up the place, trying to divert the drip-drip of rainwater by suspending plastic sheeting above the theatre floor and placing garbage cans strategically. The renovated offices upstairs went unleased.

The Burkes were able to keep the place afloat and, with renewed interest by the community, managed to gain a spot on the National Register of Historic Places. They obtained a grant and financing for renovation and eventually added a parking lot. Gradually the Nippon Kan came to life again, with everything from business meetings to kabuki plays. On two occasions the Shirayuri Children's Orchestra of Tateyama, Japan (Bellingham, Washington's sister city), came to perform—the second time in a joint performance with Seattle's own high school group, the Imperials. The Nippon Kan throbbed to lively music from wedding receptions and private parties.

A curious tradition has been maintained. The left-hand wall of the stage is covered with the signatures of those who have performed there throughout the history of the building (including the author of this book, who lectured there).

Other Interesting Buildings

Historic

ALASKA BUILDING
618 Second Avenue South

The building was constructed in 1904 for an investment group that included the Scandinavian American Bank and J.C. Marmaduke, a Missouri developer. The designers were Eames and Young of St. Louis. It was the first concrete and steel building in the city. Most of the others of the time were of masonry, brick, wood, and mixtures of materials. The building was faced by brick and terra-cotta and still is sturdy and attractive. The lobby has white marble walls and ceilings, with archways leading to the stairways. Brass light supports line each wall of the lobby.

When investment group Morton, Biehl, and Mortenson acquired it in 1959, one-third of the building, floors ten to fifteen, was occupied by the United States Coast Guard as its Northwest Regional Headquarters. It was a most suitable tenant, for clearly a maritime-related enterprise had been in the building since its construction, because the fifteenth floor windows are large portholes on the side facing Elliott Bay. One of the investors, George Mortenson, recalls that there was a huge board, perhaps 10 x 25 feet, across one wall of the fifteenth floor that showed the position of every known ship at sea, updated regularly. Unfortunately for the investment firm, the USCG moved to the Government Building later.

The fifteenth floor currently consists of several sizes of conference rooms used by the main tenant, the City of Seattle. The space once was a ballroom and was home to the Alaska Club, a private social club.

193

ARCTIC CLUB BUILDING
Third and Cherry

The Arctic Club was a social club of prominent citizens, which originally was housed at the Morrison Hotel, Third and Jefferson. The membership outgrew its building and the Arctic Club Building was erected in 1916 on the site of the original Seattle Theater. Designed by A. Warren Gould, the building provided nine stories for the club plus additional offices.

The exterior is quite handsome, faced in cream terracotta. Over the club entrance was a life-size polar bear figure (since removed), and the faces of walruses, tusks and all, were carved intermittently into the facade. The original, protuding terra-cotta tusks were removed several years ago and replaced with lighter cement replica tusks by the management, who feared that the tusks would fall on passers-by during a possible earthquake. The top floor exterior also was quite elaborate with multicolored matte glaze terracotta decor along the main cornice and spandrels.

The Arctic Club lobby was finished in imitation Caen stone. There were paneled meeting rooms on the second floor.

In 1971 the Arctic Club merged with the College Club and vacated the Arctic Building. While the building has been devoted to offices of the City of Seattle since 1973, the splendid dome room remains on the third floor. It was originally the club dining room but now is used for special events. A crystal chandelier hangs about fifteen feet down from the center of the dome. Stained glass panels alternate with broad, ornately carved ribbing about two feet wide to form the ceiling of the sixty-foot-square room. The circumference of the dome at the termination of the curved dome panels features friezes of fruits and vegetables. On one wall are eight square smaller stained glass windows, and adjacent to the domed room is an additional columned room.

Scenes on the tiles of the fireplace are of Mount Rainier and Lake Washington.

THE BRODERICK BUILDING
810 Second Avenue South

One wishes the building could talk, for here took place many of the biggest business deals in Seattle's history. Originally the Baily Building, it was one of the first office buildings built after the 1889 fire. It was completed in 1891 for William Baily by Saunders and Houghton who had built other Seattle buildings for Baily. The six-story structure was of local sandstone blocks, an early form of construction. The original owners shared (still do) a peculiar ten-foot strip of land with the adjacent Butler Hotel, now a parking garage, that was reserved for horse-drawn carts to load coal into the buildings. There were thirty-four fireplaces in the building at time of construction. The flues are still in the building, although it is illegal to light fires anymore.

For many years a tenant of the building was Western Union's Seattle office. Even within the city companies communicated with each other by telegram, much as today they are connected by fax machines, and a network of pneumatic tubes came into the offices on the top floor. Such tubes ran to the heart of the downtown business area and, for all we know, may still be there.

Today the interior courtyard of the Broderick Building is enclosed, with long windows stretching to the skylight, but in earlier years it was open to the elements. The courtyard is simple with a snack bar and tables available for employees and visitors.

Possibly the most interesting aspect of the building's history was that its next owner, Henry Broderick, one of the major leaders of Seattle for decades. Broderick came to Seattle in 1905 and, having learned shorthand, worked as a secretary for John Davis, then the largest real estate agent in Seattle. About that time, the railroad boom came to Seattle, and according to current owner Martin Smith, one day a man bustled in while Davis was out of the office. Since no one else was there, the man demanded that Broderick go with him to Fourth and Jackson, still at the edge of tidelands. He gestured sweepingly and said he wanted to buy all "that land" for the railroad. Broderick gladly assisted him. Later Broderick started his own firm and was exceedingly prosperous. Some of downtown's major exchanges of property went through his hands, among them the moving of Frederick and Nelson's store from its original Second Avenue location. His firm of 175 people merged with Coldwell Banker in 1968. He was on the Board of Regents of Seattle University and a Director Emeritus of Seafirst Bank.

Broderick was a very modest man and lived simply. He had no children and worked until his death, four months short of age ninety-five. According to Smith, he was a man of quiet good deeds, who gave money outright frequently and anonymously to those in particular need. He never learned to drive or owned a car, always taking taxis. A measure of his popularity was that, when he needed blood after an operation, a procession of taxi drivers came to offer theirs. The Broderick Building is only one visible reminder of Broderick's multifaceted life in Seattle.

CENTRAL BUILDING
810 Third Avenue South

The Central Building is interesting because it was built so that additional stories could be constructed above the ninth floor. A slab was in position there for the purpose. Projected were two additional floors over the entire building and four stories above the central portion, a sort of square tower and penthouse. The addition was never made, although the architect's drawings show how it would have appeared.

The appearance of the original building has changed little. It was built in 1913, eight stories with a penthouse at the ninth. It may have been influenced by the architectural theory of forthright, clean construction to represent American, not European style architecture. The exterior is of plain terra-cotta decorated in black with few frills and furbelows, indeed giving a modern appearance today, eighty years later. An inset exterior balcony on the third floor, with low railings flush with the front facade suggests a good location for some public speaker.

The entrance lobby utilizes white marble for floor and walls, relieved only by green and gold molding around panels in the ceiling.

The Public Defender's offices occupy the eighth and ninth floors and general offices the rest of the building.

COLMAN BUILDING
801-21 First Avenue South

Today, one of the most impressive and historic buildings remaining from old downtown Seattle is the Colman Building, still very much in use and a handsome structure facing the Sound.

Pioneer Laurence Colman's first office was on the *Windward*, a retired clipper ship on the Seattle waterfront. After the tidelands were filled and the waterfront extended, the first Colman Building was erected over or adjacent to the hulk of Colman's clipper. The six-story brick-faced commercial building with stone and marble trim is well maintained and in full use today. According to architectural historian Lawrence Kreisman, the Colman Block is an excellent and early example of the influence of Chicago commercial style on Seattle architecture. The 1889 building was planned by S. Meany as only two floors, but architect August Tidemand in 1904-06 added four floors and a new facade. Kreisman said in his book *Historic Preservation in*

Seattle that the large pivoting windows, brownstone base, and absence of most classical ornamentation reflected architect Louis Sullivan's belief that twentieth-century American buildings should honestly express their function without adhering to archaic decorative principles.

A particular feature of the Colman Building is the width of its hallways, about double that of later structures. The lobby is quite stunning with marble floors and partial marble walls with wooden cornices. A stairway worthy of a descending bride leads to the second floor, the scrolled ironwork topped by a brass rail. Polished brass water fountains grace each floor.

The waterfront location of the Colman Building was useful to the many fisheries and maritime companies that occupied the building. However, a partner of a one-time investment company that owned the building, George Mortenson, says that at one point in the 1960s, there were forty-two attorneys in the building.

Ernst Hardware Company's first store was located on the retail level of the building, but other retail enterprises fill several storefronts today. The Colman Building appears to be as sound today as it was a hundred years ago. A convenient access ramp leads to the waterfront adjacent to the northwest side of the building.

COURT IN THE SQUARE
401 Second Avenue South

Only a block from the Kingdome, the handsomely renovated Court is entered under an awning that extends toward the street. Two buildings—the 1906 Goldsmith Building and the 1900 North Coast Building—were joined by an attractive courtyard to make one office building. The restructuring took place in 1985 as part of the Pioneer Square project.

Railroad tracks formerly ran between these two buildings into King Street Station, just across the street. The courtyard consuming the defunct track space includes a concrete pool reflected in a tall mirror, large post lamps, and large potted plants. Windows to the west soar to the skylight, which opens during pleasant weather to create a garden ambience below. Each office complex of the Goldsmith Building has a small balcony festooned with hanging greenery facing into the courtyard.

B.F. DAY SCHOOL
3921 Linden Avenue North

B.F. Day School is the oldest continuously operating public school in the city. Before the school was conceived, B.F. Day paid the needed $100 three-months' rental in 1890 for three rooms at the Nichols Building in Fremont to house about one hundred students. They then offered to contribute $1,000 toward the construction of a permanent school building, but their kind offer was refused. Subsequently in 1890, B.F. and Frances Day offered to donate a block of their land with twenty 250 by 400-foot lots, for a school building. The gift was given with the stipulation that the school district should erect a brick building to cost no less than $25,000—a sum that assured a lasting structure in those days. The offer again was refused but was accepted a year later in 1891, after Fremont was incorporated into Seattle. J. Parkinson, Seattle School Architect, designed a two-story, brick school building of eight rooms, each with two tall windows set between structural members. The entire structure was 62 by 94 feet. In 1902 architect James Stephen (following Parkinson's original plans largely) designed an addition that formed the east-facing Romanesque revival arched entry and part of the north wing. In 1916, with still further expansion required, architect Edgar Blair designed another addition at both north and south completing the building as it is today.

HERITAGE BUILDING
111 South Jackson Street

The relatively small but unusual building was built of sandstone and brick in 1904. Always a warehouse since the turn of the century, the most recent such occupant was Standard Brands Paint. Following a fire, NBBJ (Naramore, Bain, Brady, and Johanson), second largest architectural firm in the United States, took over the building. The exterior was left virtually the same as the original construction, but the interior was dramatically renovated by NBBJ.

Upon entering the building through an added vestibule, one sees the red brick wall at the right continuing up the full five stories to a skylight, the original beauty of the bricks unadorned. A white zig-zag stairway angles up to the top story, giving the impression of a juncture of two separate buildings. Small balconies protruding on each floor from the left white wall create the feeling of a Mediterranean setting. An atrium tops the five stories, used for a lounge and lunch area.

NBBJ is the architectural firm involved with such interesting Northwest projects as the Two Union Square building, the Market Place Tower, and the Bagley Wright Theatre, all award winners. It has offices in Los Angeles, San Francisco, Tucson, Phoenix, Columbus, New York, and Research Triangle Park, North Carolina.

HOGE BUILDING
705 Second Avenue South

The Hoge Building is located on the site of the first white settler's cabin, that of Carson Boren. The eighteen-story building was completed in 1911, becoming Seattle's second skyscraper and the second to utilize structural steel cage construction. The Alaska Building, completed in 1904, was the first in both categories. James D. Hoge was the secretary-treasurer of the *Post-Intelligencer* newspaper and later the president of Union Savings and Trust.

Noting the severe damage sustained by San Francisco buildings during the 1906 earthquake, Hoge's architects Bebb & Mendel specified a structural design and types of materials that met seismic requirements. Builders broke all world's records for erecting the steel frame, taking only thirty days to complete the eighteen stories.

The exterior of the Hoge Building was finished with light colored brick and terra-cotta veneers. The building's base and crown were heavily ornamented in the Beaux Arts style with Corinthean pilasters, cartouches, medallions, and lions' head corbels and a substantial cornice, all of molded terra-cotta.

At the time of conception of their buildings, James D. Hoge and L.C. Smith announced a friendly competition for the tallest building of the time. The Hoge Building was eclipsed in height by the Smith Tower, completed in 1914. (See "The Smith Tower," page 183.)

LOWMAN BUILDING
105 Cherry Street

James Lowman, Henry Yesler's nephew and an owner of Lowman and Hanford, stationers and publishers, built the present building in 1907. The building was constructed on the site of Yesler's Pavilion, built by Yesler in 1865 in a corner of an orchard. For a time musical productions were held there. It was remodeled into offices in 1887 but burned in the 1889 fire.

MARION BUILDING
Second and Marion

The small office building has the dubious distinction of being two stories shorter than its original configuration, since they fell off during the 1965 earthquake.

MERRILL PLACE
318 First Avenue South

Covering an entire square block facing on First Avenue, Merrill Place is a joining of the large brick 1905 Schwabacher Hardware Building, their 1909 warehouse behind (once a performing arts hall for Empty Space Theatre), and two other smaller buildings—the 1913 Hambach Building and 1906 Seller Buildings. One would never conceive from the exterior that such an imaginative, significant complex would result. A waterfall tumbles into the inner open-air court surrounded by greenery. The top three floors have been converted into view apartments, secluded and safe. A major software company occupies a large complex of offices, and on the ground floor is the Il Terrazo Restaurant, named as a "top ten" eatery, a fine arts shop, etc.

On the Underground Tour of Pioneer Square one can still see the sign for Schwabacher Hardware. The firm supplied gold prospectors and later mining companies, logging firms, and others from Alaska, as well as locals.

MUTUAL LIFE BUILDING
605 First Avenue South

The building was constructed on the site of Henry Yesler's cookhouse for the First National Bank of Seattle. The first floor and basement rose in 1890, right after the 1889 fire. In 1897 five additional floors were added by new owners, Mutual Life Insurance Co. Later, retail store space was provided at street level. An elegant cigar store occupied

some of the space, at one time an ice cream parlor flourished, and a speakeasy operated there in the 1920s. The
building stood vacant from about 1967 to 1982, but it was
restored as part of the Pioneer Square project. While the
exterior appears similar to the original, the interior was
completely gutted and replaced by modern office construction—although some of the original trim has been retained.

THE SEATTLE TOWER
1218 Third Avenue

Originally called the Northern Life Tower, built for the
Northern Life Insurance Company in 1905 by the Morgan
Brothers, the Seattle Tower may be the most *Pacific Northwest* building of old Seattle. The architect, A.H. Albertson,
sought to reflect the massive and enduring character of the
Cascade and Olympic mountains. The exterior thus soars
straight up to the twentieth story and, from there to the
twenty-seventh or top story, moves upward in gradations.
The intent was to reflect a crag, to create a building that
seemed to grow out of, rather than be placed on, the earth.

Gradations of exterior color from iron ore color at the
bottom to a much lighter color at the top were to simulate
the changing colors of Mount Rainier from evergreen forest
to white-capped summit. Three metal spires resembling
evergreen trees complete the Northwest theme.

The splendid lobby has marble walls with insets of
bronze depictions of evergreen trees, one inset above each
elevator. The gold leaf patterning of the ceiling suggests
trees and waves. The curvature of the ceiling in relation to
the vertical walls gives an impression of a tunnel, perhaps a
tunnel through a forest. In 1931 friends placed a bronze
plaque with likenesses of the builders, the Morgan Brothers,
at the far end of the lobby. Four chandeliers of pale green
crystal panels are harmonious with the general aspect.

After serving as the headquarters for Northern Life Insurance Company for almost fifty years, the building was vacated by the company in the 1950s. New corporate owners moved the company into a new Northern Life Building a block from the company's original site. The original became The Seattle Tower, a building housing the offices of diverse firms.

Some Newer Buildings

Seattle has experienced immense growth in the past decades. Many new skyscrapers have overshadowed the original ones, which seemed massive in their time. Here are a few outstanding examples:

COLUMBIA SEAFIRST CENTER

Completed in 1985, the Columbia Seafirst Center is the tallest building, by the number of stories, west of the Mississippi River, towering seventy-six stories above Fourth Avenue. It is twice the height of the Space Needle. In addition it has a garage, retail space, offices, and six stories of below ground parking. The Columbia Tower Club on the top two floors enjoys a matchless view, but is a membership-only club.

One and one-half million pounds of Carnelian granite were used in the walls and flooring of the building. The cost of the lobby alone was about one million dollars.

TWO UNION SQUARE

The building is another recent addition to the Seattle skyline, interesting because of its unusual design. Great attention was given to designing a building that reflected the Northwest's natural environment and Seattle's industries, marine and flight. To achieve this a soft-flowing wave form repeats itself throughout the building, suggesting a sail or a wing profile, wind or water in motion. The light fixtures throughout the building are designed with the same themes in mind, as are colors of carpets and decor.

The structure is fifty-six stories high. A part of the building is a three-level, one-acre retail space surrounding a courtyard. An urban garden on the top level, plants, paths, and a waterfall create a refuge. A great waterfall cascades over real granite boulders in the center of the courtyard.

Designers used marble and woods liberally to enhance the seashore and forest feeling of the office structure, topped by a tower that is described as a crystalline box with a sloping penthouse angled toward Elliott Bay. Views from the building include the Olympic and Cascade mountains, the lakes, and the Sound.

WASHINGTON MUTUAL TOWER
1201 Third Avenue South

The fifty-five-story skyscraper was built by Wright Runstad & Company and designed by William Pederson of the New York firm Kohn Pederson Fox. The *New York Times* declared it one of the nation's three best new office buildings upon its completion in 1988. The basic design is a clean, square, modern building that utilizes stone and glass effectively. The tower takes a more historic pyramid shape to match or reflect surrounding buildings, with grillwork and strips of reflective glass that change color with the sun—bright green on sunny days, bluish-green on cloudy.

Because the Washington Mutual Tower site extended to Second Avenue and encompassed the old Brooklyn Building, designated as a Seattle landmark, builders had to strengthen the ninety-year-old structure. The Brooklyn Building was first listed in the Polk Directory in 1891, with one Sarah A. Kinnaman offering furnished rooms for rent.

Following the 1889 fire, many small residential hotels sprang up to house displaced persons.

The public spaces of the building have a hotel ambience. The Tower building has an atrium, outdoor plaza, a day-care center, fitness center, and other modern amenities.

THE SEATTLE ART MUSEUM AND THE FINE ARTS SOCIETY

Even as the rough and tough pioneer period of Seattle dominated the waterfront with gold and coal miners, loggers, and sailors, gentler pursuits began. In 1894 Ella Shepard Bush, formerly of Pennsylvania, started the Seattle Art School, attracting a group of pupils working in different media. Soon the Society of Seattle Artists was founded, and the members hosted an exhibition of their works in 1904.

Leading the movement for a more comprehensive arts organization were Will Conant, W.W. Kellogg, and Mr. and Mrs. Herman H. Field. The Seattle Fine Arts Association was organized in March 17, 1908, by forty-two people, who put together an exhibition in June of Japanese prints donated by sixty-three Seattleites.

The 1909 Alaska-Yukon-Pacific Exposition opened in Seattle, and the Fine Arts Society managed a building devoted to artworks by renowned artists. The energetic group continued to obtain traveling exhibitions of works from Oriental rugs to photographs of the Panama Canal, working out of several buildings—outgrowing each one.

In 1930 Lawrence Vail Coleman, Director of the American Association of Museums, Washington, D.C., was hired to assess the Society's need for new, permanent quarters. As a result, Richard E. Fuller, president of the Society's board of trustees, and his mother, Mrs. Eugene Fuller, offered $250,000 for construction of a new building—provided the City of Seattle would donate the land in Volunteer Park.

Thus, the handsome Seattle Art Museum came to grace the city by 1933. There were 33,000 visitors on the first day of operation.

In 1951 Mrs. Donald E. Frederick donated the early seventeenth-century *Deer Scroll*, a portion of a scroll considered a National Treasure of Japan with the remainder of the scroll in the Emperor's collection. In 1989 Virginia and Bagley Wright donated to the museum their magnificent collection of Japanese folk textiles.

Two years later the building closed for refurbishment and realignment of the art collections. The new Seattle Art Museum opened in December 1991 at First and University, and the original one in Volunteer Park reopened in 1994 as the Seattle Asian Art Museum, its collections of Japanese, Chinese, and Korean art considered to be among the most important in the nation.

The downtown museum contains fine collections of African sculpture, Central American, South American, Ancient American, and Northwest Coast Native American art. It also exhibits American and European art; Northwest art in depth; Greek, Hellenistic, and Etruscan art and coins; and Egyptian, Mesopotamian, and Islamic sculpture, metalworks, and paintings. Numerous special traveling exhibitions are featured. The new building itself is handsome.

Not a skyscraper but a structure that melts into the landscape as if growing there, the Seattle Art Museum helps to anchor the restoration of old Seattle's downtown area, extending from First to Second Avenue on University Avenue.

The architect for the building was Robert Venturi, who later received the Pritzker Architecture Prize for his design. Venturi has been called an apostle of Postmodernism, a style that makes use of the past but includes America's own Main Street feeling.

To design the building was not easy, since there is a considerable slope from First to Second Avenue, and the architect decided to use the terrain instead of excavating a boxy building backed up against a retaining wall. A graceful, terraced stairway runs the length of the building outside and is repeated inside. At ground level windows complement the reddish-buff hue of the building, each bordered by red granite edged by bright-colored, glazed terra-cotta. Colorful, shiny tiles are incorporated into the motif. Etched into the curving exterior of the building is the sign "Seattle Art Museum" in very large letters.

At either end of the gallery floors wide windows provide a panorama of Elliott Bay and the city, respectively.

Warranting exclamations of awe from visitors, a giant, black "Hammering Man" sculpture soars forty-eight feet from the corner sidewalk, a fitting tribute to Seattle as a workingman's city. Unfortunately, a sling broke as the spectacular sculpture by Jonathan Borofsky was being lowered into place just two months before the museum opened. It had to be returned to a Connecticut foundry for repairs and was reinstalled safely a few months later in 1992.

CHAPTER 5

Hotels

Historic Hotels Still Operating

THE ALEXIS HOTEL, First and Madison

The hotel building was constructed in 1901, when the Pioneer Square area was the center of business. It was known as the Globe Building, housing the businesses of the owner, J.W. Clise. It had a checkered career after the central district moved north and Pioneer Square deteriorated. The building changed hands in 1917 and was occupied by tailors, pawn shops, inexpensive restaurants, and a public market. In the 1930s it was remodeled to become the Arlington Garage that encompassed both the old Alexis Hotel and the adjacent Arlington Building. Encouraged by the popularity of the Pioneer Square renovation into a prime tourist attraction, the Cornerstone Columbia Development Company gutted and totally rebuilt the interior of the building as a hotel; only the outside walls and courtyard are old, everything inside is new. Nonetheless, the hotel is listed on the National Register of Historic Places. The architect for the renovation was Bumgardner Interior Design. The lobby is paneled with circular and square columns breaking up the space. An unusual chandelier provides an accent. A skylight above gives the lobby a cheerful aspect.

The Painted Table Restaurant off the lobby is paneled in cherrywood, as are the bar and columns supporting the ceiling. Hand-painted pottery plates rest on each dining table, the work of local artists. A large, square, wooden art deco chandelier adds to the impression of age in the restaurant.

The Arlington Building, constructed in 1901, went from being a garage, as well, to house the Alexis Hotel's Arlington Suites. One may choose from fifteen plan configurations, nine color schemes, and a variety of amenities, including fireplaces, built-in bars, custom furniture, and antiques, in the suites. Rooms are equally individualistic.

One of the more unusual guests in recent years was the Sultan of Brunei, attending an APEC meeting (Asia Pacific Economic Council).

THE CLAREMONT HOTEL, Fourth and Virginia

Owner Don Barton completed a drastic five-year renovation and return to excellence in early 1995. The Claremont was built in 1927 by Stephen Berg. Architects were Stewart & Whitley, who did not build any other building of that size in Seattle, as far as is known. Barton said that the Claremont was one of several hotels built in the 1920s, about the same time as the elegant Olympic, to take advantage of the sharply increasing population. Included were the Claremont, Mayflower, Vance, Camlin, Vintage Park (formerly Kennedy), and the Pacific Plaza. Others in the group have been renovated in recent years.

In years past the Claremont was "the" place to stay for Alaskan visitors, one of those situations where one person tells another. A particular attraction for Alaskans, who tended to stay awhile in the big city at that time, was the inclusion of kitchens in every room or suite. A huge totem pole was mounted in the center of the lobby, as was a large signboard for guests to leave messages for other Alaskan travelers. Several Alaskan governors have stayed there.

Today one enters a lobby, alternately paneled and plastered, that soars at least twenty feet to the ceiling. Antique Viennese sideboards rest on either side of the entrance. The original terrazzo brown and white floor blends well with the marble wainscoting. Marble window seats have become display niches. A second inner lobby that graced the hotel was restored. Balconies with low railings of wrought iron and dark mahogany surround the inner court, once open to the air but now enclosed and lighted above.

A few steps from the lobby, a well-windowed lounge sports a very long cherrywood bar. An arch at each end of the room of latticework adds interest. This room reeks of history. It was the Colony Club, where young adults went to dance in downtown Seattle at midcentury. The club was operated by Norman Bobrow, who was also a major promoter of jazz and contemporary singers and stage acts. Bobrow was instrumental in assisting Pat Suzuki, a little-known singer, to gain the lead in the *Flower Drum Song* about two years after doing a performance at Seattle's Moore Theater. Suzuki later lived at the Claremont Hotel. The next famous restaurant to occupy the space was Art Louie's Chinese restaurant, which now is in Ballard as Louie's.

THE FOUR SEASONS OLYMPIC HOTEL

As Seattle grew into a small metropolis in the 1920s, the city had outgrown its fine hotels. Some were beginning to crumble and fade like aging dowagers. Particularly needed was a hotel that could accommodate conventions, as none existing was large enough. The business community decided that it was imperative for Seattle to have a new, elegant hotel if it were to retain a place among cities of the world. Entrepreneurs began to consider where to build such a place.

In 1894 the University of Washington relocated to its present site, and by hosting part of the 1909 AYP Exposition site on its grounds, it gained a number of permanent buildings left over from AYP. Meanwhile, the downtown tract obtained as a territorial university site needed development—the centrally located site between Third and Fifth, Seneca and Union known as the Metropolitan Tract. The property was leased to developer James A. Moore, who retained a young lawyer, John Francis Douglas, to manage it. To Douglas, it seemed like a good hotel site.

Detractors of that site noisily agitated for locating a new hotel in Pioneer Square, in order to retain the downtown core, for business was gradually moving north to its present center. While different factions argued about where the hotel would be, Douglas took matters into his own hands. Without consulting anyone, Douglas sent a steam shovel and dump truck to the site to begin digging. The papers thought the site had been decided and ran a story to that effect. In all the confusion the matter had been decided.

But where was the construction financing to come from? With the true, bootstrap mentality called the Seattle Spirit, businessmen simply raised the money jointly to build the hotel through a sale of securities to the general public, the shares bearing the name of "Kind Words Clubhouse."

The Olympic Hotel was designed by New York architects George Post and Son and opened December 6, 1924. It was acclaimed as the grandest hotel west of Chicago. The exterior reflected the Italian Renaissance period with facades of light-colored brick and terra-cotta. As the hotel was intended to accommodate conventions, the public spaces were extra large and meeting rooms were provided.

Builders used wood paneling polished to a warm glow in the lobby and public rooms. A crystal and bronze chandelier, deep piled rugs, and ornate plaster work added to the aura of opulence.

Four Seasons Olympic Hotel Lobby

Six orchestras played at the various rooms of the Olympic for the gala opening on December 6, 1924. An estimated 2,500 guests entered the flower-filled lobby. Yellow chrysanthemums and red roses graced every table top and every corner. Chinese maids were dressed in jade

green silk. Pretty girls wandered the ballrooms selling ciga-
rettes and cigars. Entertainers in sailor garb moved from
ballroom to ballroom. A special poem was penned:

It's theirs, all theirs.
So let 'em come,
And freely make themselves to hum,
Ain't Seattle going some!
Olympic put 'er there!

Within weeks the hotel was the center of social life. Mrs.
John Douglas was responsible for introducing the popular
Monday luncheons, often followed by fashion shows. Frank
Hull and his wife hosted Sunday dinner dancing in the
Georgian Room. Major dance bands played the Olympic
with their music often broadcast over radio station KFOA.

According to Nancy Wright and Barbara Aydelott,
writing in the fall 1987 *Columbia* magazine, a men's club,
reportedly founded by William Boeing Sr., retained a group
of fourth-floor rooms. A group of prominent businessmen
met daily in the hotel's grill beginning in the 1940s, referring to themselves as the "Olympic Roundtable." *Seattle
Times* editor Col. Alden B. Blethen lived in the penthouse
with his family from 1933-39.

Wright and Aydelott wrote that Col. Roscoe Turner, the
famous aviator, brought his lion cub to the hotel and that,
when Charles Lindbergh visited, enthusiastic fans grabbed
buttons off his vest and ripped sections from his clothing
before he was rescued.

As mentioned elsewhere in this book, successful Japanese businessmen who were excluded from certain social
clubs formed their own club in rooms of the Olympic.

With the addition of 300 smaller rooms in 1929 to
accommodate traveling salesmen, there were 756 rooms
in the old landmark.

In 1955 the Western Hotels, now Westin, acquired a lease on the Olympic. In 1962 the management demolished the landmark Metropolitan Theatre around which the hotel had been built, in order to provide a large ballroom facility and a driveway entrance.

Western's lease was about to expire in 1979, and since this property was part of the Metropolitan Tract, the latter's managers wondered if the aging building would continue to be profitable and considered demolishing it. Nostalgic community leaders appealed for restoration and continued use as a hotel. Its future was brighter after it was placed on the National Register of Historic Places in June 1979. The Metropolitan Tract management leased the property in 1980 to the Urban Investment and Development Company of Chicago and Four Seasons Hotels Limited, Toronto. Working with NBBJ Group of Seattle, interior designer Frank Nicholson of Concord, Massachusetts, and residential designer John North, the partnership invested $55 million to restore the hotel's grand public spaces and integrate new construction in a compatible manner. The upper floors were rebuilt to create larger guest rooms and suites, reducing the number of rooms from 756 rooms to 451 more spacious ones. The splenderous ballroom that had been built in the space formerly occupied by the Metropolitan Theater was demolished and replaced by a drive-in entrance courtyard.

Lawrence Kreisman described the restoration in his book *Historic Preservation in Seattle*: "A new Garden Court Lounge was constructed with five two-story Palladian windows similar to windows of the public rooms elsewhere in the hotel. A new glass-walled spa complex was added on a second-floor terrace facing south, its form influenced by nineteenth and early twentieth century conservatories. Additional meeting rooms were designed to complement the elegantly restored Spanish Ballroom and its adjacent foyer.

Other public spaces, including the lobby and the Georgian dining room, were restored and updated with the finest materials available, including imported oak paneling, eleven kinds of marble, handwoven carpets, antiques, and richly textured fabrics. Restoration included the original silverware, with coffee pots, chafing dishes, and candelabra. The exterior required tuckpointing and cleaning brick, and replacing missing cast iron trim and marquee fascia with a glass reinforced polyester resin to simulate cast iron. Glass reinforced concrete replicated damaged terra-cotta."

Glittering events continued to be held at the Four Seasons Hotel. One such event was the 1990 Annual St. Valentine's Chamber Music Fundraiser featuring the Broadway Symphony and Seattle Chamber Singers. The fifty-hour marathon began in the lobby on Friday, February 16, at 7:00 P.M. and continued until Sunday, February 18, at 9:00 P.M. Madrigal singers and Mozart string quartets held forth in the public areas, and Brahms was played in the Georgian Room.

The Four Seasons celebrated the seventieth anniversary of the Olympic/Four Seasons on December 6, 1994. The event was dampened somewhat by an unusual snowstorm that prevented members of a choir scheduled to sing from attending, and some special guests from venturing out. Nonetheless, it was a beautiful and meaningful affair. Twenty-five historical photos graced the walls. Albert Kerry Jr., age ninety-one, signed the guest book. He had signed the Four Seasons opening day guest book in 1982, and his father was the first to sign the guest book of the original Olympic Hotel opening in 1924. Robert Denny Watt and Brewster Denny represented the pioneer Denny family. The Four Seasons provided an enormous cake in the shape of the hotel. Altogether it was a fitting tribute to the grand old hotel, center of social activity for so many years, and moving toward a century of continuing service.

THE MAYFLOWER PARK HOTEL, Fourth and Olive

The hotel got a new lease on life during the establishment of Westlake Center, the delightful downtown shopping center, with the Metro station below the street. The Mayflower Park abuts on the Center with a direct walkway now into the hotel.

It was the Bergonian Hotel in 1927 and was then renamed the Mayflower Park under owner Stephen Berg, who also built the East Hotel and the Claremont. In 1933 it was renamed the Mayflower Hotel and after World War II was purchased by the Western Hotels as one of their original group. Now the hotel is again the Mayflower Park owned by Marie and Birney Dempcy.

It has an air of opulence with a truly magnificent five-tier crystal chandelier that almost overwhelms the first lobby and check-in desk. A second mezzanine lobby, off the first one just a few steps, is furnished comfortably almost as an oversized sitting room with couches and chairs, a grand piano, quietly elegant hangings, and carved gold molding above paneling.

SORRENTO HOTEL, Ninth and Madison

Surely one of the city's most impressive small hotels, the Sorrento was built in 1909 in time for visitors to the Alaska-Yukon-Pacific Exposition. Samuel Rosenburg, a clothing merchant, was the owner and Harlan Thomas the architect. He patterned the hotel after his impressions of the Sorrento, Italy, Sorrento Hotel. It was built in a V-shape with two wings embracing a private circular driveway graced by an Italian fountain and surrounded by a wrought iron fence, a very Continental entrance. The brick, seven-story hotel was decorated at the sixth story by intermittent medallion-like terra-cotta works. Four towers enhanced the Mediterranean or Italian Renaissance design of the Sorrento.

The interior has been modified considerably, but the basic design remains. A small entry with check-in desk leads into the lobby called the Fireside Room, which doubles as a dining room and a sitting room with a fireplace. A massive column is the core of the round room, paneled as are the walls with fine Honduran mahogany and graced with brass light fixtures. The room originally had large windows facing Elliott Bay that greeted incoming guests with a matchless view of the city and the Olympic Mountains, but since the view was later obscured by newer buildings, the windows were replaced with paneling. The fireplace was tiled with a Mediterranean scene in green and white, relieving the sheen of the surrounding wood. Potted plants, a profusion of small tables, and upholstered chairs today allow a multi-purpose use where lunch may be served or cocktails and hors d'oevres of an evening.

The keystone of the Sorrento Hotel was always its top floor restaurant, Top of the Town, which featured the entertainment of singer Betty Hall Jones for many years. Jones was remembered for her fancy hats, a different one each performance. Many proms and special events have been held at the Top of the Town, elegant even after its hotel portion became somewhat run down between the thirties and fifties. In 1960 the hotel was sold to Morton, Biehl, and Mortenson and Associates, who leased it back to the seller, John A. Metzger, for operation. In December 1981 other new owners, Michael J. Malone and Robert Burkheimer, restored the hotel to its former splendor. The remodeling resulted in seventy-six individually designed rooms and suites created from the former 150 rooms. Today partners Mike Malone and Craig McCaw operate the Sorrento. In 1990 they again refurbished the guest rooms and added a penthouse suite. Rooms and suites may have damask fabrics, patterned carpeting, roman shades, carved chairs, and other rich appointments, each room or suite different.

In its earlier decades the hotel received such guests as the Vanderbilts and the Guggenheims, who enjoyed staying in suites at the Sorrento. Indeed, Suite 408 is still supposed to be haunted by Cornelius Vanderbilt's ghost. Eileen Mintz, public relations person for the hotel, called in a psychic to give her opinion on this rumor and reported that the psychic felt very disturbed in that room and wanted to leave. The presence purportedly moves things around and makes unexplained noises, but most guests do not find him threatening.

A different kind of presence is an unknown species of small birds that return to nest under the rafters each spring for about three months—as regularly as the swallows that come back to Capistrano.

After refurbishing, the hotel attracted well-known guests such as Lily Tomlin, Beau Bridges, Raymond Burr, and business magnates whose privacy was respectfully protected. In 1994 Meg Ryan, Tom Hanks, and other members of a production company were in the hotel during shooting of scenes for the movie *Sleepless in Seattle*.

The main dining room, the Sorrento Grill formerly, then the Dunbar Room, and now the Hunt Club, was always a favorite meeting place for businessmen, as well as guests. Today its cuisine is faultless with an equally warm ambience in the design. True to the name, the restaurant serves wild game dishes—buffalo, venison, pheasant, duck, and shellfish—as well as a regular menu.

An interesting footnote is that, not long after building the hotel, Samuel Rosenburg traded the hotel for Bear Creek Orchard of Medford, Oregon. He placed his two sons, David and Harry, in charge of the orchard—the David and Harry known today throughout the world for direct-mail fine fruit boxes and baskets.

Not-So-Old Interesting Hotels

THE EDGEWATER HOTEL, Pier 67

The Edgewater is not an old hotel, having been built in the 1950s, but the setting is unique. One end of the graceful lobby is a ceiling-to-floor window that frames a panoramic view of Elliott Bay and the Olympic Mountains. The bottom of the window seems to disappear into the water, for the hotel is literally on the water; indeed, in prior days, the hotel advertised that guests could fish from the windows. They could, indeed, until safety regulations put an end to this charming pastime. A wayward guest crawling out the window would have landed in the water.

The Edgewater continues its love affair with water in a long restaurant with windows on the waterside. Not only is the scenery impressive, but one can watch the ships, boats, and ferries milling around and large planes descending over Elliott Bay on a flight path for Sea Tac Airport.

THE WESTIN HOTEL, 1900 Fifth Avenue

The hotel itself is unusual in design. The site is very historic. The fourteen-story Benjamin Franklin Hotel opened there in 1929, adjacent to the imposing Orpheum Theatre. The Benjamin Franklin was an expensive hotel with rates as high as three dollars per night, but guests endured the price because it was the hub for social activity, and they could enjoy the theater presentations, a real vacation in one place.

The very next year Western International Hotels (Westin Hotels & Resorts later) acquired the hotel. Things remained static for a time until 1948, when Western replaced the hotel's Outrigger Lounge with a more exotic Trader Vic's restaurant.

Twenty more years passed, the aging Orpheum was razed in 1968, and in 1969 the forty-story cylindrical tower of the first Washington Plaza hotel complex opened on the site, affording views from all rooms. It was the first major hotel to be built in Seattle for forty years. The architectural firm was John Graham and Company, the contractor Howard S. Wright & Company.

The Washington Plaza became so popular that a twin tower was erected on the site of the razed Benjamin Franklin Hotel, this one forty-seven stories. An 18,000-square-foot grand ballroom, indoor swimming pool, meeting rooms, and restaurants were housed in the base building that joins the two towers. The name was changed to the Westin Hotel in 1981.

Courtesy of the Westin Hotels

Historic Hotels That Are Long Gone

THE BUTLER HOTEL was the leading hotel of the early decades. It was a six-story structure at Second and James, and a walkway led from the Pioneer Building to the hotel to make it convenient for businessmen to meet their guests at the Butler. The vast dining room was bisected by a series of arches to separate the men's and women's dining sections. The proprietors were German immigrants Dietrich Hamm and Ferdinand Schmitz, gracious hosts. Before the days of the Butler's fame as a dine-and-dance mecca, soft dinner music was provided for years by Nicholas Oceconomacos (called "Connie Mack" by his close friends) and an ensemble. When it became an aging dowager, the Butler Hotel's six stories were modified to become a two-story garage. If only the remaining walls could talk, what stories of early-day shenanigans would be revealed!

◆ ◆ ◆

The C.C. CALKINS HOTEL on Mercer Island is long departed but was a rather ostentatious hotel for its time. It was an early destination resort for vacationing Seattleites, since it took a steamer ride to reach Mercer Island in 1902.

Calkins was a century ahead of his time, for he not only built a resort hotel, but his real estate ideas paralleled those of modern developers who build homes around golf courses or other natural attractions. Charles Cicero Calkins acquired a huge tract of land on Mercer Island, just south of where eastbound Interstate 90 now touches land, with only $300 capital. He subdivided the land surrounding the resort into lots, sold them, and recouped his capital plus considerable profit.

According to one historian the hotel had seventy-five rooms (another said only twenty-four rooms plus several parlors), four cottages, and a greenhouse not only to supply flowers for the dining room and lobby, but also as a showplace for exotic plants and flowers. The grounds surrounding the place were beautifully landscaped, as well. The hotel boasted elaborate architecture with a turret topping the castle-like structure.

The interior was equally posh, including a ballroom, dining room, and several small parlors. A grand staircase led from the entry to the second story. For the enjoyment of guests the hotel had a boathouse and Turkish baths.

The Calkins Hotel was popular from the beginning. Visitors got a feeling of "getting away from it all" when they boarded the steamer *C.C. Calkins* at Leschi Park for the trip to Mercer Island. Celebrities came. President Benjamin Harrison stopped at the Calkins during a boat trip around Lake Washington in 1891.

Calkins seemed to be prospering at last, after ventures in other states had failed, when his wife Nellie left him in 1890 and went East with their daughter Ruby. Ruby literally rolled out a second-story window from her bed (placed next to the window on a hot night in Atlanta, Georgia) and died of her injuries that same summer. The national economy faltered in 1891 and crashed in 1893, so that Seattleites had no money for frivolities like enjoying a weekend on Mercer Island. Calkins was unable to collect some of his land sales proceeds. He left the area in 1894.

The Calkins Hotel went through several subsequent ownerships. Dan Olden tried unsuccessfully to operate it as a hotel. Eugene C. Lawton bought it in 1902 and leased it to a Major Cicero Newell for operation as a school for delinquent boys. When news of Newell's cruel treatment of his charges became known, the school was closed and it became a private sanitarium for alcoholics and drug addicts for a couple of years. In 1905 it was a boarding house, and for a brief year it became a hotel again when Dr. J.J. Leiser bought it—only to have it burn down in 1908.

◆ ◆ ◆

DENNY HOTEL/WASHINGTON HOTEL. In the 1880s developers realized that the city needed an imposing hotel if visitors to the city were to be impressed enough to locate new businesses there. Arthur Denny and others announced in March 1889 that they would build a castle-like 500-room hotel atop Denny Hill. Fortunately, it did not exist before the June 1889 fire or it might have been consumed. It was designed by Stanford White of New York. The hotel was almost completed when the 1893 financial crisis stopped construction; it stood vacant for another ten years until James A. Moore acquired and completed it, renamed it the Washington Hotel, and prospered. Dominating the hill, the hotel sported turrets, spires, and towers like a nineteenth-century castle. Management advertised the hotel rather grandly as the scenic hotel of the world. The dining room featured as many as five gourmet entrees, with complete dinners for seventy-five cents. To get to the hotel from the business district, one boarded a cable car at Third and Pine to ascend the two hundred feet to the entrance, only a block away "as the crow flew." Although splendidly appointed and situated in the center of six acres of beautifully landscaped gardens, the Washington was torn down in 1906 to permit the Denny regrade, or flattening of Denny Hill. (See photo on page 10.)

◆ ◆ ◆

THE OCCIDENTAL HOTEL, rebuilt after the 1889 fire to be the Seattle Hotel, was located at the convergence of James, Yesler, and Second Avenue. (See "Old Places, New Uses.")

CHAPTER 6

Old Theatres

Beginnings of Theatre in Seattle

Seattle has a long history of interest in drama and the arts, far beyond that of most cities. As unwelcome a comparison as it may be for modern actors and actresses, the true roots of theatre in Seattle lie in the vaudeville theatres of questionable scripts and, worse yet, the box houses of the "Tenderloin District," a seamy area around Pioneer Square that thrived in Seattle's 1880s and 1890s. As Seattle cleaned up its corruption, the interest in stage productions remained and regular theatres took over around Pioneer Square and also moved northward to the respectable areas that now constitute downtown Seattle. Both performers and their scripts became mainstream, instead of from the bump-and-grind circuits.

A phenomenon embraced by operators like John Cort and John Considine, box houses were born of the extreme lack of decent women and the oversupply of lonely men in early Seattle. There simply were not enough Mercer Girls or unattached Indian ladies to go around. The box house gave those lonely males a lascivious venture into the world of female companionship. A typical box house consisted of a stage and runway, bar, and curtained boxes where patrons could see the activity but have privacy. The boxes were comfortably furnished with upholstered couches, and patrons could order drinks delivered to the box. Some of the stage performers tended to prance through their routines, then disappear into one of the boxes. Their activities within were left to individual decision, sometimes no more than friendly conversation. When the sale of liquor was outlawed at such establishments, the box house failed. Mayor Phelps, who sanctioned the liquor ban, was unusual, for most of the city authorities of the 1880s and '90s were corrupt, often virtually dependent on the payoff for their living expenses.

John Considine was one of the most prominent box house owners, as flamboyant a character as any in frontier legends. Driven out of business by the liquor ban, he returned about Gold Rush time when a newer mayor closed his eyes again to the "Tenderloin." Considine acquired the People's Theater in a basement and bought an interest in nearby Billy the Mug's saloon at Second and Washington. Above the tavern he opened the Owl Club Rooms, where gambling held sway. For about five years, all seemed rosy for Considine. He tried to protect his empire by supporting friendly politicians, but Seattle gradually managed to overcome the bulk of corruption that had made it known as one of the wickedest cities in the United States. Considine's wings were clipped a bit in June 25, 1901, when he actually got into a running gun battle with the new crusading police chief, W.L. Meredith, and killed the man at Guy's Drugstore at Second and Yesler. Considine was acquitted on the grounds of "continuous struggle," a term that suggested self-defense.

Eventually Considine moved on into legitimate theatre productions; he acquired an interest in Seattle's first motion picture theatre, Edison's Unique Theater, and staged live stage acts there, as well. In 1904 he and two others built the Orpheum Theater (not the handsome Orpheum that

stood at Westlake and Fifth). These
ued to expand their holdings throughc
managed or controlled more than fort.
fornia to Washington. Considine also be
Hollywood productions and became resp

Considine acquired a keen competi
Pantages, who came to open the Crystal 1.
very much a "shoestring" vaudeville and m.
house. But he was able to expand and encroach .
ine's virtual monopoly; in fact, by 1920 Considine
most bankrupt. Pantages acquired some of Consi.
properties, adding them to his stable of theatres that gi
into a vast chain covering the United States and Canada.

As Seattle began its crusade for a cleaner town, legitimate theatres opened to attract mainstream productions
with decent performers and clean scripts, productions from
New York stages, vaudeville acts to which a man could take
his gentle wife or daughter without shame. The Alhambra
Theater booked stage shows and melodramas. The Dream
Theater was one of the first to show the best of the new
motion pictures and held pipe organ music concerts, as well
as used the organ as background music (since "talkies" were
still a long way off). The Metropolitan, surrounded by the
Olympic Hotel, the Music Hall (only demolished in 1991),
the Orpheum, and other major theatres thrived from the
twenties to the sixties and even later.

Seattle's Own Architect

Before enumerating some of the more interesting
theatres, it is imperative to note that a Seattle architect,

Priteca, was responsible for many local theatres
nal ones, as well.

sman B. Marcus Priteca showed design talent as
s fourteen years of age. At nineteen he received a
rship from the Royal Institute of Edinburgh to enable
to travel to the United States for further study. Since
wanted to see the Alaska-Yukon-Pacific Exposition, he
ne to Seattle, where he was persuaded to stay on by
rchitect E.W. Houghton, who offered him a job as draftsman. It was the first step to a long, illustrious career.

Priteca did not stay long as a draftsman but quit to open
his own office two years later. In 1911 he received a contract
from Alexander Pantages to design a San Francisco theatre.
Pantages was to become the dean of the vaudeville theatre
business.

Priteca remained the sole architect for Pantages
Theatres from 1911 to 1929, after which the circuit was
dissolved. His offices remained in Seattle—for fifty years
within the old Pantages Theatre, later known as the
Palomar. During his lifetime he designed 60 major theatres
and 160 minor theatres for clients throughout the nation.
He also designed Longacres Racetrack.

Four Interesting Theatres Still Standing

COLISEUM THEATRE Building, Fifth and Pike Street

The building was remodeled in 1993-94 to open November 19, 1994, as a retail outlet for the Banana Republic.

The theatre was designed by architect B. Marcus Priteca
for owners C.D. Stimson and Joe Gottstein. The grand

opening celebration was on January 8, 1916, with matinee idol Wallace Reid attending.

The Coliseum was one of the nation's first theatres to be designed specifically for screening motion pictures. Designers also incorporated features that would make it possible to convert the Coliseum into an opera house, but this never happened.

The Coliseum was constructed of steel and reinforced concrete. The Fifth Avenue facade was set back from the street to accommodate a row of retail shops. The Pike Street side had no setback; shops were contained within the main structure. The exterior was of solid white terra-cotta with its design executed so as to retain the outline under illumination. On both sides the building sported arches and niches with scrollwork of fruit, flowers, and leaves. Above the arches were garlands draped between bullock's heads, a motif that originated in the friezes of Roman temples. Below the cornice, the name of the theatre appeared in Roman-style incised letters COLISEVM. Originally the recesses contained small white lights. The cornice also was studded with hundreds of tiny lights, so the building was quite spectacular at night. During remodeling for the Banana Republic the exterior was refurbished and, above the retail level, appears much the same as designed.

Revolving colored lights flashed from the marquee of the Coliseum Theatre. Above the corner ticket booth was a large coffered half dome crowned by a cupola of art glass, surmounted by a cluster light. The cupola was destroyed in the 1940s, and the half dome and marquee were replaced in 1950 by a more modern marquee with a neon-lighted revolving cylinder. On top of the cylinder was a gold-colored replica of the "Oscar" (given for various types of movie-related excellence). Unfortunately, it weathered badly and was removed in 1966.

Owners Stimson and Gottstein spared no expense, and the Coliseum boasted many firsts in theatre construction. The innovations included a nursery for small children, the first mezzanine, the first orchestra to accompany silent movie productions, and the first passenger elevator capable of transporting twenty-seven persons from the main floor to mezzanine to main balcony.

The domed ceilings were patterned in mosaics of rich blue tiling. The general decor was Egyptian above the proscenium arch and on walls. There was a small fountain, playing on glass globes illuminated by colored lights, on each side of the stage. Between them were the elevated orchestral pit and the organ console. The Moller pipe organ was the largest theatre organ of its day, and the organist could "rattle the rafters."

Hardwood seats were upholstered in leather and were placed to provide plenty of leg room. One hundred fifty box seats, or loges, equipped with comfortable chairs of German rattan occupied the curved mezzanine balcony. A form of air-conditioning, unusual for that day, was provided.

The Coliseum was renovated in 1950, and searchlights probed the skies to advertise a grand opening on December 29, 1950. The aging building was named a Historic Landmark in 1966, but the Coliseum continued to serve Seattle until 1990.

As indicated earlier, after lease by the Banana Republic, the exterior of the old Coliseum Theatre was cleaned and restored in 1994. The interior was reworked for the retail store, but vestiges of the original wall etchings were retained as much as possible. Although closed off, parts of the theatre remain in an unused section of the building.

5TH AVENUE THEATRE, 1308 Fifth Avenue

Currently the host to musical theatre productions and guest performances, the 5th Avenue Theatre and the Skinner Building in which it is located were designed by respected Seattle architect R.C. Reamer. The theatre opened in 1926 and was drastically refurbished in 1980.

The design was extremely ornate with an overall Chinese architectural design, capitalizing on Seattle's avowed position as "Gateway to the Orient." The theatre was modeled after the Summer Palace, the Temple of Heavenly Peace, and the Throne Room of the Imperial Palace in Peking's Forbidden City. Construction features included heavy timber columns, beams, and coffering for which Imperial Chinese architecture was known. (Reamer used heavy timbers and beams in his design of the Old Faithful Inn in Yellowstone National Park, as well.)

The design team included Gustav Liljestrom, a protegee of Cecil B. DeMille, who had sponsored gallery exhibitions of the artist's works. Liljestrom had been trained in China before he became the chief designer at the S. & G. Gump Company of San Francisco, famous for its hotel and theatre interiors. Liljestrom supervised the interior decorative painting.

One of the auditorium's most spectacular features was the great, coiling dragon presiding over the domed ceiling, which was a nearly exact replica of the dome from the throne room of the Forbidden City. In the Grand Foyer, great lacquered pillars held up the mock-bamboo roof of the heavenly temple. Foo dogs stood guard on either side of the original cage box office, but now they guard the lobby staircase. Every care was taken with each detail of the art so that, to many, the 5th Avenue Theatre was the chief example of Chinese architectural design in the United States.

The first production company was Fanchon & Marco, which staged such acts as *Boyce Combe and the Sunkist*

Beauty Review and a photoplay *Young April* by Cecil B. DeMille. A crush of people trying to gain entrance attended opening night September 24, 1926, a queue extending over seven city blocks.

Films began to replace live theatre, but James Q. Clemmer, one of the Northwest's great film exhibitors, added a touch of "live" to the film showings. The great Wurlitzer pipe organ rose from the center of the orchestra pit to burst forth at a precise, suspenseful moment in a movie being shown. He costumed the staff to match the style of the feature currently being shown, and in the lobby he placed "Jim Q," a large talking teddy bear that greeted the children. Keeping the faith, when teddy's voice broke down, he was reported to be recovering from toy surgery.

The increasing popularity of television and the trend toward smaller neighborhood theatres contributed to the decline of the 5th Avenue's popularity. The 2,400-seat theatre became unprofitable and closed in 1978. Two years later, when developers proposed to gut the interior to make way for a shopping mall or offices, local theatre fans and businesses came to life and protested that it was less costly to renovate the magnificent 5th Avenue Theatre than to build a new performing arts facility. No existing facility could replace the theatre. Forty-three businesses and individuals banded together to form the 5th Avenue Theatre Association, a non-profit organization. The association underwrote the loans required for renovation, as well as the losses to be expected during initial months of operation.

Richard McCann, a University of Washington graduate in music composition and the School of Architecture, had worked for and later assumed leadership of the firm of B. Marcus Priteca. His knowledge of historic theatres made him a natural to undertake the renovation.

In order to provide greater seating comfort, the number of seats was reduced to just over 2,100. The slope of the main floor was sharpened for better viewing. Some of the decorative plaster moldings and columns had rotted and were restored. The original bright reds, blues, greens, and yellows of the Chinese painted designs had deteriorated and the paint was flaking off. A Los Angeles designer stenciled the designs onto canvases, then painted them to match the originals, and the canvases themselves were installed directly onto the ceiling. Otherwise, the basic splendid design of the theatre remains.

Lighting fixtures, ventilation, carpeting, furnishings, and dressing rooms were redone. The control technology for stage lighting and audio systems was modernized.

The 5th Avenue Theatre had a gala reopening on July 3, 1980, as ostentatious as the 1926 original gala. There were balloons, firecrackers, lion's head dancers by the Chinese Youth Club, a fashion show of ancient Chinese robes, and a display of northern Chinese instruments. A parade of vintage limousines with dignitaries moved slowly up Fifth Avenue led by the Chinese Community Girls Drill Team. KCTS-TV operated live from the lobby during intermission of the opening production, the musical *Annie*. Other touring shows followed, as well as concerts, lectures, and presentations. In 1989 the 5th Avenue Music Theatre Company, a resident non-profit theatre company, was established to produce and present the best musical theatre entertainment in a subscription series. Located in the center of the the city, the theatre continues to host top names and enjoy full houses.

MOORE THEATER AND HOTEL
1932 Second Avenue

Designed by E.W. Houghton in 1907, the theatre and hotel were planned for completion to house tourists coming to the 1909 Alaska-Yukon-Pacific Exposition. Both businesses are still operating.

Land developer and financier of several Seattle build-
ings, James A. Moore was simultaneously building the New
Washington Hotel and the Moore Hotel when he added the
Moore Theater to his list of projects at the urging of James
Cort, then manager of the Northwestern Theatrical Asso-
ciation. The theatre opened December 28, 1907 with a crowd
of 3,000; obviously there was standing-room-only, for the
theatre was built to seat only 2,500. The opener was *The
Alaskan*, a comic opera written by Harry Girard and Joseph
Blethen, hosted by James Cort himself.

The Moore Hotel portion had already opened in April,
and the layout of the building was unusual, in that the hotel
partially surrounded the theatre.

The exterior of the seven-story Moore Theater and Hotel
Building was quite restrained, finished with white ceramic
glazed tile and beige terra-cotta trim. The interior of the
theatre oozed opulence. The overall theme in the lobby and
auditorium was taken from Italian and Byzantine styles.
The foyer floor (carpeted later) was of a hexagonal pattern
composed of gray and red marble and onyx. The theatre
opened from the right side of the lobby and rose the full
seven stories of the building. A huge steel girder extended
the width of the theatre to largely support the weight of the
balcony, so no interfering columns blocked the view of the
stage. Allegorical figures representing the arts of music and
dance decorated the supporting beams below a central,
lighted dome.

The auditorium had twenty-six private boxes, which
were removed later. The original seating capacity was
reported at 2,500; however, it may have been overstated.
Indirect lighting was achieved by colored glass set behind
scrollwork bands. As late as 1980, a national survey placed
the Moore as having the best acoustics on the West Coast.

Performers liked the comfort of having a hotel on site;
they could enter the theatre without going outside. Today

we might call the Moore a destination resort, for there was a salt water natatorium in the basement of the building, as well as entertainment in the theatre. Patrons did not seem to mind the posts planted in the swimming pool, a necessary bracing for the hotel and theatre floors above. The "Turkish and Russian baths for men and ladies," with massage and dressing rooms, were popular well into the 1950s.

Possibly confusing to theatre buffs, the Moore was known as the Orpheum Theatre (because it was on the Orpheum Circuit) from 1923 to 1927. It was briefly the President and then the Moore again. Under manager Cecil Schultz in 1935, enthusiasts say that the theatre reached its full potential, with attractions such as the Dance Theater Series, the Great Artist Series, and such.

During the ensuing years, the theatre was the leading cultural house in the city, hosting such celebrities as Marie Dressler, Ethel Barrymore, Anna Pavlova, Sergei Rachmaninoff, and Feodor Chaliapin.

The theatre was the center for major traveling productions such as *The Merry Widow, The Return of Peter Grimm*, and *Music Master*. At midcentury the live theatre circuits became less prevalent, and the Moore was used for three years as a revival center, then hosted a wide variety of events such as boxing, road shows, movies, and the popular rock production *Hair*.

Around 1977 the theatre was in danger of demolition, but the Seattle Landmarks Board hoped to see it designated a Seattle Landmark. At the time of application the Moore was the only theatre in Seattle remaining a "hemp house," the lines for scenery pulled by ropes and by hand. The owner, George Toulouse, at first objected but consented nine years later. In February 1986, the City Council passed an ordinance designating the Moore a Seattle Landmark. Operated by the Seattle Landmark Association, the theatre still hosts traveling theatrical presentations and other attractions. It retains much of its original design. The hotel is a modestly priced operating business; the swimming pool stands empty in the basement.

PARAMOUNT THEATRE, 901 Pine Street

The Paramount opened as the Seattle Theatre in 1928 at Ninth and Pine (Not the same as the Seattle Theatre on Third and Cherry that operated from 1892-1915.) and reopened in March 1995, after a long, dark period. It was designed by architects Rapp and Rapp, who were responsible for the New York Paramount and many other motion picture theatres in the nation, in collaboration with Seattle's own B. Marcus Priteca and F.J. Peters. Hollywood's Adolph Zukor of Paramount Studios was in the forefront of creating theatres as historic and dramatic settings for theatrical and musical fantasy.

The theatre covered half a city block, facing Pine Street. Portions of the eight-story building were and are used for office space. The theatre's central box office was flanked on each side by three multipaned double doors. A triangular marquee projected over the front, and three large semicircular windows rose above the entrance. The exterior of the building was fairly restrained, but it had rows of windows on the higher stories, plus decorative trefoil arches and terra-cotta cornices that balanced the dark red brick veneer of the facades.

Like so many theatres of that "magic palace" age, the theatre was ornate inside. The overall architectural style was predominantly French Renaissance. Rapp and Rapp used the Palace of Versailles for inspiration. Entering the foyer a patron was greeted by a graceful stairway curving from the first-story balcony along beige and black paneled marble walls. The stair railings were of ironwork and wood. A large crystal and gold chandelier was suspended from the ceiling of the three-story foyer.

In his book *Historic Preservation in Seattle*, Lawrence Kreisman stated:

"A progression of spaces leads from box office to colonnaded foyer and into a grand hall with two magnificent bronze and crystal chandeliers high overhead and three tiers of balconies. The boldly ornamented auditorium utilizes inverted domes with hidden lights, draperies, and textured walls and ceilings with many carved ornamental surfaces to create distortion-free sound."

The seats sloped sharply toward the stage, which was flanked by two more bronze and crystal chandeliers. All the mirrored, sparkling surfaces gave the patrons a feeling quite in keeping with the "magic palace" approach.

The Paramount Wurlitzer orchestra pipe organ was the largest in the world when it was installed. The Wurlitzer Publix No. 1 was designed by Jesse Crawford, pianist at Sid Grauman's Million Dollar Theatre in Los Angeles, for the Publix Theatres chain, aimed at large theatre auditoriums. This type of organ could be played to imitate many orchestral instruments with the use of two or more manuals, foot pedals, and preset stops. The organ is still in place.

On opening night, the program featured organists "Ron and Don" (Renaldo Baggott and Don Moore) at the organ to accompany the production. During the ensuing years many famous organ celebrities such as Henry Keats, Buss McClelland, Gaylord Carter, and Eddie Clifford were employed to entertain the audiences. During the 1960s the organ was played during major motion picture premiers held at the Paramount. In 1971 the American Theatre Organ Society held its Sixteenth Annual Convention in Seattle, using the Paramount organ as a feature.

The magical lure of such magnificent theatres was transitory. As Ben Hall stated in his book *The Best Remaining Seats* (1961):

"It was a brief era, as golden ages go, swept in on a floodtide of splendor, fantastic architecture, music, laughter and dreams. It began and ended in the decade that lay between Prohibition and Depression and it brought pleasure and escape from boredom to a whole generation of Americans who wanted desperately to believe in make-believe."

The Great Depression closed the 3,000-seat theatre temporarily. When it reopened, it was strictly a movie house, except for the special organ concerts mentioned above. During years of changing ownership and management, nearly all of the original sculpture, ornate furniture, and paintings disappeared, although the Wurlitzer was left intact. In 1981, under new ownership of the Volotin Investment Company, the theatre was refurbished under the supervision of Ray Shepardson. This was largely cosmetic—cleaning, new carpet, upholstery, upgrading the sound system, etc. The Paramount opened October 1981 as a live concert hall and operated until its sale to the Seattle Landmark Association in 1992. Under SLA's management it underwent extensive renovation and additions to the stage to accommodate the most elaborate traveling shows. The overall appearance is much the same as the original. The Paramount reopened in March 1995, with the hit, *Miss Saigon*.

Note: Anyone interested in old theatres (not necessarily in Seattle) might wish to contact the Theatre Historical Society, P.O. Box 767, San Francisco, CA 94101.

CHAPTER 7

Seattle Trivia

Some Random Firsts for Seattle

Frye's Opera House was Seattle's first, built on First and Marion at a cost of $125,000 in 1883-84. It could seat 1,300 people, probably most of the population of the time. Among its presentations were: *Little Red Riding Hood*, *The Mikado*, and *Macbeth*. One of the University of Washington's earlier commencement exercises was held there. Unfortunately, it burned in 1889.

◆ ◆ ◆

Squire's Opera House, named for Watson C. Squire, later a United States Senator, built in 1879 on First between Washington and Main, was considered the first real theatre building in Seattle. It was constructed with rare taste in design, but it had a serious problem with ventilation so that patrons almost fainted during performances. It closed within two years, was remodeled into the Brunswick Hotel, and burned in 1889.

◆ ◆ ◆

The first theatre of the vast Pantages chain was opened by Alexander Pantages at Second and Seneca in 1904 and operated until 1914.

◆ ◆ ◆

The first radio station in Seattle was KJR, opening in 1922. KRSC, later KING, opened in 1948 as the first television station.

◆ ◆ ◆

The first brick building in Seattle was built by Dexter Horton at First and Washington streets. Only 28 x 72 feet and one story tall—and only the front was brick—it was called "the brick building" for many years. Horton operated a store there, which he sold to Atkins & Shoudy's in 1866.

◆ ◆ ◆

The daughter of George McConaha was the first female born in Seattle, September 18, 1852. The first male child was Orion O. Denny, July 17, 1853, born to Arthur A. and Mary A. Denny.

◆ ◆ ◆

The first divorce in King County was that of Dr. David S. Maynard on December 2, 1852, severing the ties to the wife he left in Ohio. Maynard also was the first to issue a marriage certificate as justice of the peace in King County on January 23, 1853, for the marriage of David T. Denny and Louisa Boren.

◆ ◆ ◆

The first election, held in Seattle in 1853, sent Arthur A. Denny as delegate to the Oregon territorial legislature.

◆ ◆ ◆

The first hotel was the Felker House which opened in 1853 and was burned in the 1889 fire.

◆ ◆ ◆

Dexter Horton opened Seattle's first bank in April 1870, in a one-story frame building at First and Washington. He built the building after he had sold his store to Atkins & Shoudy, then went to San Francisco for a couple of years. He returned in January 1870 and brought a steel safe with him. Local merchants got in the habit of storing their money in it—a do-it-yourself method of storing or removing their sacks. So Horton started a bank.

◆ ◆ ◆

In 1866 an Independent Order of Good Templars was formed for the promotion of temperance. The first Chief Templar was Reverend Whitworth. Others were Rebecca Horton, David Denny, and Louisa Denny.

◆ ◆ ◆

A Seattle Brass Band formed in 1860. Lonesome for the music of his native Germany, George Frye interested twelve youths in joining a band, obtained the music, instruments, and a teacher, and soon had an acceptable sounding group. They played for every important event and continued to be an active group until the 1920s.

◆ ◆ ◆

The Seattle *Gazette* published its first newspaper Dec. 10, 1863. J.R. Watson, who referred to himself as "Our Ollapod," printed some sample copies in Olympia and the small paper took hold. It only was published when there was sufficient news but it was supposed to be a weekly. The newspaper evolved into the *Intelligencer* and the *Post-Intelligencer*.

◆ ◆ ◆

Seattle's first water system was installed in 1865 by Charles Terry and Henry Yesler, who were given the exclusive right to furnish water. It came from springs in the hills back of town and was distributed in V-shaped flumes elevated above street. Later water was sent through hand-bored logs, a system active until 1886.

◆ ◆ ◆

Dr. Maynard ran the first hospital in 1863 with himself as superintendent, surgeon, and physician, and Mrs. Maynard as nurse. She also was in charge of a "lying-in" department. Maynard's home "old Felker house" was also the city's first hotel.

◆ ◆ ◆

Churches: The Brown Church seems to have been the first church, but one known as the White Church also existed almost as soon as the town was organized. Both were Methodist. The Seattle First United Methodist Church organized in 1853. The first Catholic church opened in 1868, called The Church of Our Lady of Good Help. The Plymouth Congregational Church came along in 1869 as did the First Baptist Church. The Presbyterian church was added in 1876. The first Episcopal congregation was Trinity, with its initial gothic-style church built in 1870 at Third and Jefferson. It burned in the 1889 fire, but was replaced at a different location.

◆ ◆ ◆

The first church wedding was held in the White Church in 1865, joining Clarence Bagley and Alice Mercer, youngest of the four Mercer sisters. The ceremony was performed by Rev. C.G. Belknap.

◆ ◆ ◆

Congregation Bikur Cholem was organized in 1899, Seattle's first Jewish congregation. Its name translated means "Society for the Visitation of the Sick." The congregation was one of Sephardic Jews.

◆ ◆ ◆

The first cemetery was on land donated by David Denny, where Denny Park was located 1931. Bodies were later moved to Masonic Cemetery or Lake View Cemetery near Volunteer Park.

◆ ◆ ◆

Jane Eads, a Chicago newspaper reporter, was the first commercial airline passenger of Boeing Air Transport (later United Air Lines). On July 1, 1927, she went from Chicago to San Francisco in twenty-three hours.

◆ ◆ ◆

In 1894 Seattle became the first municipal body to own a public utility, when they purchased the Spring Hill system.

◆ ◆ ◆

In 1893 the Great Northern Railroad entered Seattle.

◆ ◆ ◆

In 1893 today's site of the University of Washington was acquired, and in 1894 the cornerstone of Denny Hall was laid.

◆ ◆ ◆

The women of Washington Territory were granted suffrage in 1883, but the right was rescinded in 1897. A bill granting the right was passed by the legislature in 1909 and ratified in 1910.

◆ ◆ ◆

The first automobile, an electric-powered one, reached Seattle in 1900. The first auto dealer, Whitford Rapid Vehicle & Motor Launch Company, was operating by 1901.

◆ ◆ ◆

The University of Washington staged its first crew race with the University of California on Lake Washington in 1903.

◆ ◆ ◆

The Mountaineers Club was organized in 1906.

◆ ◆ ◆

The first issue of the *Seattle Daily Times*, which evolved from the *Times*, *Call*, *Press-Times*, and other smaller rags, was published August 7, 1896.

◆ ◆ ◆

The Chicago, Milwaukee, and St. Paul Railroad came into Seattle in 1909.

◆ ◆ ◆

Union Station was completed in 1911.

◆ ◆ ◆

Swedish Hospital was founded in 1911.

◆ ◆ ◆

The Fisher Flouring Mill opened in 1911 and grew to be the largest west of the Mississippi River. In 1955 it had 600 employees.

◆ ◆ ◆

Jefferson Park was the site of the first public golf course in the United States, opened in 1915.

◆ ◆ ◆

The Ship Canal between Lake Union and Lake Washington was opened for navigation in 1917.

◆ ◆ ◆

On February 20, 1913 the Daughters of the Nile, headed by Mrs. Walter M. Krows, was founded. Its aim was to assist the Shriners Hospitals for crippled children.

◆ ◆ ◆

As early as 1955, Seattle may have been the pleasure boat capital of the world.

◆ ◆ ◆

Seattle College, now Seattle University, was founded in 1891.

◆ ◆ ◆

I. Magnin & Company opened a store in Seattle at Sixth and Pine in 1954.

◆ ◆ ◆

The University of Washington's first baccalaureate degree went to a woman, Clara McCarthy, in 1876. Her name is on a dormitory at the university.

◆ ◆ ◆

Seattle's first major fair, the Alaska-Yukon-Pacific Exposition, opened in 1909. The grounds sprawled across what is now the University of Washington's campus.

◆ ◆ ◆

The Alaska Building was Seattle's first skyscraper, fourteen stories, built in 1904.

♦ ♦ ♦

Western Union completed its first telegraph lines to Seattle on October 26, 1864. In 1929 the first branch office of Western Union in Seattle was opened in the Triangle Hotel at 551 First Avenue South. The office was linked to WU's main office at Second and Cherry by pneumatic tubes.

♦ ♦ ♦

The first major highway bridge in Seattle was the George Washington Memorial Bridge on Aurora Avenue North completed in 1932. It was also the first fixed span bridge. It permitted tall ships to pass underneath without the necessity of a time-consuming bridge opening.

♦ ♦ ♦

Around 1920-30 a new kind of stage presentation called the "theatre in the round" was tried out at the penthouse of the T.F. Murphys on top of the Meany Hotel.

♦ ♦ ♦

The Ryther Child Center was begun and has become a pioneer in treating children with mental and emotional problems. It began as the personal project of Mrs. Ollie H. Ryther, who took in needy children and, in 1915, incorporated the Ryther Child Home.

♦ ♦ ♦

In 1926 Bertha Landes became mayor of Seattle, the first female mayor of any city in the USA. She had no particular political ambition but was a woman devoted to public service. Prior to 1920, she was president of the Seattle Federation of Women's Clubs. In 1921 she was involved with the Women's Exhibit for Washington Manufacturers. Appointed to the mayor's committee on unemployment, she ran for and won a post on the city council, elected thereafter as council president. She became acting mayor in 1924, won an election in 1926, but was defeated in 1928. The *Seattle Post-Intelligencer* commented on her first day in office in terms typical of the attitudes of the day, saying she "will hang up her big droopy hat with the smart coral facing and her black satin cape-coat with the beige fox collar, clear the flowers off the desk and begin. . ." (quote from August 7, 1963, commemorative edition).

◆ ◆ ◆

Seattleite and scientist Dixy Lee Ray became Washington's first female governor in 1977-81, in fact, the state's only female governor to date. Forthright, some would say even crusty, she encouraged the development of nuclear power and pooh-poohed its dangers compared to other means of power generation.

◆ ◆ ◆

In the 1940s, Ole Bardahl developed and sold the lubricant products and additives marketed as "Bardol" or "Bardahl." For twenty-one years Bardahl racing cars competed at Indianapolis, then "Miss Bardahl" won five Gold Cups and six National Championships, a familiar sight at Seafair hydroplane races.

◆ ◆ ◆

The first baseball field was built at Madison Park in 1890.

◆ ◆ ◆

The first known Seattle photographer was E.A. Clark. At least two of his photos are preserved, of Sarah Yesler and of Yesler's home, both taken in 1859. Clark died in 1860 at only thirty-two years of age.

◆ ◆ ◆

The first charitable institution in Seattle was formed on April 3, 1884, by fifteen women that included the ilk of Sarah Yesler and Babette Gatzert. The new Ladies Relief Society is now Seattle Children's Home. Although not restricted to helping children, the first attention was given to orphans and friendless children. The Dennys donated land for the first home that opened in 1886 for thirty children. The home still operates as Seattle Children's Home but has moved four times.

◆ ◆ ◆

Seattle's first private golf course was in Wallingford, a three-hole course laid out in the mid-1890s. A tent served as a clubhouse, and the course literally was in the middle of a cow pasture.

◆ ◆ ◆

The oldest (not necessarily first) saloon in Seattle is the Central Saloon. It *looks* like the kind of place gold prospectors, sailors, and lumberjacks patronized, with dark walls and furniture. It was a popular hangout in the 1970s for counter-culture people and was the campaign headquarters for Tiny Freeman's bid for a congressional seat, running as an anarchist Republican. The popular February Mardi Gras dubbed "Fat Tuesday" also was an idea born in the saloon. Since 1976 there has been a Pioneer Square week-long celebration of a Seattleized Mardi Gras with many musical events. For a time the Central was the center of grunge music in Seattle, but at this writing it features blues. It is an upbeat place under the ownership of Ken "Jomo" Ward and Guy and Brenda Curtis, and is noted for its food, too.

◆ ◆ ◆

The oldest (but not necessarily the first) restaurant is the Merchants Cafe facing Pioneer Square. The site was one that Doc Maynard gave to Henry Yesler in the 1850s. Yesler sold it to Terry in 1857, and in 1864 a two-story clapboard house sat on the site. It burned in 1889, and John Hall Sanderson then put up a building at a cost of $15,000, a great deal of money in that day. Gallagher Chambers Company, Wines and Liquors opened for business. In 1890 Mary Gartland operated a cafe in the basement of the building. In 1892 Charles Osner bought the Chambers business and changed its name to The Merchants Exchange Saloon, retaining it until sold to F.X. Schreiner in 1898 as The Merchants Cafe. It operated continuously by Schreiner's nephew John until he died in 1964. The cafe was closed until 1972, when it was refurbished and reopened by Howard and Gregg Rolie (Gregg was a member of the bands "Santana" and "Journey"). After two other turnovers of ownership, Gary Smalling took over in 1985.

At some time, the owners installed a thirty-foot standup bar that came around Cape Horn on a schooner. There are hooks on the outside alley wall used to lower beer kegs to the basement room. The safe and gold scale are originals. Today the restaurant is on the National Register of Historic Places. The building has two stories and a basement dining room that ooze history. The first-floor walls are of heavy carved wood and stained glass. Both walls and a partition have tongue-and-groove wainscoting. Booths are antiques. On the lower level all the original uneven brick is exposed; it was in the area where many buildings were partly or wholly buried by the regrade.

◆ ◆ ◆

The first downtown condos were the Royal Manor, Eighth and Seneca (1973), and the Royal Crest, Third and Lenora (1975), built by Morton, Biehl, and Mortenson. One reason for the construction was the effort to keep people and business downtown. Morton was chairman of the Mayor's In-City Living Task Force.

◆ ◆ ◆

Northgate Shopping Center was the first shopping mall in the United States, as far as can be determined.

◆ ◆ ◆

Seattleite Jim Whittaker was the first American to climb Mount Everest in 1963. During the trip he lost thirty-five pounds.

Gone But Not Forgotten

The Rainier Hotel was built between Columbia and Marion, Fifth and Sixth avenues within eighty days after the 1889 fire. It was a huge, three-story "plus" building with cupolas and a covered promenade on the ground floor. But it was a loser and eventually was remodeled as an apartment house, surviving until 1910.

◆ ◆ ◆

Today's senior citizens remember the Trianon Ballroom fondly, some as the site of their first romances. At Third Avenue and Wall Street, the ballroom was of impressive Spanish style architecture built in 1927. An outside balcony was dubbed the "spooning area." The ballroom featured famous dance bands such as Benny Goodman, and radio stations frequently broadcast "live" from the ballroom. The popular night spot did not close until 1956, becoming a Gov-Mart store. In 1969 the building was remodeled for the tenant, American Games.

◆ ◆ ◆

Luna Park at Alki was the Coney Island of Seattle from 1907, when it opened, to the early 1930s. It featured a giant figure eight roller coaster, Chute-the-Chutes Water Slide, the Giant Swing, Canal of Venice, merry-go-round, carnival style games, a salt water natatorium (indoor swimming pool) and dance hall. A further attraction was possibly the longest bar in Seattle. Seattleites found Luna Park a grand place to cavort of a weekend, especially since Alki boasted one of Seattle's best and fairly sandy beaches. Unfortunately some felt Luna Park to be an immoral influence. Its history was checkered; it opened and closed several times, depending on who was running the city. In 1931 the natatorium was the victim of an arsonist, and several of the major rides were gone. Gradually the facilities were razed or fell into the water. At low tide some of the pilings that supported them can be seen today.

The Stockade was a summer resort on Alki Point from the early 1900s to 1936. It was built and operated by Alfred and Lorena Smith in 1902 on the site of the Denny party's original settlement, Sixty-third and Alki approximately. Access then was by ferry from Seattle, or by a rambling plank road. Friends Mr. and Mrs. William J. Bernard lived at the Stockade while their home next door was being completed in 1904. The Smiths and their children helped to bring rocks from the beach to build the fireplace for the Stockade. H. Martin Smith closed the Stockade in 1936 when the big Alki Natatorium closed during the Depression. An apartment building stands on the site of the Stockade today. In 1907 the Bernard property next door to the Stockade became known as the Fir Lodge, a clubhouse for the new Seattle Auto and Driving Club, then it was a riding club with one horse, and then a restaurant—the Alki Homestead. From the beginning, it was known for its chicken dinners served family style, a tradition continuing today, although today other entrees are also available.

◆ ◆ ◆

A familiar sight on Elliott Bay and later Lake Union was the fire boat *Snoqualmie*. It was a ninety-one-foot tug built after the 1889 fire at the insistence of Mayor Robert Moran. She was moored at the foot of Madison Street and served the city well until 1927, when she was replaced with a newer craft. For several years thereafter she monitored activities on Lake Union, then, after a short career as a Seattle-Alaska freighter, burned in Kodiak in 1974.

◆ ◆ ◆

The red tower with the words "Frye Bacon and Ham" was a familiar sight along Airport near Boeing Field's present location. Charles Frye and partner Bruhn had a meat packing plant there. Frye had a ranch in northeastern Montana where he raised cattle and pigs, which wound up in his packing plant. He maintained a non-union shop, and for this reason, organizers were known to call him "Kaiser" Frye during World War I times. Frye was no relation to the prominent pioneer Roberta Frye Watts or to George Frye. Charles lived at Seventh and Columbia, where he hung a big art collection that outgrew the house, so he laid plans for the Frye Museum. However, he died in 1940, leaving control of his estate to Walser Greathouse. In February 1943 a bomber taking off from Boeing Field on a test flight crashed into the meat-packing plant and destroyed it; virtually nothing was saved. Greathouse rebuilt and continued the business. Greathouse carried out Frye's plans for a museum, opening it February 8, 1952. The museum housed Frye's considerable art collection, plus ongoing acquisitions to the present. After Walser Greathouse's death in 1967, his wife Kay was a moving force for the museum.

◆ ◆ ◆

Between 1894 and 1904, bicycling caught on in Seattle. Responding to the popularity of the sport, the city built an entire network of trails, clubhouses, restaurants, and restrooms just for bicyclists. Bicyclists enjoyed about fifty miles of paths and four race courses. There were at least forty sales and repair shops devoted to the bicycle trade. The only part of the trail network remaining is on Interlaken Boulevard between Del Mar Drive East and Twenty-fourth Avenue East. Serving the bicyclists were several dealers and a weekly cycling column in the newspaper. Among bicycling clubs was the Queen City Bicycle Club,

◆ ◆ ◆

Horse racing was staged on First Avenue during the 1868 Fourth of July celebration.

◆ ◆ ◆

A man named Robert Patton invented a hat with an attached small umbrella. Soon Seattleites were calling him the "Umbrella Man." He became the model for a popular weather report cartoon. Another contingent of people credit bootlegger Roy Olmsted with this invention.

◆ ◆ ◆

The Ranch on Aurora, old Highway 99, was a wild and wicked, well-patronized roadhouse during Prohibition days—which in Seattle lasted, to an extent, into the 1950s.

◆ ◆ ◆

Yesler Wharf was the center of activities for earliest Seattle, a place where sternwheelers and ocean-going sailing craft docked. Most wharves were burned in the fire of 1889, but not Yesler's.

◆ ◆ ◆

A man named McDowell once had a barge on Lake Washington to deliver coal to shoreside homes.

◆ ◆ ◆

Madison Park is on the site of J.J. McGilvra's 1860 homestead. A 500-seat pavilion was a popular place for dancing and band concerts from 1895-98. The park had formal gardens and walkways through the trees. There were baseball fields for semipro or amateur games, a boathouse, theater, and a racetrack of sorts for harness and regular racing on the site of today's Broadmoor district. The National Guard practiced on a parade field called Battalion Hill, enjoying the rapt attention of crowds of spectators (from a photo posted in the Red Onion Tavern today). Management provided platforms which could be rented by vacationers as a dry tent site. Small houses owned by the University of Washington for storage of equipment by the U/W crew, who practiced on the lake, have been remodeled and enlarged and still can be seen along Forty-first Street. White City Park, an amusement park, thrived adjacent to Madison Park. Unfortunately, White City also was a hangout for prostitutes who had little cribs along the dock. Boats offered cruises of Lake Washington. The Anderson Steamboat Company operated as early as 1906. An auto ferry went from Madison Park to Kirkland until 1953. Bob Matson was the captain of the ferry on the Madison-Kirkland run. Crowds from Seattle would attend the Mercer Island dance pavilion or the annual Bellevue Strawberry Festival.

◆ ◆ ◆

Leschi Park was one of the most popular destinations for weekenders from 1888 until the cable car era ended. It still is a popular park with a large marina. Downtown theatre manager John Cort opened the Lake Washington Casino in 1890, part of the Leschi complex. Four years later the Yesler Avenue Street Cable Railway Company took over the casino and renamed it Leschi Park Pavilion, staging vaudeville shows, concerts, and plays. In 1906 Sara Bernhardt starred there in *Camille and Sophia.*

From the cable car's terminal, steps led down the steep slope 200 feet to the lake. There were boats for rent, a swimming beach, a zoo, a hotel, and cabins—some of which were rented by the hour. The Leschi Landing was home port to lake steamers and an excursion boat, the *Fortuna.* The hotel had a large dance hall, and on a holiday weekend, perhaps 50,000 people patronized the park and hall. An auto ferry, *Leschi,* from Leschi to Meydenbauer Landing at Bellevue and to Medina, started service in 1913 and operated until the opening of the Lacey Murrow floating bridge. The *Leschi* stopped running in 1940 and was moved to the Madison Park-Kirkland run, which ceased operations August 31, 1950. The 250-passenger steamer *Dawn* made twelve stops along the west shore of Mercer Island alone.

◆ ◆ ◆

In the Good, Better, Best bar of the Lakecafe, the former captain of the ferries *Dawn* and *Leschi,* Frank Gilbert, is immortalized by a full-size bronze statue created by Everett artist Maggie Weir. Gilbert spent much of his retirement time talking with old cronies in Benson's Cafe, the former name of Lakecafe. Patrons winding up their evenings frequently declare, "Let's buy one for the captain."

◆ ◆ ◆

The Benson family opened the first restaurant at Leschi in 1880; it was named Bob's, Spinnaker, and Hindquarter before its current name of Leschi Lakecafe. The restaurant has light fixtures salvaged from the old Olympic Hotel and has many paintings of sailboats on its walls.

◆ ◆ ◆

Across the street from the Leschi Lakecafe is the site of Omar's, a coffee shop that sold hamburgers for ten cents and a short whiskey for a quarter. Next door to Omar's was a fish market, but its owners' real business was bootlegging it is said.

◆ ◆ ◆

A Female Suffrage Society organized in 1871. Among its members were Mrs. Henry Yesler and Lizzie Ordway, a Mercer Girl. One of its famous lecturers was Susan B. Anthony, who spoke in the small Pioneer Square area church known as "The Brown Church."

◆ ◆ ◆

Television watchers miss the wacky Rainier Beer television ads of the 1980s, involving bottles that resembled people cavorting on the beach . . . or the one riding a motorcycle that roared off to the voiceover of "Rraaiinneeer Bbeerrr."

◆ ◆ ◆

The 1950s-'60s sometimes were called the golden age of children's programs for television in Seattle. Here are a few that any Seattleite from thirty to fifty would remember:

J.P. Patches, the beloved clown on KIRO-TV, who also did birthday parties, special events, and fund-raisers, hosted the longest-running children's program in American history.

Captain Puget (Don McCune) and his sidekick, First Mate Salty, played for awhile by Ivar Haglund, aired on KOMO-TV in the 1950s-late '60s. The children who came to Ivar's restaurants identified with Ivar as Salty, not the proprietor of the place.

Don McCune (Courtesy of Linda McCune)

Wunda Wunda, the good witch played by Ruth Prins, was the star of a television show on KING-TV for children. Probably any Seattleite who grew up here could still sing the "Wunda Wunda Song."

King's Clubhouse on KING-TV featured Stan Boreson from 1953-67. His show crossed all age lines, especially his hilarious takeoffs on the Scandinavians, and included clowns, animals, and goofy stunts that sometimes drew the station's personnel into the acts.

257

Sheriff Tex was the forerunner of them all, running 1948-51 on KING-TV and keeping viewers in stitches in the 1950s-60s. His comedy acts wound up on records and cassettes, still available.

◆ ◆ ◆

The Colored Ladies Society was organized in December 1889, the first organization of black women. The first African-American Episcopal Church was organized in 1891.

◆ ◆ ◆

"Captain Burrows—Summer and Winter Pleasure Resort." This was the sign for a popular fishing resort where the Black River leaves Lake Washington. Captain Ferry Fay Burrows and his wife Martha came from Missouri in 1897 to a small cabin at the south end of Lake Washington belonging to Burrows' father. Later the family built a houseboat from which to operate. Seattleites came to rent a rowboat, skiff, or canoe at a price of twenty-five to fifty cents and could make a wonderful catch of trout and silver salmon in a couple of hours. Martha Burrows put on a home-cooked meal of chicken and biscuits for hungry fishermen. The Burrows had about fifty small boats for rent and later ran a tug, *Janet L*, to tow log rafts.

◆ ◆ ◆

During World War I, the Seattle Minute Men, a paramilitary organization made up of business and professional men (including the highly respected Thomas Burke) and approved by the mayor and chief of police, monitored the level of patriotism in the city. One teacher was fired for failing to pass a quiz on the topic of patriotism, and eventually six were dismissed. One reason for the undue attention given to the school system was that Anna Louise Strong, an avowed pacifist and socialist, had become a school board member.

Also under attack were two textbooks on European history, said to be pro-German.

◆ ◆ ◆

The Seattle Street Railway made its appearance in 1884, a three-mile set of rails with a terminal at Battery and First Avenue. Powering the streetcars were teams of horses. Five years later the line was electrified.

◆ ◆ ◆

Ravenna Creek, a babbling stream bordered by woods, once wandered through the countryside and into Lake Union. It is still there but was rerouted into a city drain.

◆ ◆ ◆

Gasworks Park along the north shore of Lake Union was, indeed, the site of a gasworks established there in 1907 by the Seattle Gas Company. Gas was generated for cooking from a coal-fired plant which then switched to oil. In 1956 natural gas deposits made the plant obsolete and it languished, polluted and ugly, until the city bought it in 1962. They hired architect Richard Haag whose design has won awards for his retention of some gas towers amid the rolling lawns as reminders of technological change.

◆ ◆ ◆

On the Duwamish River flats in 1892 the Brothers of Our Lady of Lourdes built a four-story chapel, dormitory, and library plus other buildings. They landscaped the grounds and installed a garden and orchard for self-suffi-ciency of the order. The mission was a failure and was abandoned in 1919. The chapel was razed in the 1920s and other buildings remodeled to become Our Lady of the Lourdes Parish Church. The brothers had built a Grotto of Our Lady of Lourdes of the West which did remain and was the center of a community feast of St. Anthony annually until 1970, when the parish hall and grotto were bulldozed.

◆ ◆ ◆

In Depression years there were several shacktowns or Hoovervilles in Seattle. One consisted of about five hundred rickety dwellings centered around today's Royal Brougham and East Marginal Way.

◆ ◆ ◆

Armories have come and gone in Seattle. The 1894 armory at Fourth and Union was demolished in April 1904 to make way for the *Post-Intelligencer* building. The latter was designed by E.W. Houghton and built by Stirrat & Goetze, contractors. It was four stories tall, had business offices on the first floor, new presses in the basement. Each reporter had his own desk and typewriter and the editorial department occupied the top floor. The composing room consisted of eleven Merganthaler lintotype machines. Beside the presses were eight carloads of paper. Erastus Brainerd had been named editor-in-chief in January 1904. He was instrumental in bringing about the election of Albert E. Mead as governor in 1905. The Seattle National Guard Armory met the wrecker's ball in 1968 to make way for better roadways around Pike Place Market. It could have passed for a European castle complete with moat, as far as appearance, because of its turrets and embattlements. The structure was designed to house the regimental headquarters of an infantry regiment and one battalion of infantry with a signal corps unit. In 1929 it had been used to house a complete regiment of artillery. The facilities for drill were not adequate. Preservation efforts to rescue the building failed as the turn-of-the-century structure was in less than perfect structural condition. This was not helped by the fact that it was swept by a 1962 fire, and that the wrecker had smacked it a few times before the contract for its demolition was totally approved. A new armory was dedicated April 15, 1939, a $1.25 million block-square structure bounded by Third, Harrison, Nob Hill, and Thomas. Curiously it, too, would be in the wrong place—on a site appropriated for the Seattle World's Fair. It was built with Works Progress Administration (WPA) money and employed 300 men. It was a fairly forthright building, its only significant ornamentation being two huge concrete eagles that soared above the entrance steps. It was situated on a plot 256 by 300 feet and was four stories high at the front. The huge building had a drill hall on the first floor, a 1-1/2 acre area with a ceiling seventy feet high. The ceiling was unusual in that it was built to allow for expansion, contraction, snow loads, and wind resistance—what constructors called a "floating ceiling." A spectators' balcony surrounded the drill hall with seating for 1,000 people. Hardly any noise escaped from the building, insulated with 120,000 square feet of acoustical materials. A sub-basement under the garage basement housed an ammunition vault for storing arms and ammunition. There was a soundproof rifle range capable of handling twenty-eight shooters aiming at targets seventy-five feet away. The armory was also intended as a center for visiting servicemen and local guardsmen. It had a large swimming pool, recreational facilities, and sleeping accommodations for up to 600 men.

◆ ◆ ◆

The BROADWAY HALL BUILDING at 1120 Broadway was demolished in 1960. The terra-cotta building with a graceful archway was built in 1905 as a combination apartment house, office, and theatre building and was piped for gas lights. It was a showplace in its early days, housing the Gramercy Theater, renamed Cinema 21. The theatre's walls were covered with important silk hangings; furnishings and decor was Louis IV period. In the late "teens" the second floor was converted into two ballrooms, scheduled for everything from high school proms to Junior League charity affairs.

◆ ◆ ◆

The Eagles Auditorium at Seventh and Union has been remodeled as the home for ACT (Contemporary Theater).

◆ ◆ ◆

Jensen's Beach opened in 1877 between Pike and Union streets near today's Aquarium. It had twelve bath houses where swimmers could rent suits and towels.

◆ ◆ ◆

A favorite early swimming hole for youngsters was a sandy beach north of Columbus Street.

◆ ◆ ◆

In the 1880s there was a Budlong's Boathouse not far from Colman Dock. The proprietor built boats and rented rowboats and small sailboats. The Puget Sound Yacht Club was established there in 1886 and held its first cup race in August. The 1889 fire burned Budlong's.

◆ ◆ ◆

Seattle's first waterfront park was developed by the Port of Seattle in 1915. It was on the roof of the port's Bell Street terminal and included a solarium, salt water pool, and a children's playground. It was intended to be used by children and their moms after shopping at the nearby Pike Place Market, but it had to be closed in the 1920s when its patrons were mostly sailors and female companions of dubious reputation.

◆ ◆ ◆

The Ladies Mite Society was organized in 1865 to secure lecturers on temperance and other reform topics. One of its members was Mrs. Charles Terry.

◆ ◆ ◆

The Elliott Bay Yacht Club and other such clubs operated from Brighton Boathouse at the foot of Battery Street in 1894. A considerable small boat marina developed there by 1902. It was the site of regattas and other activities during the Alaska-Yukon-Pacific Exposition. Elliott Bay Yacht Club merged with the Seattle Yacht Club in 1892 and operated from a clubhouse near the West Seattle ferry.

◆ ◆ ◆

At the turn of the century, there were excursion boats on Elliott Bay, one with a steam calliope, another with a nickelodeon.

◆ ◆ ◆

The Alaska-Yukon-Pacific Exposition was exceedingly popular. On opening day June 1, 1909, 39,216 people attended. There was a military parade, speeches, and a congratulatory telegram from President Howard Taft.

◆ ◆ ◆

The Aqua Theater was a popular spot on warm summer days. Located at the southwest side of Green Lake, it was an amphitheater with a stage, separated from the seating by water, all in the open air. Productions such as *The Student Prince* were staged. It was gone by the late 1950s.

◆ ◆ ◆

It is not gone nor yet forgotten. The Blue Moon Tavern on Northeast Forty-fifth Street was the gathering place and watering hole for all manner of free thinkers, intellectuals, and just plain students bent on a lively evening. It was opened in

1934 by Henry J. Riverman. When the Blue Moon was threatened with destruction in 1989, patrons and friends energeti-
cally tried to get the tavern declared an official landmark.
Unsuccessful, they settled for a reprieve by the landlord that
left the building in place, at least for the time being.

Note: The author is indebted for some of the aforemen-
tioned items to author Hershman *et al.*, *Seattle's
Waterfront* and to Ralph B. Potts, *Seattle Heritage*. (See
bibliography.)

Old Places, New Uses

A grand hotel in about 1864 was the Occidental, in a
triangle then formed by James, Yesler, and Second Avenue
in the heart of today's Pioneer Square. It was a clapboard
house of thirty rooms and became the gathering place for all
town doings from political rallies to strawberry festivals. It
had a good livery stable and a billiard table. Board cost fifty
cents a meal, one dollar an entire day, or six dollars a week.
In 1865 entrepreneur John Collins arrived in town and
bought a one-third interest in the Occidental. During the
early 1880s Collins (who seemed to be the sole owner then)
built a new Occidental Hotel, a handsome building with ash
and black walnut paneling. The ground floor was occupied
by the Puget Sound National Bank. Collins expanded his
hotel to accommodate as many as four hundred guests, but
lost the building in the 1889 fire. Again Collins rebuilt,
renaming it the Seattle Hotel, home of many major events
until it was torn down in the 1960s and replaced with a
parking garage that is still there in the triangle formed by
James, Yesler, and Second Avenue. It is referred to by some
as the "Sinking Ship Garage."

◆ ◆ ◆

Famous madam Lou Graham's house (not home) in the old Washington Court Building is presently occupied by the Union Gospel Mission. Graham was known as the "hostess with the mostest."

◆ ◆ ◆

In 1913 a building was constructed for the Washington & Oregon Railway and Navigation Company on what is now First Avenue and Royal Brougham. It was a transshipment warehouse for products from ship to rail, rail to ship. Massive fir beams and columns up to eighteen inches square supported the three-story building. The exterior was of red brick. Still in excellent condition, the remodeled warehouse is now the headquarters of Hart Brewing Company, plus an assortment of small offices on the upper floor. Abandoned rails still lie adjacent to the building.

◆ ◆ ◆

Dexter Horton Bank moved from Pioneer Square to across from the Seattle Public Library.

◆ ◆ ◆

Nordstrom's is located in the old Alhambra Theater building.

◆ ◆ ◆

The Cherry Street Parking Garage was once the Grand Opera House of 1900.

◆ ◆ ◆

The U.S. Assay Office, so busy during the Yukon Gold Rush, became the social center of the German Club, Deutsches Haus, in 1935.

◆ ◆ ◆

The Home of the Good Shepherd, built in 1906 as a home for young women by the Sisters of Good Shepherd, 4647 Sunnyside Avenue North, was used for office and studios by Pacific Northwest Ballet until about 1993.

◆ ◆ ◆

The West Queen Anne Elementary School, 515 West Galer Street, was completed in 1896. Since 1981, it has served as a condominium.

◆ ◆ ◆

The University Methodist Episcopal Church built in 1909 today is a small retail mall.

◆ ◆ ◆

Wallingford Center, 4416 Wallingford Avenue North, was originally the Interlake Public School, built in 1904. The Center has rental units and retail spaces today, ranging from restaurants to gift shops.

◆ ◆ ◆

Guy Phinney, real estate developer, built a wonderful English garden for his home and family around 1891. In 1899 that garden was acquired by the city to become Woodland Park Zoo.

◆ ◆ ◆

The bed of the old Seattle, Lake Shore and Eastern Railroad is now the Burke-Gilman Trail.

◆ ◆ ◆

Bread of Life Mission in the 1890 Matilda Winehill Building at First and Main was a retail store and hotel.

◆ ◆ ◆

The Leyte Hotel at 614-24 South Jackson Street was renovated to become the Far East Building with a diversified tenancy in 1984. It is most unusual, with two pre-1909 wood frame structures forming the top two stories, and a bottom floor built much later.

◆ ◆ ◆

The Crystal Pool was one of Seattle's most popular recreational spots in the 1920s and 1930s. It had an indoor pool, boxing matches on Tuesday nights, and was a roller rink for a time. The Bethel Temple purchased the property at 2033 Second Avenue in 1943 and remodeled it as a church.

Names in Seattle

DUWAMISH FLATS, DUWAMISH RIVER. Adapted from an Indian word *dewampsh* meaning "the people living on the river."

DENNY WAY. A major street named for Arthur Denny and/or the Denny family, who were among the first party of permanent settlers of Seattle. Arthur Denny's 320-acre claim is now the heart of downtown Seattle. Actually, David Denny was in Seattle earlier than Arthur, having scouted the place for possible settlement.

THE LACEY V. MURROW FLOATING BRIDGE. Murrow was the engineer for the building of Seattle's first floating bridge across Lake Washington.

BELLEVUE. The word in French means "good view."

COAL CREEK PARKWAY leads toward the site of the old coal fields at Newcastle.

EVERGREEN POINT FLOATING BRIDGE. Washington is known as the "Evergreen State." But the bridge was renamed the Governor Albert D. Rosellini Bridge.

DENNY REGRADE. In the early days of Seattle, Denny Hill was as steep as Capitol Hill or other heights. Loggers brought downed trees to its cliffs and slid them down the slope to Yesler's Mill on the waterfront, resulting in the term "Skid Road," often corrupted to "Skid Row."

HARRISON, JACKSON, JEFFERSON, MADISON, and WASHINGTON streets were named for presidents of the United States.

KING COUNTY got its name from the thirteenth vice president of the United States, William Rufus King.

THE MAGNOLIA DISTRICT has madrona trees. George Davidson of the U.S. Coast and Geodetic Survey misidentified the trees he saw.

BOREN AVENUE. Carson Boren was one of the original party of settlers and staked claims with Denny. Before long he left Seattle and acquired timber lands.

TERRY STREET. Charles Terry and brother Lee Terry were part of the original party of settlers that came to Alki. The party consisted of: Mr. and Mrs. Arthur Denny, Mr. and Mrs. John Low, Mr. and Mrs. Carson Boren, Mr. and Mrs. William Bell, Mr. David Denny, Miss Louisa Boren, Mr. Charles Terry, Mr. Lee Terry. Louisa Boren, sister of Carson, married David Denny.

BELL STREET. Mr. and Mrs. William Bell and their daughters were among the original settlers of Seattle.

DEXTER HORTON BUILDING. An early entrepreneur who joined with Arthur Denny in several enterprises, including the Dexter Horton National Bank.

BAGLEY WRIGHT THEATER. Daniel Bagley was a Methodist minister who moved to Seattle in 1859. He was especially instrumental in obtaining the territorial university for Seattle, later the University of Washington, where the Metropolitan Building, Four Seasons Hotel, etc., are located. The theater is named for a descendant and art connoisseur Bagley Wright.

YESLER WAY. Named for Henry Yesler, who came to Seattle in the fall of 1852 looking for a sawmill site. He built the mill, a cookhouse, and hall that became Seattle's first community center, and he became Seattle's first mayor in 1869.

COLUMBIA STREET. When the founding fathers of Washington Territory and Washington State debated its name, one popular choice was Columbia.

THE CINCINNATUS CLUB. A progressive club to which many of the prominent businessmen of the 1930s belonged. Among its aims was a campaign to return the Republicans to power.

ELLIOTT BAY, ELLIOTT AVENUE. Captain Charles Wilkes named the bay in 1841 for either midshipman Samuel Elliott or Rev. J.L. Elliott, chaplain.

ALKI POINT. Alki was an Indian word meaning "by and by."

PORTAGE BAY is along the channel between Lake Union and Lake Washington. Before the Montlake Cut was dug, Indians had to portage canoes from one lake to the other.

BALLARD. In 1890 W.R. Ballard operated a shingle mill in the area incorporated that year as Ballard.

MAYNARD BUILDING. Of the early settlers, perhaps Dr. David S. "Doc" Maynard was the most charismatic. He was friendly to everyone and enjoyed a particular comradeship with Chief Seattle. The Maynard Building is in Pioneer Square, still in use today.

THE FRYE MUSEUM. Charles Frye was a meat-packer—Frye and Bruhn. He was an art connoisseur and his home became so crowded with artworks that he drew up plans for a museum, which was built after his death.

HIRAM CHITTENDEN LOCKS were named for the Army Corps of Engineers designer who built them.

HOOVERVILLE. A designation in many cities for shacks and substandard housing occupied by the unemployed of the Great Depression. Seattle's Hooverville was mostly along the tide flats, where there were old, abandoned buildings dating back to the original settlement.

JOSHUA GREEN BUILDING. Green was the president of the Puget Sound Navigation Company. He owned many vessels of the "Mosquito Fleet," small ferries that served residents along Puget Sound. The fleet was the forerunner of the Washington State Ferry system. Green also purchased the Peoples National Bank founded by Bailey Gatzert in 1927 and ran it very profitably.

LESCHI PARK. Leschi was a local Indian leader who actively fought to drive the settlers away from Seattle during the brief Indian war of 1856. As Leschi left Seattle in defeat, he burned many buildings such as the Plummer's sawmill on Black River.

KIRKLAND. Named for Moses Kirkland.

RENTON. Captain William S. Renton built a steam sawmill at Alki Point in 1853, but he soon found that the point was prone to strong northerly tides and strong winds. He moved the mill to Port Orchard. In the mid-1870s he developed coal mines at Renton.

MERCER STREET. Asa Mercer was the young man who went east to scout out marriageable females to come to Seattle, the "Mercer Girls."

SENECA STREET. Probably named after Seneca, Kansas, a Midwest town that was home to an early settler.

PHINNEY RIDGE. Guy C. Phinney laid out a 286-acre claim in that area.

ROYAL BROUGHAM WAY was named for a popular *Post-Intelligencer* sportswriter around the time that streets were being rearranged to accommodate the Kingdome. Brougham also was known for his zany promotional events that occasionally went awry, e.g., an eighty-pound model airplane with a six-foot wingspan that was supposed to overfly a group honoring Boeing, but crashed into the salads of diners.

SPRING STREET. There once were springs in that area used by the pioneers.

VOLUNTEER PARK honored the First Washington Infantry after they returned to Seattle from the Philippines in 1901.

GEORGETOWN was named by a proud grandparent, Julius Horton, brother of Dexter, who platted land in the area in 1890. George Horton became a physician and was Seattle City Coroner 1891-94.

WOODINVILLE was named after W.D. Wood, 1897 mayor.

QUEEN ANNE HILL. The first house on the hill was of Queen Anne style architecture, built by Herman Chapin. Others built additional homes of the same style and soon the area became known as Queen Anne Town, then Queen Anne Hill.

LAKE WASHINGTON was named by Thomas Mercer after George Washington.

LAKE UNION was named because of the hoped-for union of the two natural lakes.

CAPITOL HILL. Arthur Denny reserved a six-acre portion of his donation claim to be used as a state capitol, but Olympia, not Seattle, was chosen for this honor. Others believe his claims did not extend to Capitol Hill, and that it is named after James A. Moore, a Seattle developer who also had a development in Denver, Colorado, called Capitol Hill.

GASWORKS PARK on Lake Union is named for the Washington Natural Gas Company plant formerly located there. Gasworks Park is one terminus of the Burke-Gilman Trail. The land for the park was purchased in 1962.

GREEN RIVER is named for the color of the water and of some of the rocks in the stream bed.

HIGHLINE DISTRICT. Many years ago there was a Highline Road that clung to the ridges somewhat back from the waterfront. It went from Seattle to Tacoma.

HOOKER STREET. Developer Albert M. Brookes wanted to name the streets in his plat for Civil War figures. In 1891 he named Thomas Street for General George H. Thomas but was forced to change it, because there already was another Thomas Street. He named the street after General Joseph Hooker. Hooker was known for patronizing the camp followers of his troops, who were dubbed "Hooker's Division." The name began to be applied to all prostitutes thereafter. In Seattle's case, though, the street was named for the general.

INTERLAKEN BOULEVARD that runs near and in Washington Arboretum originally was part of the bike path system of the late 1890s mentioned elsewhere in this book. The word means "between the lakes," and the boulevard is between Lakes Washington and Union.

LEARY WAY. John Leary came to Seattle and was admitted to the bar in 1871. He practiced law until 1882, then went into journalism. He bought the *Seattle Post* which later merged with the *Intelligencer* to become the *Post-Intelligencer*. In 1889 Leary filed a plat that included the street.

MEDINA was named after the sacred city of the Moslems in Saudi Arabia, where Mohammed is buried.

MEYDENBAUER WAY. William M. Meydenbauer filed a forty-acre claim in 1869 on Lake Washington but only used it as a summer getaway. He was known for his savory wares at the Eureka Bakery.

OLIVE WAY is named for Olive Bell, daughter of the pioneer family, but she moved away from Seattle when she was only ten years old.

PAR PLACE in north Seattle was part of the 1929 Golfcrest plat. Lakeside School was located on that tract.

REDMOND was named for Luke McRedmond who located there in 1871. The settlement was originally called Salmonberg.

Note: The author is indebted for some of the above name derivations to books by Doug Cardle and Ralph B. Potts (see bibliography).

Did You Know That. . .

Lake Washington used to drain through the Black River near Renton.

◆ ◆ ◆

For the early part of the century, cable cars ran up and down the Denny Regrade, not unlike those of San Francisco. Cars ran from downtown to parks on Lake Washington: Madison, Madrona, and Leschi. The four cable car lines were: Yesler Way, James Street, Madison Street, and Front Street. The latter was electrified around 1900 but the other three remained cable cars until 1939-40.

◆ ◆ ◆

The big E on top of the waterfront Edgewater Hotel is noted on nautical charts as an aid to navigation.

◆ ◆ ◆

In February 1916 twenty-nine inches of snow fell on Seattle. Residents were skiing on the streets. The weight of the snow caused the St. James Cathedral dome to collapse with a roar and also the roof of the West Seattle Christian Church to fall.

◆ ◆ ◆

You could ride elephants with a basket on their backs at Woodland Zoo in the 1960s.

◆ ◆ ◆

Ferries connected Madison Park and Kirkland in 1890, and by 1900 there was passenger service between Madison Park and Bothell. After 1911 ferry routes were established between Seattle and Bellevue, Mercer Island, and Vashon Island.

◆ ◆ ◆

Yesler Hill was known as "Profanity Hill," because walkers used blue language climbing the steep paths and streets to its two highest points—234 feet at Seventh and Spruce and 256 near Broadway and Tenth.

◆ ◆ ◆

The totem pole in Pioneer Square was stolen from the Tlingits of Alaska. In 1899 a boatload of prominent citizens went to southeast Alaska to survey the situation centering around the gold prospectors' needs. They planned to fish and have some fun, too. The city fathers included the likes of Jacob Furth, banker; J.W. Clise, president of the Chamber of Commerce; J.P.D Lloyd, rector of St. Mark's Episcopal Church, and others. At 4:00 A.M. one morning while anchored near Ketchikan the party went ashore and took a tall totem pole from a Tongass Island graveyard. When they got it home, with special ceremonies, they implanted it in Pioneer Square. The U.S. Government did not consider it a prank, and a marshal came from Alaska to arrest all of them for stealing government property. A federal grand jury in Juneau indicted the perpetrators, and the media and citizens had a field day alternately laughing and being outraged by the incident. After much maneuvering the guilty were dismissed, and since it was not government property but Indian property, the Tlingits agreed to accept $500 for the pole. They got even, though. In later years the pole deteriorated and the Tlingits charged what was called an exorbitant fee to carve and send a replacement.

◆ ◆ ◆

Freeway Park is all that was installed of a 1961 plan conceived by one Paul Thiry to make a tunnel of the I-5 freeway for some distance and create a new north-south street along this covered portion as a tree-lined esplanade and entrance to the city of Seattle.

◆ ◆ ◆

Seattle has known some dramatic weather extremes. In 1861 the temperature fell to -4 degrees. Some lakes were frozen six inches deep, and two feet of snow fell. Conversely, a temperature of 114 degrees was recorded in 1866. No rain fell from July 1 to October 30, 1868.

◆ ◆ ◆

The Seattle Golf Club was originally located in Laurelhurst.

◆ ◆ ◆

Five United States presidents visited Seattle prior to 1920. President Rutherford Hayes came by steamer in 1890 with his wife and son. General Tecumseh Sherman was also aboard. He visited the Port Blakely sawmill and moved on to the Port Madison sawmill, where the Democratic owner would not permit the president to land. President Benjamin

Harrison arrived in 1891 and received a warm welcome from fleet ships decked out in bunting. He took a trip around Lake Washington on the old paddlewheeler *Kirkland*. President Theodore Roosevelt was met on May 23, 1903, by an honor guard of bunting-laden ships and a crowd of thousands. The boisterous "Teddy" made some rousing speeches and was received with equal enthusiasm. President William Howard Taft visited briefly on September 29, 1909. He was cheered during a motorcade. The next day he went to the AYP, played golf, had lunch, and went to Tacoma. President Woodrow Wilson came in 1919 and went by motorcade through Seattle. Uptown (approximately today's central business area) he received cheers, but as his car came along Second Avenue, workmen were hostile in an audience that included pacifists and "Wobblies." They stood politely but silently, an unnerving experience for President Wilson.

◆ ◆ ◆

Lake Washington was called *Hyas Chuck* or "Big Lake" by the Native Americans. It was then called Lake Duwamish and Lake Geneva before Mercer named it after George Washington.

Places

THE MONTLAKE CUT

In pioneer days a connection between Lake Union and Lake Washington was envisioned to admit ocean-going vessels to the interior lakes. Early in the century there was a six-foot-wide log flume between the two. The Army Corps of Engineers constructed the waterway in 1917, but it has served mostly private, smaller craft. Most commercial boats, especially freighters and steamers, use Harbor Island or Elliott Bay facilities. Montlake Cut becomes a merry place during University of Washington football games, because private boats and a handful of charter boats come to the games by boat. The cheers of crowds fill the air along Montlake Cut, since Husky Stadium is adjacent to the waterway. Today there is a scenic trail on the south side of the waterway, connecting the University of Washington's Arboretum Trail with the West Montlake Park on Portage Bay. It was designed by the Army Corps of Engineers and the Seattle Garden Club in 1970 and designated a National Recreation Trail in 1971. At the east end of the trail is a forty-foot totem pole carved by John Wallace, a Haida chief and donated to the city of Seattle in 1983. The north side of the Montlake Cut is bordered by the Burke-Gilman hike/bike trail.

THE *WAWONA*

The historic ship *Wawona* is docked at the south end of Lake Union. She was a lumber carrier, 156 feet long with a 36-foot beam, one of the fleet of all-sail lumber carriers that plied the waters largely between Puget Sound, the Columbia River, and San Francisco Bay. After 1914 the *Wawona* was used for years in the Bering Sea fishery industry. During World War II she served as a barge. Now she is a floating museum, open to the public.

OLD HOUSES

Along 812-28 Twenty-third Avenue are six beautifully restored row houses built during 1892-93 in a late Victorian style once common to low-income houses in Seattle. Considered historic, the homes have protective covenants to preserve their architectural style.

ELLIOTT BAY BOOKSTORE

Twenty-two years ago a bookstore opened in Pioneer Square, a seemingly unlikely place then inhabited chiefly by down-and-outers. Under Walter Carr's careful guidance, the Elliott Bay Bookstore today is an icon. It started small in the historic Globe Building, one of the first in Pioneer Square to be renovated, but today it is mammoth, rambling below to a basement and on into adjacent buildings. Nooks and crannies, wooden floors in places, and a restaurant all are part of Elliott Bay. The browsers range from scruffy, self-styled intellectuals to secretaries on their noon lunchtimes, and the double-breasted suit crowd. Owner Walter Carr said that Elliott Bay is one of the first to combine food and books. Perhaps the first was Keppler's in Menlo Park, California, a used bookstore that offered coffee and pastries; or Peabody's, Baltimore, also a used and serious antiquarian bookstore, that had a bar and coffee shop.

Seattle is known as a city of readers, perhaps first in the nation. Elliott Bay simply caters to everyone at a basic level. It has a devoted following, a wonderful plus for the many authors who appear there for book talks and readings—authors that include Erica Jong, Tracy Kidder, Tom Robbins and the like. Rick Simonson hosts as many as seven or eight readings per week.

FORT LAWTON, Discovery Park, Magnolia area

The installation was established in 1898 on 700 acres of land donated by local citizens, when the United States was concerned about intrusions during the Spanish-American War. It was named after General Henry Ware Lawton, who served in Cuba and was killed in the Philippines in 1910.

Designers of the grounds were aware of the spectacular site, a height with a sweeping view of Puget Sound, the Olympic and Cascade mountains. The building were laid down beside a wide street and featured the clean architecture of Greek Revival mode. Gracious officers' quarters, barracks, post exchange, and gymnasium were situated around an oval parade ground.

Before World War I about 500 horses were stabled at Fort Lawton, awaiting dispersement all over the world for peaceful tasks. The fort was a training ground before and during World War I and an embarkation point.

During peacetime there were military parades, concerts, and special events, well attended by civilians as well as military personnel.

After the beginning of World War II, the fort shifted quickly into a wartime status. Government contractors threw up additional temporary wooden buildings, a few of which are still in use by Discovery Park personnel. Over one million soldiers were trained, processed, and sent to the Navy's port of embarkation at Pier 91 (south side of Magnolia area) for overseas war duty. Returning soldiers and families also came back through the fort. Again during the Korean conflict 1950-53 the fort became a P.O.E.

Throughout those years Fort Lawton served as the command post for Air Defense until 1974, when the 49th Artillery Group was inactivated. The post also was headquarters for the Tenth U.S. Army Corps until 1968; this commanded Army Reserve and ROTC units for the Northwest region.

In 1964 the Secretary of Defense declared about 85 percent of the fort to be surplus. Four years later, the Tenth Corps was inactivated and a new 124th Army Reserve command under the Sixth Army was created with headquarters at Fort Lawton. It commands units in Washington, Oregon, California, and Nevada.

The Army started to reduce the fort by demolishing a three-story hospital that overlooked the Sound. At this point, Seattle historical societies objected and were able to get the core buildings on the National Register of Historic

Places. They have been sealed securely but the exteriors are painted and maintained.

A large segment of Fort Lawton's grounds was given to the City of Seattle in 1972-74 to become Discovery Park. Since government lands that are withdrawn from use are offered to native people, too, a coalition of Western Washington tribes acquired a block of land and built an impressive center on it—the Daybreak Star.

The residences on the fort have been maintained and are still occupied by military families, both Army and Navy.

KUBOTA GARDENS,
Rainier Avenue South at Fifty-fifth Street

Acquired by the City of Seattle some time ago, the Kubota Gardens still involve the Kubota family management. Fujitoro Kubota, a Japanese immigrant from Kochi Prefecture, remembered the lovely old temples and gardens of his native land. In 1906 he started a gardening and landscaping business at the present location and began later to specialize in the art of creating Japanese gardens. By 1929 he had acquired five acres and gradually created a demonstration garden for his potential clients. It included a rock garden, pond, rose garden, lily gardens, and lawns. Even though he was interned during World War II, he returned to rescue his garden from the weeds. The area is now a park with twenty acres of woodlands and trails, plus another fifteen acres surrounding the park as a buffer, and includes ten ponds, a stream, native flowering shrubs, and such.

RUBY MONTANA'S PINTO PONY

A little girl in a little town—Ruby Montana in El Reno, Oklahoma—had her picture taken on the pinto pony of a traveling photographer in 1933. She hung the photo in her room and dreamed that the pony would come to life and gallop into her life. It never did, but Montana's shop near Pioneer Square has a collection of "stuff" that amounts to a walk down memory lane. Montana's success with her shop has finally enabled her to buy that pony or horse she always wanted.

GOODWILL INDUSTRIES MEMORY LANE MUSEUM, 1400 South Lane

A display of antiques hangs from the ceiling of a barn-like building, items such as sausage grinders, spinning wheels, high button shoes, a stuffed armadillo. On certain Wednesdays the store holds a vintage fashion show at noon.

SHOREY'S BOOKSTORE

For over one hundred years customers have searched for books at Shorey's. With over a million items in stock, Shorey's is one of the largest antiquarian bookstores in the world.

It All Started in Seattle

Seattle businesses that began in Seattle and spread beyond the borders of Washington include:

THE BOEING COMPANY, known worldwide. See page 123 for a profile of William Boeing. And it all started here in Seattle.

◆ ◆ ◆

THE BON MARCHE. The year after the great fire of 1889 Edward Nordhoff and his wife Josephine came to

Seattle to seek a milder, more healthful climate for their ailing daughter Eleanor. When Edward could find no job, he and his wife leased a small one-story frame building at First and Cedar Street. With their life savings of $1,200, they bought merchandise to set up a store with the grand name of The Bon Marche Nordhoff & Co. As a youth Nordhoff had gone from Germany to work in a Paris department store. Nearby was another department store called The Bon Marche, established in 1852. He was impressed with the merchandising method of arranging like goods by departments and dreamed of opening his own Bon Marche—which he did.

1902 newly enlarged Bon Marche at Second & Pike (Courtesy of the Bon Marche)

The young couple did all the work themselves, with Josephine often holding the baby as she waited on customers. She learned Chinook in order to serve Indian people. A curious idea by Edward was effective. Until he brought sacks of pennies from back East (acquired during a buying trip), change had been given to the closest nickel. Now The

Bon Marche advertised items for nineteen cents or forty-nine cents, and people took the streetcar to Belltown, which was not downtown, just to take advantage of the slightly lower prices. The Bon reimbursed their fare. Despite the 1893 financial collapse, the Nordhoffs hung on.

In 1896 they moved to a store on Second and Pike, located near where street cars and cable cars turned. Riders could see The Bon Marche's window displays as the car made this maneuver. Then came 1897 and the discovery of gold in the Yukon. Prosperity followed. However, in 1899 Edward died of tuberculosis, leaving Josephine, age twenty-seven, with three young children. She was a capable business woman and ran The Bon Marche until she married Frank McDermott in 1901.

By 1902 a major addition was made over and above the original Second and Pike corner, with The Bon Marche continuing to operate even as construction ensued.

Josephine Nordhoff died of cancer on February 7, 1920, at age forty-eight. Her husband Frank McDermott, Edward's brother Rudolph Nordhoff, and a valuable executive, Frank McL. Radford continued to successfully operate The Bon. The entire block between Pine and Stewart on Third Avenue was purchased and a four-story building constructed—the present location of the downtown store. The style of the building was art deco, a popular design of the time, 1927. Seattle's first escalators were installed. Before the new store opened, the principals sold the store to Hahn Department Stores, New York (it became Allied Stores Corp. in 1933). Management appointed Frank McL. Radford the president of The Bon Marche.

Expansion into branch stores began with the Everett store in 1949, the Northgate Mall store in 1950. Yakima, Tacoma, Bellingham, and others followed. The original downtown store became the largest department store west of Chicago in 1955. In 1976 the name of the store was changed simply to "The Bon," since that is what patrons called it anyway, but the official name of The Bon Marche was restored in the 1980s.

In 1995 The Bon Marche had forty contemporary stores and four home stores. And it all started here in Seattle.

◆ ◆ ◆

ERNST HOME CENTER, INC.'s first store was in the Colman Building, Seattle. The company targeted do-it-your-self homeowners and is a leading home improvement, hardware, and garden retailer.

In 1994 the firm had seventy-seven retail outlets in eight states and continues to grow. In 1991 it began the concept of a superstore prototype that had 42,000 square feet of selling space, one way of combatting the inroads of competitive regional warehouse stores. The company also is expanding into much smaller secondary markets, serving communities that are too small to attract the warehouse store but large enough to need an Ernst style store. And it all started here in Seattle.

◆ ◆ ◆

FLETCHER GENERAL CONSTRUCTION has undergone several name changes, but two pioneer Seattle firms make up the bulk of it. The J.A. McEachern Company was founded by brothers Dan and Jack in 1911. The company was awarded the Bell Street Terminal Project by the Port of Seattle as its first contract. For fifteen years thereafter the J.A. McEachern Company was involved in major construction and shipbuilding ventures. In 1926 the firm entered into a partnership agreement with General Construction Company to build concrete irrigation ditches for the U.S. Bureau of Reclamation. Among the major ventures thereafter (solely and in other partnerships) were the construction of the Owyhee Dam in Eastern Oregon; shipbuilding with

Henry J. Kaiser, Todd Shipyards, and others; concrete for Shasta Dam, California; the Hungry Horse Dam, Montana; Shilshole Bay Marina and the Cargill Elevator, Seattle.

Meanwhile, Seattleite Howard S. Wright had a construction company that included Howard E. Wright and George J. Schuchart. Wright constructed the Puget Sound Pulp and Timber Company mill in Bellingham, the Navy docks in Bremerton, the Space Needle in Seattle, hangars for Moses Lake's Larson Air Force Base, pulp mills for Sitka and Ketchikan. Wright and other companies joined General to become Fletcher General Construction. The firm has been instrumental in the building of ninety-one dams and numerous other major projects. The company has offices in Irvine and Walnut Creek, California; Hadlock, Tacoma, Vancouver and Seattle, Washington. And it all started here in Seattle.

◆ ◆ ◆

JAY JACOBS was a local man who played football for the University of Washington. He started working at The Bon as a furrier and soon resigned to open his own store on Fifth Avenue. Jay and his wife Rose gradually added accessories, then dresses. In the early 1950s they identified that the junior size customer had special needs and opened a second store specializing in "Juniors" at Northgate Shopping Center, the nation's first mall. Management added menswear in the 1970s, and the stores have won awards of excellence for both juniors and young men's clothing. Jay Jacobs stores numbered 288 at their peak, slightly lower today, and are located in all fifty states. And it all started here in Seattle.

◆ ◆ ◆

NBBJ, Heritage Building, constitutes the initials of four architects who have shaped the skyline of Seattle. In 1943 Naramore, Bain, Brady, and Johanson joined forces to secure a large World War II naval contract. The partnership combined the know-how of building for three specific needs:

housing, health care, and education. The new firm designed a total support community for one the nation's shipyards. Since then, the firm has designed diverse projects from schools to skyscrapers, including the following in Seattle: Market Place Tower, Bagley Wright Theatre, Fluke Hall at the University of Washington, Two Union Square, and others. The popular Sun Mountain Resort was a remodel by NBBJ. Today the firm employs over 500 people in eight American cities and in Tokyo, Japan. And it all started here in Seattle.

◆ ◆ ◆

PACCAR INC. was started by William Piggott Sr., in 1905 as Seattle Car Manufacturing Company to produce railway and logging equipment in West Seattle. A fire destroyed the plant in 1907 and the business relocated in Renton the following year. Since railroads, logging railroads, and extensive logging enterprises thrived in the Pacific Northwest, the company prospered, too. It was particularly known for building the first sturdy railroad equipment to carry massive logs and for the first connected trucks (supports for rail cars, not motor trucks).

In 1911 the name of the company was changed to Seattle Car and Foundry Company, and as part of a merger with Twohy Brothers of Portland in 1917, it became Pacific Car & Foundry.

Back in Anderson, Indiana, the Dart Truck Company was building early motor trucks, and eventually became a division of Paccar Inc. Paccar entered the truck business by acquiring Kenworth Motor Truck Company of Seattle in 1945.

Through a reputation for building good heavy equipment, and through mergers and acquisitions, Paccar Inc. today has factories and outlets all over the world and is a publicly held corporation. However, Charles M. Pigott, a member of the founding family, still is a major stockholder. And it all started here in Seattle.

◆ ◆ ◆

THE RAINIER BREWING COMPANY. In 1878 a German immigrant brewmaster, Andrew Hemrich, founded a small brewery on Airport Way. He brewed three different brands of beer as Seattle Brewing and Malting Company, and Hemrich's premium label was Rainier Beer. The loggers, miners, and fishermen had a legendary frontier thirst, and the company prospered until Washington State initiated prohibition in 1916. At that time, Hemrich's company had grown to be the sixth largest brewery in the world and had moved to a handsome brick building in Georgetown, south of its original location. The brewery became a feed lot, but the buildings stand today as a warehouse and ice house.

After repeal of prohibition in 1933, Fritz and Emil Sick purchased the original Airport Way brewery and managed to regain the Rainier brand from the California Brewery by the late 1930s. Meanwhile, the Sicks produced Rheinlander beer, and then Rainier, as well.

After the death of Emil Sick in 1964, Sicks' Century Brewing Company went through several name changes, amalgamations, and ownerships—in the process, becoming Rainier Brewing Company. Currently the firm is owned by Hicks, Muse & Company.

Rainier is known all over the world with countless distribution points. And it all started here in Seattle.

◆ ◆ ◆

REI RECREATIONAL EQUIPMENT, INC., was formed in 1938 by twenty-three Seattle mountain climbers led by Lloyd Anderson. Their initial purpose was to locate quality climbing equipment from Europe at the best possible prices.

They formed a cooperative to achieve it, following the Rochedale, England, cooperative principles of collective ownership, open membership, competitive pricing, and profit distribution through an annual patronage dividend.

The company has had only four presidents: Lloyd Anderson 1938-71; Jim Whittaker, the first American to reach the summit of Mount Everest, 1971-79; Jerry Horn 1979-83; and Wally Smith 1983-.

The first full-time retail store was opened in 1944 in Seattle, the second in 1975 in Berkeley, California. The first East Coast expansion started in 1987 in Reading, Mass. Today REI has forty-one retail outlets in the United States and has been named twice as one of the "100 Best Companies to Work For in America." And it all started here in Seattle.

◆ ◆ ◆

STARBUCKS COFFEE is discussed under "The Coffee Revolution," page 74. And it all started here in Seattle.

◆ ◆ ◆

UNITED PARCEL SERVICE

Nineteen-year-old Jim Casey started the American Messenger Delivery in 1907, a time when communication between offices was personal, for phones only existed in public places. A dozen messenger services operated in competition, but Casey offered twenty-four-hour service, staying up all night himself to serve the customers. His messengers and he used bicycles and motorcycles for deliveries. After four years he asked his brother George to join him.

Before long the American Messenger Delivery merged with Evert McCabe's Merchant Parcel Delivery, retaining that name. By 1914 the firm had seven Yale motorcycles equipped with carbide headlights so they could run at night.

Their early projects were not confined to delivery of messages and parcels. Messengers took baggage to the depot or a tray of food to a late-working employee. A messenger was hired by a jealous wife to locate a stray husband.

The company added Charles Soderstrom, an accounting whiz. The MPD started deliveries for retail stores, acquired a fleet of trucks, and delivered furniture and almost anything to anywhere. After the outbreak of World War I, when store employees were scarce, more stores hired their delivery services. MPD moved to a location that had a loading dock, so trucks could back up for easier loading.

In 1919 the brothers Casey acquired a company in Oakland and changed the name of their combined firms to United Parcel Service. To give a concept of pricing, in Oakland a delivery up to six blocks cost fifteen cents, to San Francisco $1.25.

Only three years later UPS added Los Angeles and installed conveyor belts in Seattle and Los Angeles to handle the parcels more efficiently. In 1925 four out of the five major Seattle department stores used UPS for deliveries. Service to Portland came in 1927, and in 1928 Soderstrom converted the entire fleet of trucks from Stuart, Metz, and GMC to 1928 Model A Ford trucks.

UPS attempted to use United Air Express in 1929 for deliveries from the West Coast to the East Coast, but the Great Depression caused the service to cease in 1931. It was 1929, also, when the four founders (two Caseys, McCabe, and Soderstrom) turned management over to a board of managers. By 1934, despite the Depression, UPS was well established in the major cities of the west coast and was eyeing the Midwest. After World War II the expansion of UPS accelerated. Service to New York from San Francisco began in 1956, for UPS Air was reborn in 1953 on the West Coast. Deliveries for department stores were de-emphasized, and general service to homes and businesses was the main thrust of the 1950s. In 1975 UPS became the first package delivery company to serve every address in the forty-eight contiguous states.

To cover the area of Seattle originally served by American Messenger Delivery today requires 900 PCs, 2,000 portable computers, 1,300 electronic data collectors, 600 semi-trailers, 100 semi-tractors, 300 package trucks, and 4,200 employees!

The total UPS fleet numbers 120,000 vehicles. In striving for accident-free driving, the company awards its accident-free drivers a twenty- and twenty-five-year honor, a listing in the Circle of Honor with the driver's photo hanging in the company offices.

On Second and Main, birthplace of Casey's AMD that became UPS, the Annie E. Casey Foundation created a beautiful Waterfall Park with a special plaque to honor the men and women of UPS.

Today the main office of UPS is in Atlanta, Georgia, but it all started here in Seattle.

◆ ◆ ◆

Others include Schuck's Auto Supply, now a part of Northern Automotive Corporation; Unigard Insurance Company; Pay 'n Save, now merged into Payless; and many more that started here in Seattle and grew beyond belief.

Bibliography

Anderson, Eva Greenslit. *Chief Seattle*. Caldwell: The Caxton Printers, Ltd., 1950.

Baxter, Portus. Materials in Dubuar Scrapbook No. 80, p. 49, in Special Collections University of Washington Libraries, Seattle.

Berner, Richard C. *Seattle 1900-1920*. Seattle: Charles Press, 1991.

Best, David Grant. *Portrait of a Racetrack*. Redmond, Wash.: Best Editions, 1992.

Boeing Archives. In-house materials about William L. Boeing.

Brewster, David and David M. Buerge, editors. *Washingtonians*. Seattle: Sasquatch Books, 1988.

Broderick, Henry. *Mirrors of Seattle's Old Hotels*. Seattle: Dogwood Press, 1965.

Calhoun, Anne H. *A Seattle Heritage*. The Fine Arts Society. Seattle: Anne H. Calhoun, 1942.

Cardle, Doug. *About Those King County Names*. Seattle: Coastal Press, 1989.

Case, Frederick. "How Dry It Wasn't," *Pacific Magazine*, October 10, 1983.

Chittenden, Gen. H.M. "The Lake Washington Canal," Seattle Chamber of Commerce paper, date missing.

Clark, Norman H. *The Dry Years*. Seattle: University of Washington Press, 1965.

Daniel Guggenheim Medal Citation. "William Edward Boeing," New York, 1936.

deBarros, Paul. *Jackson Street After Hours*. Seattle: Sasquatch Books, 1993.

Dodge, Dennis. "Tough times, happy days form legend of Longacres," *Daily Racing Form*, Northwest edition, September 21, 1992.

Dorpat, Paul. *494 More Glimpses of Seattle*. Seattle: Paul Dorpat, 1982.

_____. "Golden Potlatch," *The Seattle Times*, Sunday Times Tourist and Trade Number, July 28, 1935.

_____. *Seattle Now and Then*. Seattle: Paul Dorpat, 1984.

Downey, Roger. "The Pride of Dorothy S. Bullitt," *Channels* (KING-TV), September/October 1985.

Droker, Howard. *Seattle's Unsinkable Houseboats*. Seattle: Howard A. Droker, 1977.

Dudar, Helen. "A welcoming new museum for the city on the Sound," *Smithsonian*, April 1992, pp. 47 ff.

Duncan, Don. *Meet Me at the Center*. Seattle: Seattle Center Foundation, 1992.

Faber, Jim. *Steamer's Wake*. Seattle: Enetai Press, 1985.

Ficken, Robert E. "Seattle's Ditch," *Pacific Northwest Quarterly*, January 1986.

"The 5th Avenue," Theatre Historical Society Annual for 1984. San Francisco and Seattle: Theatre Historical Society and the 5th Avenue Theatre, 1984.

Gates, Bill. "How to Make a Small Fortune in Software," E-mail. *New York Times* Special Features.

Gellatly, Judy. *Mercer Island Heritage*. Mercer Island: Mercer Island Historical Society.

Goodman, Michael E. *Seattle Supersonics*. Mankato, Minn.: Creative Education, Inc., 1993.

Hall, Ben M. *The Best Remaining Seats*. New York: Da Capo, 1988.

Hershman, Marc J. *Seattle's Waterfront*. Seattle: Waterfront Awareness, 1981.

Hickok, Ralph. *The Encyclopedia of North American Sports History*. New York: Facts on File, 1991.

Hitzges, Norm. *The Norm Hitzges Historical Sports Almanac*. Dallas: Taylor Publishing Company, 1991.

Jones, Oran D. "Coliseum Photoplay House, Seattle," *The Architect*, July, 1916.

KING-TV. Miscellaneous in-house data re. Dorothy S. Bullitt.

Kreisman, Lawrence. *Historic Preservation in Seattle*. Seattle: Historic Seattle Preservation and Development Authority.

_____, *The Stimson Legacy*. Seattle: Willows Press, 1992.

Longacres Park. "End of an Era," commemorative yearbook, September, 1992, copy at Washington Thoroughbred Breeders Association, Inc., Kent, Washington.

Lovoll, Odd S. *The Promise of America*. Minneapolis: University of Minnesota Press, 1984.

McCallum, John D. *Dave Beck*. Mercer Island, Wash.: The Writing Works, 1978.

Microsoft Corporation. In-house information on William Gates and Microsoft Corporation.

Morgan, Murray. *Skid Road*. Seattle: University of Washington Press, 1982. 1st pub. by Viking Press, Inc., in 1951.

Mumford, Esther Hall. *Seattle's Black Victorians 1852-1901*. Seattle: Ananse Press, 1980.

Nakane, Kazuko. "Paul Horiuchi, A Profile," *Reflex*, February/March 1995.

Nelson, Gerald B. *Seattle*, New York: Alfred A. Knopf, 1977.

Newell, Gordon. *The Green Years*. Seattle: Superior Publishing Company, 1969.

Newell, Gordon and Don Sherwood. *Totem Tales of Old Seattle*. Seattle: Superior Publishing Company, 1956.

Nicandri, David L. *Italians in Washington State*. Tacoma: The Washington State American Revolution Bicentennial Commission, 1978.

Nordstrom, John. *The Immigrant in 1887*. Manuscript at Nordic Heritage Museum, 1950.

"The Northern Life Tower, Seattle," *The Architect and Engineer*, December 1929.

O'Connor, Harvey. *Revolution in Seattle*. Seattle: Left Bank Books, 1981.

Owen, John. *Press Pass*. Seattle: P.I. Books, 1994.

Phillips, Reynolds. "William E. Boeing," *Boeing Magazine*, November 1956.

Pierce, J. Kingston. "Go East, Seattle," *Eastsideweek*, April 1, 1992, pp. 13 ff.

Pike Place Market media information and other materials.

Potts, Ralph Bushnell. *Seattle Heritage*. Seattle: Superior Publishing Company, 1955.

Rambeck, Richard. *Seattle Seahawks*. Mankato, Minn.: Creative Education, Inc., 1991.

Robinson, John S. "The Grande Dame of Seattle Broadcasting," *The Weekly*, July 21, 1982, page 23.

Rothaus, James R. *Seattle Mariners*. Mankato, Minn.: Creative Education, 1987.

Sadis, Stephen. "The Miracle Strip," a videotape, 1993.

Sale, Roger. *Seattle Past to Present*. Seattle: University of Washington Press, 1976.

Satterfield, Archie. *The Seattle Guidebook*. Chester, Conn.: The Globe Pequot Press, 1975 with updates to 1991.

Sears, Bill. "How the dome miracle became reality," *Seattle Kingdome Commemorative Magazine*, March 1976.

Seattle/King County Convention & Visitors Bureau. "News about the King County Domed Stadium," July 1974; "King County Multipurpose Stadium," Nov. 1974; "King County Stadium," June 1975. Newsletters.

"History of Seattle Steam," typewritten information from Seattle Steam Company, Seattle.

"Seattle Underground," pamphlet. Seattle: Underground Tours, 1968.

Shorett, Alice and Murray Morgan. *The Pike Place Market*. Seattle: Pacific Search Press, 1982.

"Emil Sick," Bicentennial biographies, *Seattle Post-Intelligencer*, March 19, 1976, page A7.

Slauson, Morda C. *Renton from Coal to Jets*. Renton: Renton Historical Society, 1976.

Smith, Al. "Seattle After Dark, 1922-49," photographic exhibition at Museum of History and Industry, Seattle, 1994-.

Spiedel, William C. *Sons of the Profits*. Seattle: Nettle Creek Publishing Company, 1967.

Stephens, Dave. *Ivar*. Seattle: Dave Stephens, 1982.

Syring, Richard H. Special series on David Beck, *Bremerton Sun*, Feb. 20-22, 1957.

Taylor, Quintar. *The Forging of a Black Community*. Seattle: University of Washington Press, 1994.

Tonkin, Nancy. "Renovation of a Movie Palace," *Puget Soundings*, January/February 1980, pp. 14 ff.

Tsutakawa, Mayumi and Alan Chong-Lau. *Turning Shadows Into Light*. Seattle: Young Pine Press, 1982.

Tsutakawa, Mayumi. "Kanreki: The 60th Anniversary History of the Japan-America Society of the State of Washington 1923-1983," Japan-America Society of State of Washington, 1983.

U.S. Army Corps of Engineers. "Lake Washington Ship Canal and Hiram M. Chittenden Locks," informative brochure.

Van Lindt, Carson. *The Seattle Pilots*. New York: Marabou Publishing, 1993.

Veirs, Kristina, ed. *Nordic Heritage Northwest*. Seattle: Nordic Heritage Museum, 1982 (copyright Veirs).

Warren, James R. "Building the Ship Canal and Locks," Seattle: *King County and its Queen City: Seattle*, 1981.

_____. *Seattle*. Woodland Hills, CA: Windsor Publications, Inc., 1981.

Warren, James R. and William R. McCoy. *Highlights of Seattle's History*, Seattle: Historical Society of Seattle and King County, 1982.

Watson, Emmett. *Digressions of a Native Son*. Seattle: The Pacific Institute, Inc., 1982 (copyright Watson).

_____. *Once Upon a Time in Seattle*. Seattle: Lesser Seattle Publishing, 1992 (copyright Watson).

Watt, Roberta Frye. *Four Wagons West*, Portland: Binfords & Mort, 1931.

Willingham, William F. *Northwest Passages*. Seattle:
Seattle District, U.S. Army Corps of Engineers, 1992.

Zingg, Paul J. and Mark D. Medeiros. *Runs, hits, and an
Era: the Pacific Coast League, 1903-58*. Urbana,
Illinois: Published for the Oakland Museum by the
University of Illinois Press, 1994.

Media guides from Seattle Seahawks, Seattle SuperSonics,
Seattle Mariners.

Selected issues of newspapers: *Seattle Times, Seattle
Post-Intelligencer, Argus, The Coast*.

Museums, archives, special sources: Nordic Heritage
Museum, Museum of History and Industry, Special Collections University of Washington, Washington Thoroughbred
Breeders Association, Seattle Public Library, Fraternal
Order of Eagles, The Army Corps of Engineers files, Japan-
America Society files, Fort Lawton's National Guard
archives, Department of Transportation historical files,
Hiram M. Chittenden's historical and explanatory materials, Wing Luke Museum, Bellingham Public Library
pamphlet files, numerous files at Seattle Public Library,
files of Department of Transportation, Seattle office, Metropolitan Tract offices, and KING-TV.

People: Junius Rochester, Greg Lang, Gary Henson, Norma
Jean Cugini, Al Bek, Jean Godden, Mary Jane Hashisaki,
Walter Carr, Gary Henson, Victor and Marcia Rosellini,
George Mortenson, Cheryl and Donovan Burkhart, Mark
and Denise Swerland, Martin Smith of the Broderick
Building, Kingdome staff, representatives of the Seattle
Mariners, Seahawks, and SuperSonics, Governor Albert D.
Rosellini, Bill Sears, George Hancock of Hart Brewing
Company, Emmett Watson.

Index